Women's Aggressive Fanta

Women's Aggressive Fantasies examines the roles of aggressive fantasies and impulses in contemporary women's lives. Such impulses have previously been overlooked by psychoanalysis, feminism and depth psychology when, as Sue Austin argues, they should occupy a central position.

Drawing together apparently disparate strands of theory from feminism, critical psychology, contemporary psychoanalysis and post-Jungian thought, this book succeeds in providing a new insight into the phenomenon of women's aggressive energies and the images which express them. A collection of vignettes from women's day-to-day lives are used to demonstrate how the management of aggressive fantasies plays a significant role in women's self-experience and their position in society. These fascinating, moving and, at times, shocking, extracts demonstrate how aggressive fantasies form the basis for psychological, relational and moral growth. This book will help clinicians engage with the fantasies and draw out their therapeutic value. In particular, the author examines the crucial role of aggressive fantasies and energies in women's sense of embodiment, and in recovery from severe and chronic eating disorders.

Women's Aggressive Fantasies provides a valuable insight into the role of aggressive impulses in women's sense of agency, love and morality, which will fascinate all those involved in the practice or study of psychoanalysis, critical psychology and gender studies.

Sue Austin is a Jungian analyst specialising in working with people with severe and chronic eating disorders.

Women's Aggressive Fantasies

A Post-Jungian Exploration of Self-Hatred, Love and Agency

Sue Austin

Routledge
Taylor & Francis Group

LONDON AND NEW YORK

First published 2005 by Routledge
27 Church Road, Hove, East Sussex, BN3 2FA

Simultaneously published in the USA and Canada
by Routledge
270 Madison Avenue, New York NY 10016

Routledge is an imprint of the Taylor & Francis Group

Typeset in Times by
RefineCatch Ltd, Bungay, Suffolk
Printed and bound in Great Britain by
TJ International Ltd, Padstow, Cornwall
Paperback cover design by Lisa Dynan

British Library Cataloguing in Publication Data
A catalogue record for this book is available
from the British Library

Library of Congress Cataloging-in-Publication Data
Austin, Sue.
  Women's aggresive fantasies : a post-Jungian exploration of
self-hatred, love and agency / Sue Austin.—1st ed.
     p. cm.
  Includes bibliographical references and index.
ISBN 1–58391–909–0 (hbk)   ISBN 1–58391–910–4 (pbk)
1. Women—Psychology.   2. Aggressiveness.   I. Title.

  HQ1206.A868 2005
  155.3′33—dc22   2004024985

ISBN 1–58391–909–0 (hbk)
ISBN 1–58391–910–4 (pbk)

For Mike

Contents

Figures

Acknowledgements

This project owes an incalculable debt to all the women, too numerous to mention individually, whose eyes lit up with delight when I told them about my interest in women's aggressive fantasies. At times, their enthusiastic responses have kept me going when all else has failed.

Another group of people who deserve special thanks are the women who contributed material to the project. For the sake of confidentiality I can only give their pseudonyms: Adele, Dolores, Doris, Ella, Helena, Isla, Jane, Juliette, Margaret, Mary, Nina, Rosa, Sara and Vivienne. The project would have been impossible without their support and contributions. Loyalty to their contributions was one of the other significant factors in my keeping going with the project, and I only hope that I have done justice to their texts in the ways that I have worked with them.

My thanks also to my analysands who gave permission for me to refer to moments from our work together.

And of course, I need to thank the people at *Psychology Press* who made this book possible: Kate Hawes, Routledge editor, for taking it on as a publishing project in the first place, Claire Lipscomb and Helen Pritt for editorial support, Kristin Susser for production management, Lisa Dynan for cover design and Frances Paterson of *Olive Grove Indexing Services* of Thirroul, N.S.W., for inspired indexing. Sincere thanks also to Hugo Crago for proofreading.

Other people have made specific contributions and I would like to thank them.

My partner, Mike, for just about everything, but not least of all: love, humour, integrity, companionship, technological backup, proof reading, and for being him.

Associate Professor Leon Petchkovsky, for the long-haul task of helping me to put my mind together and for being his extraordinary self.

Giles Clark for helping me focus my feelings and thoughts and for helping me to get that lot into language. Also my thanks for his capacity to continue relentlessly and for his inspiring conviction that the basis of the clinical project is that madness can (must?) be recycled.

Peter Fullerton for engaging, arguing and struggling with me with such patience and incisiveness, for sharing his clinical brilliance, and for helping to sort out some of the most stuck and muddled parts of this book.

Dr. Jill Welbourne for having common-sense, and outstanding expertise in the field of eating disorders and for being a supportive and generous colleague.

Professor Andrew Samuels, for his inspiring work in adjacent areas which he made available to me, and for his insightful responses to my work. Also my thanks for his unwavering support over many years.

Professor Renos Papadopoulos, for his sustained interest in my work through his editorship at Harvest.

Professor Valerie Walkerdine, for inspiration, support and the ground-breaking work she has done.

Donald Williams and Dolores Brien at The Jung Page (http://www.cgjungpage.org/) for sponsoring an internet seminar in October 2000 based on a paper of mine. A good deal of the final shape of this book came out of what I found myself thinking about as a result of that seminar. Also my thanks to all who participated in the seminar: I learnt a great deal from it.

Dr. Susan Rowland for her contributions to the post-Jungian field, and for her help and encouragement.

Dr. Raya Jones for her useful insights into some of the theoretical subtleties in Jung's work.

Phil Ackman for helping me understand the difference between a PhD and a book, and for pointing out what I needed to concentrate on.

Philip Latey, for keeping the mortal remains functional, and for sparring around ideas in enlivening ways.

Dr. Tony Swain and Dr. Erin White for supervision of the earlier PhD version of this project.

Michael Welbourne, for much needed and much appreciated proof reading of the PhD version of this project.

Cliff Bostock for introducing me to the work of Leo Bersani.

All my other friends and colleagues who have put up with me and encouraged me though the project. My specific thanks to: Romayne Jesty, Lesley Walding, Kathy Clark, Leone Knight, Vanessa Hannan, Angie Kenyon, Mi Weekes, Linda Milton, Ann Cotterell, Mayling Hargreaves, Sam Burgess, Bernadette Ackman, John Merchant, Leslie Devereaux, Alison Clark, Risé Becker, Allan Tegg, Sue Jenssen-Clare, Sue Holmes, Trish Shervington, Cassandra McNaught, Felicity Hartigan, Sally McBride, Stefanie Kenyon, Kate Chambers, Melanie Temple, Polly Tamplin, Maria Fitzgerald, Gerri Mehra-Slevin, Robyn Townsend, Doreen Wainer and anyone else who I may have missed out. I am deeply grateful to you all for your tolerance and patience.

I also want to take a few lines to thank all the rock musicians and stand-up comedians I have spent so much of my time listening to and watching and whose creative use of their aggression has been an inspiration and source of endless delight. Thanks to you all for being prepared to recycle your own madnesses and those of the world in such lively and connective ways.

Thanks also go to the people who gave me 'the breaks' that it takes for a very working-class, London girl/woman to get far enough through the education system to start a PhD, let alone finish one and then turn it into a book. Of special mention are Dr. David Hirshmann, Dr. Tony Butler, Professor Mike Berry and Professor Garry Trompf. Of extra special mention is Dr. Andrew Harrison, to whose generosity I owe a very great deal indeed.

PERMISSIONS

The author and publishers wish to thank the following for granting permission for earlier versions of parts of this book to be used here. Specifically:

Harvest: *Journal for Jungian Studies*, Vol. 50, No. 2 (Karnac, London) for 'Desire, fascination and the Other: some thoughts on Jung's interest in Rider Haggard's "*She*" and on the nature of Archetypes', parts of which appear in Chapter 1.
Also: Vol. 45, No. 2 (Karnac, London) for 'Women's aggressive fantasies: a feminist post-Jungian hermeneutic', parts of which appear in Chapters 1 and 4.

International Journal of Critical Psychology, Issue 7: 'Therapy', for 'The troubled and troubling discourse of infant observation', parts of which appear in the Chapter 1.

The Australian College of Psychological Medicine, Issue 27, February 2004, for 'Images from psychodynamic psychotherapy with people with long-term, severe eating disorders', parts of which appear in Chapter 6.

Women-church: An Australian Journal of Feminist Studies in Religion, Vol. 28, Autumn 2001 for 'A post-Jungian perspective on anger, aggression and femininity', parts of which appear in Chapters 2 and 4.
Also: Vol. 33, Spring 2003 for 'Jung and Rider Haggard's "She who must be obeyed": some thoughts on gender, power and fascination', parts of which also appear in Chapter 2.

The committee for the 1st Asian Pacific Eating Disorders Congress for their forthcoming publication of selected papers from the 10–14 November 2002 Melbourne Congress (edited by Graham D. Burrows, P. Bosanac, and Pierre

J. V. Beumont) in which a paper of mine entitled: 'Please hang in with me: the long haul of working with people with severe and chronic eating disorders' appears. A number of the word images from Chapter 6 of this book are drawn from that paper and presentation.

I would like to thank Bram Dijkstra for permission to reproduce the paintings used in Chapter 2. These pictures are taken from his fascinating book *Idols of Perversity: Fantasies of Feminine Evil in Fin-de-Siècle Culture*, Oxford: Oxford University Press (1986) and are reproduced with the permission of the author.

My thanks to Fernand Figueroa who gave me permission to use a case vignette of his in Chapter 6. This vignette was taken from a 'Jung Page' online seminar in May 1999. Also, I would like to thank the two women who gave me permission to use their dreams in Chapters 1 and 7.

Finally, I particularly want to thank Margot Bandola and Canns Down Press Ltd for permission to use Margot's lively and delightfully whimsical pictures 'Custard, Darling?' and 'Woman With Spanner'. 'Custard, Darling?' appears in Chapter 4 (Figure 4.2) and 'Woman With Spanner' is the cover picture for this book. These pictures (and others by Margot Bandola) can be found at http://www.cannsdownpress.co.uk/artM.A.htm.

Chapter I

A different way of looking at aggression

AGGRESSION AS A POINT OF CONNECTION

For women, aggressive fantasy can act as a point of breakthrough in the realms of relationship and agency. Of specific interest to me is the point where relationship and agency appear to clash, leaving women with what appears to be a choice between the two. I argue that a capacity to hold and direct aggressive energy for the good of relationship is a significant human achievement, and that an increasing capacity to do so correlates with an increasing capacity to build and sustain lively relationships without compromising oneself or one's values.[1]

In order to help the reader get their bearings with these ideas, I will start by illustrating my theme with a short story by Helen Garner, 'The Feel of Steel 1' (2001) from a collection called *The Feel of Steel*. I quote Garner because of the clear way she describes her discovery of the potential embedded in her aggressive energies. She also makes links between her aggression and her capacity to experience the Other more fully, and she indicates a connection between her aggression and her sense of agency. Garner outlines an early encounter with the sport of fencing at age 15, describing her teacher in the following terms:

> What Mr Fadgyas had at his disposal was a way of focusing and direct-ing aggression: of making fighting beautiful. The aggression in me, however, was deeply buried. Though I was quick on my feet, I was scared – not of getting hurt, but of attacking.
>
> (2001: 173)

Garner went on to flirt with fencing, but eventually lost interest through 'a couple of inglorious competition bouts'. Her interest was, however, re-aroused in her 50s, through her sister Judi (who had also been involved in fencing as a young woman) who faxed her an advertisement for 'Fencing for Older Adults'. Garner describes her second lesson:

> Judi and I pulled on masks and breastplates, stepped on to the piste and crossed swords. I went for her. She blocked me. I went again. It was thrilling. Adrenalin streamed through me. I wanted to attack, to be attacked, to have to fight back. I remember the lunges, the sliding clash of metal, how the sword hand rises as the foil-tip hits the target. It was glorious. We both burst out laughing. We only stopped because she didn't have a glove: I almost struck her hand and she flinched back. We lowered the blades. She pulled off her mask. Her eyes were bright, but I saw with a shock how gentle her face was, how feminine, under the cloud of hair.
>
> (2001: 174)

What is being described here is more than the pleasure of physical exertion, or even the thrill of fighting. Garner is exploring the edges of her identity as a woman, and in particular, the places where that identity breaks down in interesting and enlivening ways. The breakthrough that she is pointing to is that the disciplined, aggressive tussle of fencing connects her to her sister's gentleness and, I would suggest, not only her sister's beauty and humanity, but also to something important in herself. Through the shocking recognition of the immediacy of her sister's aliveness Garner is connected to her own aliveness.

This kind of heightened apperception of the Other (and of oneself through the splendour of the Other) is a moment of passionate love. That it can come through the disciplined and focused use of aggressive energy is the point that I will be exploring in this book. Garner recognises the rarity and value of what her aggression offers and concludes:

> That's what I want. I want to learn to fight, but not in the ordinary wretched way of the worst of my personal life – desperate, ragged, emotional. I want to learn an ancient discipline, with formal control and purpose. Will my body hold out? I hope it's not too late.
>
> (2001: 175)

Garner's short story was brought to my attention by an analysand – a woman in her 60s, who felt that Garner's description echoed a crucial aspect of her own struggle. My analysand, whom I shall call Amy, had brought up her children more or less single-handedly, having been left by her partner when the children were young. Amy had structured her career around her responsibilities to her children and came into analysis saying that she had been angry all her life, and felt that now, for the first time ever, she had space to explore that. When, some time into analysis, she came across Garner's story she was very drawn to the idea of learning to fight, but, as Garner says, not in the ordinary, desperate, ragged, emotional way, but in some other way, for which she had no language or images. Like Garner's, Amy's aggression was buried, and she was scared of her desire to attack. Amy could see, however, that something about her buried, unmapped aggression might provide a link to the sense of aliveness and capacity for greater intimacy with others that she sought, and Garner's short story seemed to be gesturing towards these links too.

Amy's concerns echoed the many conversations I have had with women analysands who describe themselves as having always been angry, or having been angry for decades. Her comments also resonated with something from my work with women with long-term, severe eating disorders, which is my area of clinical specialisation. These clinical interactions have been amplified by everyday dealings with women and men: a few months ago I had a conversation with the real estate agent from whom we were buying our new home, and she spoke of how her life had changed when her sister gave her a book on women's anger to read in her 50s. A few months before that I had a social conversation with a woman in her 60s who, in addition to looking after her terminally ill husband, running her business and being a mother to her now grown-up children, wrote short stories. Our conversation was pleasant, but fairly run-of-the-mill polite until I asked her what she was working on. She lit up with enthusiasm when she told me that she had just written a story about a woman who commits a murder and gets away with it. It turned out that she had written numerous stories about women's 'badness' and that doing so was her great passion.

In response to these vignettes, I found myself asking the Jungian question: what are these aggressive energies for? But I wanted to give it a feminist twist: what are these aggressive energies for, both in terms of inner, psychological priorities and in terms of identity formation (or perhaps refusals of the categories of identity themselves)? How do these dynamics interact with the ways in which female identity operates and is circulated in Western culture? (that being the culture which I have direct access to).

As a tactic for trying to answer these questions, I have drawn from Moira Gatens the notion that for feminist theory to be effective, it has to operate as a patchwork quilt, drawing what it needs from wherever it can be found. In this way it is possible to move beyond existing bodies of thought to say something meaningful about women's experience (1991: 1).

BROADENING THE DEFINITION OF AGGRESSION

Thus my choice has been to focus on what women's aggressive energies *are for*, rather than what they *are*. As well as being a standard Jungian tactic for engaging with unconscious material, this is also a deliberate political move, which I make in response to the fact that defining aggression or the energies associated with it is an unavoidably political act. Gerda Siann spells out the extent to which this is the case:

how a particular individual selects an approach or paradigm for [classifying or understanding aggression] depends on a host of factors. These range from those that might perhaps be regarded as situational, such as culture, era and discipline, to those that are more idiosyncratic, such as the value systems that the individual endorses and his or her temperamental disposition. Thus, to take an example, it seems to me impossible to extricate a deep belief that aggression is largely innate, and therefore inevitable, from the political implications of that belief. And it seems equally likely that those individuals who present an approach to aggression which argues for one clear and unambiguous root, whether it be innate or environmental, are likely to be people who find ambiguity not only theoretically unsatisfactory but personally threatening.

(1985: 225)

Aggression has been defined through a number of discourses, including anthropology, ethology, psychology and criminology. As Siann indicates each discourse emphasises different aspects of aggression, but almost invariably they take as given the *status quo* assumption that men 'do' aggression, sometimes 'to' women, although mostly 'at' each other in order to get something they want. As Campbell observes, '[m]en own aggression. They do not recognise the legitimacy of any other expression of it but their own' (Campbell, 1993: 54). Women's acts of aggression are seen as aberrant and pathological. Women's place in the schema of aggression is usually to be seen as the natural 'victims' of male aggression, males being thought to be innately more aggressive. Occasionally, women are cited as having aggression which is related to their hormonal cycles or to protectiveness towards their children, but women's aggressive energies remain somehow contrary to an assumed 'natural' order.[2]

Unsettling these assumptions to make room for accounts like Garner's has involved working from a much broader notion of aggression. Women's aggression is so rarely expressed in straightforward, externally focused, measurable ways. Another way of putting this might be that the traditional definitions of aggression are structured in ways which exclude and render invisible the locations and styles of women's aggression. Indeed, even talking about women's aggression is problematic – so little of it is clearly visible, and even less of it creates the kind of impact needed to rate on traditional scales as 'aggression'. Hence my choice to blur the language slightly and refer to 'women's aggressive energies' and 'women's aggressive fantasies' when I want to say something about women's experience, and 'aggression' when I want to refer to more traditional definitions, usually structured around male socialisation. Occasionally, I refer to women's aggressive energies as aggression, but usually only when I feel that the context makes it clear that I mean the enlarged concept of aggression that I am seeking to develop.

Women's aggressive energies show themselves in no-go zones of identity:

places where female identity cracks or breaks up, and it is not always obvious that the resultant fragments are connected. I suggest that shards of women's inner lives such as self-hatred, erotic rape fantasies and elements of eating disorder (and disordered eating) contain a connective, and potentially transformative unconscious thread of aggression.

Numerous authors have examined the actions of 'monstrous women' – women who kill or act sociopathically.[3] Again, however, this takes us back into traditional, masculine socialisation-focused models of aggression. I am more interested in the aggressive energies of ordinary women – where these energies turn up in their inner dialogue, in their fantasies, dreams, fears and longings, how this relates to the ways in which women live their lives, and what choices are available to them on a moment-to-moment basis. In order to bring these kinds of aggressive energies into focus I take as a starting point Andrew Samuels' definition of aggressive fantasy:

> Aggressive fantasy promotes a vital style of consciousness . . . Aggressive fantasy has much to do with our desire to know; it is not, in itself, completely bloodstained and unreflective. . . . Aggressive fantasy can bring into play that interpersonal separation without which the word 'relationship' would have no meaning. In this sense, aggressive fantasy may want to make contact, get in touch, relate. . . . Aggressive fantasy forces an individual to consider the conduct of personal relations. When one fantasizes an aggressive response to one's desires on the part of the other, one is learning something about that other as a being with a different but similar existence to one's own. Without aggressive fantasy, there would simply be no cause for concern about other people and so aggressive fantasy points beyond ruthlessness to discover the reality and mystery of persons. 'It is only when intense aggressiveness exists between two individuals that love can arise'.
>
> (1989: 208–209, quoting Storr)

Samuels' definition opens up a more interior, psychological understanding of aggression, but it also emphasises the relational, moral dimensions of aggressive fantasy as it brings us up against the Otherness of the Other. These dimensions emerge in Garner's account because what she offers is not a bald account of the thrill of aggression, but the psychological possibilities which emerge from engaging with her own aggressive energies and fantasies.

In a follow-on essay, 'The Feel Of Steel 2' (2001a), Garner finds out that she is expected to fence in the Inaugural Veteran's Section of a State fencing competition. She tries to get out of it, but her coach will not let her. The day of the competition arrives with muggy, 30°C weather, and she pulls on the mask – heavier than her practice one, with darker wires, smaller holes and a more spongily padded bib than she is used to. Garner describes sweat trickling through her hair, and dripping off her as she dons the layers of competition clothing. She faces a Sherman tank-like man from the country, who swats her blows like a mosquito. Just as we expect her to start to withdraw in the face of anticipation of a humiliating, ugly defeat, she writes: '[h]e wiped me out. I shook his hand in bliss' (2001a: 205).

Then, as the tournament went on:

> The longer we fenced in the awful heat, the cooler my head became. I felt *daring*. I didn't care if I lost but I went all out to win. My mind, normally so scattered and fleeting, tuned itself to my body. I grasped for the first time in my life what tactical thinking might be, how I could vary my attacks, feint and wait and spring a surprise. I saw in a series of bright flashes what was required, what I might one day be capable of, if I stuck at this.
>
> (2001a: 205–206; original italics)

Garner's text points to the extraordinary transformation which comes from being able to play over her own aggressive desires again and again, until there is a shift in her capacity to think. Garner's commitment to exploring her own aggressive energies and the outer edges of her capacity to stay with them enables her to keep going without being overcome by shame, humiliation, sense of helplessness, frustration or despair. Through this, I would suggest that she is able to be totally absorbed in the moment – without self-judgement or self-criticism. She simply no longer cares what the Other thinks of her. Garner has forged an amalgam of aggression and curiosity – a passionate desire to learn about herself, which she is exploring relationally. Hence, perhaps, her bliss while shaking hands with the man who has beaten her, and has provided her with the opportunity to learn something vital (in both senses) about herself.

Most importantly, Garner is not interested in winning – simple notions of competition and power are not her focus. Instead, she is after a different kind of power: genuine power 'within', rather than power 'over'. Thus she describes getting a bronze medal for her participation as a moment of 'radiant companionship'. Garner is not exploring aggression in order to beat others, but to come closer, to know herself and others better.

This fits with Amy's trajectory in analysis; what emerged for her was that in order to find out what she wanted in life and to be better able to support her adult children emotionally, she needed to get into muscular emotional and psychological tussles with people, and that she longed for friends to meet her in this and to engage with it as a central aspect of relationship and love. I suspect that it is also part of what black feminist Audre Lorde is asking for when she makes her plea to white women to confront her chronic anger (Tietjens Meyers, 1997: 212), and what Lorde is also talking about when she writes that anger between peers births change (Tietjens Meyers, 1997: 204).

Garner wisely explores the limits of her aggressive capacities in a place where the gradients are favourable: a fencing class is much safer than being a female teacher dealing with violent children or adolescents, or in a violent domestic situation. I suggest, however, that ordinary women explore their own aggressive energies and fantasies in less apparent ways all the time, and often in unfavourable circumstances. While circumstances may vary, there is an area of overlap, which is the frame of mind in which aggressive energies are most likely to flip over into a vehicle for breakthrough. This emotional space is often arrived at through some form of disciplined psychological work and Radical Buddhist nun Robina Courtin sketches a Buddhist perspective on the kind of emotional framework in which such a breakthrough is possible.

While being interviewed on Australian national radio, Courtin explains that the Buddhist emphasis is on learning to distinguish between the negative, neurotic, I-based use of energy and other potential uses of the kind of strong energy which can manifest as anger, or, if configured differently, as compassion. She lists the characteristics of energy coming from such a negative state of mind as:

> it comes from a huge sense of I, it comes from fear, it's narrow, it's a sense of separateness, and it wants to harm.
>
> (Courtin, interviewed by Rachel Kohn, 2003)

Garner's story describes the non-neurotic, positive use of strong energy – her aggression is expressed with a minimal sense of I, very little fear, great breadth of vision and willingness to engage as fully as possible, and without the desire to harm herself or the Other. From this place, aggression becomes a point of connection and expansion.

The female psyche offers a vast array of points of engagement with these energies, many of which are hard to see as the start of potentially valuable journeys, because of the way in which female identity has traditionally been viewed. As mentioned earlier, self-hatred can offer just such a point of engagement, although it can be hard to recognise it as such, and hard to keep a clear eye on the seeds of agency embedded in it. This book offers a way of seeing the value in these points of connection through aggressive fantasy, and some ways of thinking about how to take up the invitations they offer.

HIDDEN AGGRESSION AND AGENCY

But before embarking on an exploration of the covert images of women's aggressive energies which dominate the chapters that follow, I want to introduce some overt images to amplify the aggression-agency link I am making. A woman who had read a paper of mine contacted me and recounted the following dream. The dreamer is larking about with some friends, as though at the end of a school term (but as adults). They create an explosion and run for their lives. Later conversations reveal a rumour that someone suicided in the explosion – remains were found. The dreamer is very concerned about whether or not to confess, and whether she will be caught if she does not. She is also worried by some splashes of the explosive material on her body, which she notices later and feels that others must have seen. The horror of the dream left the dreamer profoundly unsettled.

Another woman who participated in a seminar described a dream in which she saw an unknown man standing at the edge of a cliff. He lifted his hand to wave at her in a non-threatening way. She suddenly found her body being lifted into the air, against her will so that she was arranged like a torpedo, with her right arm stretched out like a battering ram. She felt her face contort in murderous hostility; her body was carried by an incredible force straight ahead towards this man, intent in killing him, even though she had no desire to do so.

In a similar vein, David Hart describes the following incident that occurred in the life of a male analysand of his:

> This man was on vacation far away from home and from analysis, in fact on a trek in the mountains of Nepal, when a decisive event occurred. He was resting in a mountain pass over an abyss when there walked by him a Sherpa carrying an immense load of baggage. My client had a sudden, almost over-powering urge to push this little man off the pass and into the abyss. He struggled with the temptation and the moment passed: the Sherpa went by. But he was left with a shattering realization of what he could actually do to another person, not merely, as before, of what others were always doing to him . . . he had a new and vivid sense of himself *as the agent of his life and not merely as a reactive victim.*
>
> (1997: 97–98; italics added)

Note again the connection between aggressive fantasy and agency. Furthermore, awareness of one's capacity for destructive expressions of aggression does not necessarily make one more violent: in the case of Hart's analysand, it brings to his attention the violence done by imagining oneself to be merely a reactive victim. As Samuels suggests, aggressive fantasy becomes the basis of moral consideration.

I would say, however, that such interpretations, while true for both genders, are often much harder to access and build on for women. Again, this is because of the structure of female identity and the way in which femaleness has been taken to be synonymous with non-aggression (as both have traditionally been defined). Clearly this traditional arrangement is false: women do have aggressive energies, and struggle to find ways of engaging with them and learning about the amalgams they can form.

Often women's aggressive fantasies and impulses are well disguised, barely acknowledged, and encoded in what might, at first sight, appear to be a fantasy of romance; close inspection, however, reveals intricate systems of expression and management of aggression. Tania Modleski comments on the appeal of Harlequin Romances:

> A great deal of satisfaction in reading these novels comes, I am convinced, from the elements of a revenge fantasy, from our conviction that the woman is bringing the man to his knees and that all the while he is being so hateful, he is internally grovelling, grovelling, grovelling . . .
>
> (1984: 45)

More frequent are women's 'victim' fantasies, and it is these which dominate this book because they are the more traditionally socially sanctioned (and therefore far more common) vehicle that women use to explore aggression. My reasons for being loath to label women's 'victim fantasies' masochistic are discussed later. What needs to be said at this stage is that labelling them in this way obscures a link I want to draw to the foreground, that is, the connection between women's aggressive fantasies and women's sense of their own agency. Through her discussion of a dream of her own, Marie Louise von Franz, an early analysand and subsequently fellow analyst of Carl Jung, provides an important clue for thinking about these matters which forms the basis of Chapter 2. von Franz's dream is a classic 'victim' dream, but she makes the link between it and her creativity and agency, and in so doing, I suggest that she takes responsibility for the aggressive energy in the dream and the question of the self-destructive amalgams it had formed.

APPRECIATING AGGRESSION

Ultimately, it is women's hidden levels of aggression and aggressive fantasy that I am most interested in. Specifically: why does women's aggression end up being expressed so often in self-hateful, and apparently masochistic imagery? How do such shapings and expressions conceal, promote or destroy possibilities of agency? How can such imagery be engaged with so as to bring out the creative, connective, enlivening possibilities that Garner encounters in her own aggressive energies?

But before proceeding with this exploration, I need to outline some positions and assumptions which exploring women's aggressive fantasies have led me to. First, a key dimension of understanding individuals' struggles with themselves and others is the breadth and depth of their repertoire for creative engagement with their own aggressive energies and those of others, as well as the extent to which they can use these energies in enlivening and relational ways. Here I take my measure from Bersani's reading of Freud which is that in *Civilization and Its Discontents* we 'don't move *from* love *to* aggressiveness . . . rather, love is redefined, re-presented, *as* aggressiveness' (Bersani 1986: 20–21, original italics). Translating this into everyday life, one might say that a hallmark of a good relationship is the capacity to enjoy a really muscular, 'down to the wire' disagreement from time to time, and know that it is not only safe to do so, but that committed, aggressive engagement is an expression of one's own deepest love, and, likewise, that of the Other's deepest love too.

The second assumption is that 'aggression' is shorthand for certain kinds of energies which are, in themselves, 'value neutral', but tend to focus around the relentless nature of aliveness and desires for agency. Again, Samuels provides an insight when he quotes Tom Steel: 'aggression wants to bite, tear, smash, explode, find alternatives and push on to new territory' (1993: 163). This comment points out the creative possibilities and push towards embodied agency which dwells within aggression, alongside its destructive and annihilatory potentials. What matters are the amalgams formed between aggressive energies and other energies, and the degree of consciousness which can be brought to them. For example, an aggression/love/curiosity amalgam could express itself as creative passion. Alternatively, an aggression/hatred amalgam might express itself as an outburst of physical violence in certain circumstances, or violent withdrawal in other circumstances. Here, I am including in the term 'circumstances' the gender and social position of the protagonist(s): it is socially more acceptable for men to express an aggression/hatred amalgam in violence, while it has traditionally been more acceptable for women to express such an amalgam as a cutting withdrawal.

Repertoire of expression and use of aggression is so central to identity that it is even possible to argue that its range and style of performance are key indicators of a person's gender, class, ethnic background and choice of sexual object. The phenomenon of middle-class, professional men going to soccer matches in order to be involved in brawls between fans may be a kind of subculture tourism – making excursions into groups where the rules around where and how aggression (and also violence) can be expressed may be quite different to those attached to other areas of their lives.

The third point develops from the preceding suggestion that the process of defining aggression is political. As a consequence, the definitions of aggression, which are embedded in psychological theories, are also political entities, carrying with them social values and assumptions about what constitutes the best social order, and the ideal citizen. When I started this project, I looked to object relations theories of aggression for understanding. Eventually I gave up, realising that I could learn more about aggression and the range of emotional amalgams it can form from popular culture than I could from reading object relations theorists. Two particular sources of insight stood out: the first was stand-up comedians, much of whose effectiveness seems to me to rest on a capacity to engage with their own aggressive energies and the aggressive dynamics of their audience with style and daring. Different performers handle these aggressive energies differently, channelling them towards different ends, moving them through different amalgams and different tones in idiosyncratic ways. Also of note is how often stand-up comics weave their humour together around places where our performance of identity fails.

The second source was listening to rock music from as many bands, styles and eras as possible, but with a focus on those who were most creative and diverse in their engagement with amalgams of aggressive energies. Indeed, careful listening reveals rock as something of a random, but broad-ranging exploration of amalgams of aggression, and the different kinds of energetic and erotic effects these amalgams can be used to produce. What comes through in rock music and is missing in object relations is the raw pleasure associated with the sheer aliveness of aggressive energy. The energies associated with amalgams of aggression are pleasurable in their own right, and this is what Garner expresses so well. These pleasures resist and outmanoeuvre bourgeois anxieties about aggression and desire, anxieties which are revealed by the object relations desire to move rather too quickly towards positions which are considered more psychologically 'developed'. Above all, rock music shows how aggression is not just 'aggression' in the object relations way. It is 'aggression and frustration', or 'aggression and a desire to explore power and sexual charisma', or 'aggression as part of the thrill of being alive', and so on.

OBJECT RELATIONS AND WOMEN'S AGGRESSIVE ENERGIES

This kind of *appreciation* of aggression, its potentials, its amalgams and pleasures is a sensibility which is missing from object relations and a comment from Samuels provides an account of why this was so:

> Object relations theories unwittingly perpetuate the political *status quo*. The findings of depth psychologists are, inevitably, embedded in a particular cultural and sociopolitical matrix and hence cannot avoid taking on a prescriptive as well as a descriptive project. Object relations theories focus on intrapsychic and interpersonal explanations for personality development and dysfunction. They tend to rule out sociopolitical or other collective aspects of psychological suffering. The version of personality that object relations presents, with its accent on the decisive part played by early experiences, maternal containment, and the move toward the depressive position or stage of concern, is, in many senses, little more than a reproduction of the kind of personality that the culture which surrounds object relations already valorizes.

> (1993: 275–276)

My interest is in how and where these energies are felt and lived by ordinary women, and the challenge of finding a language for exploring these matters, which does not import the conservative identity politics of object relations. Samuels' definition of aggressive fantasy (quoted earlier) is an important first step towards this because it opens up a way of thinking about the inter-relationship between the interior, psychological dimensions of a woman's experience of her own aggressive energies, alongside the ways in which iden-tity politics seek to set the parameters of her experience of herself and the world around her.

Shortly, I will resume my critique of object relations, but first, I want to return to the theme of how the production of gender has been entwined with the definition and positioning of aggression, and introduce some illustra-tions. These processes of mutual definition are central to the creation and stabilisation of Western identity as we know it. As the parameters of identity change over time, the standards and practices around women's expression of aggression and agency change with them.

Consider how, in Jane Austen's eighteenth century *Pride and Prejudice*, Elizabeth Bennett is discussed in terms of ridicule by the young women who are her social superiors. Her 'crime' is to walk across the fields to Netherfield Park to visit her sister who is sick there, and arrive with a good deal of mud on her petticoats (1987: 81–82). The women, who are wealthy socialites, recall the state Elizabeth's clothes were in when she arrived, and make fun of them. But the member of their party who is most important socially, Mr Darcy, fails to join in this 'sport'.

On the contrary, his comments indicate that when Elizabeth arrived, he had not noticed the state of her clothes, but saw, instead, that the exercise had brightened her eyes (1987: 82). Austen writes '– A short pause followed this speech, and Mrs Hurst [one of the society women] began again' (1987: 82). At this point Mrs Hurst resumes her character assassination of Elizabeth and her family. The pause of Mrs Hurst's surprise which Austen puts before this resumption of the attack is a mark of surprise, possibly shock, that Elizabeth's agency – her desire to be the source of her own thoughts, actions and movement – did not make her an object of ridicule for Mr Darcy too. It should have made Elizabeth unacceptable to any right-thinking man, but Mr Darcy's response rather takes the wind out of Mrs Hurst's sails. In order to be recognisable as a 'good' young woman, Elizabeth should have been performing her role within its socially ascribed limits, displaying her frailty and fine sensibilities in a suitable fashion.

At a subsequent meeting, the other society lady (Miss Bingley) teases Eliz-abeth, saying that Elizabeth despises cards, and is a great reader, taking no pleasure in anything else. Again, this is an attack on Elizabeth for being independent-minded. One of the great appeals of *Pride and Prejudice* to a woman is that Elizabeth's wilful self-reliant agency, with its honest, sharp-eyed edge of intelligent feistiness actually makes her more attractive, not less, to Mr Darcy. Here is spirited determination and the aggression which underlies it being recognised as love, and forming the basis of a fairy-tale happy ending, instead of damning Elizabeth to spinsterhood.

By Victorian times this fantasy of women's physical and emotional frailty had become a significant plank in the argument against giving women the vote. Janet Sayers points out that Edward Cope, the American naturalist and palaeontologist, argued that the propriety of women's suffrage was out of the question since women were physically incapable of carrying into execution any law they might enact (1982: 70). Even more explicit was the English bacteriologist Sir Almroth Wright who argued that since women could not effectively back up their votes by force they had no right to parliamentary franchise (Sayers, 1982: 70). By defining femininity as synonymous with non-aggression, only male persons (those whose access to aggression is classed as 'natural') have a right to a say in the governing of the realm because only they can fight for the realm. Through this fragment we see how the defining of aggression and femininity in relation to each other has been part of creating the space in which masculinity has been defined, along with the allocation of different realms of power to men and women. These fantasies of difference are then read back into sexed bodies and naturalised – given the status of 'natural' and 'true' – with extensive systems of meaning being built off the back of them.

As I will argue in subsequent chapters, these structures of identity impact the conscious and unconscious landscapes which we experience as our psyche. My use of aspects of Jung's work is based on the way in which his sense of interiority as a landscape meets this view and provides a vehicle for its exploration. Most importantly, there are aspects of Jung's work which can be drawn together to provide psychoanalytically-based tools for accessing the felt, embodied and usually largely unconscious workings of these structures of identity. Accessing these workings, and the political struggles embedded in them provides a way of engaging psychoanalytically with material which lies outside the socio-political *status quo*. This matters because it is the domain where women's aggressive fantasies and energies currently reside.

In Chapter 2 I will return to this Jungian image of the psyche as a landscape which is encountered through processes such as dreams, active imagination[4], or analytic and therapeutic relationships which are structured deliberately to try to make that landscape more accessible. Jung's own work, as well as that of many of his pupils, is deeply problematic in terms of the identity politics which it inherits, and I also take this up in Chapter 2. Nonetheless, a strand can be drawn out from Jung's work and that of his followers which supports a radical, contextualised approach to the psyche and I weave this together with selected threads of post-structuralist and post-modern thought.

But before doing so, it is necessary to flesh out more fully why my work does not use object relations theory as a primary frame of reference, and instead only draws on certain aspects of it. Put simply, there are significant philosophical and practical problems with the lack of space within object relations to examine the fantasies of womanhood and motherhood on which the theory rests. These fantasies about female identity have political histories and political objectives which reside in the 'unconscious' of object relations, closing off important thinking spaces. In order to discuss these objectives, I will sketch in some aspects of the history of object relations.

Lisa Appignanesi and John Forrester comment that Helen Deutsch's reinterpretation of Freud became the new Freudian orthodoxy after the Second World War (Appignanesi and Forrester, 1993: 440). Deutsch's view was that femininity was synonymous with passivity and masochism, and Elizabeth Badinter draws out what this meant in terms of the period's orthodox psychoanalytic view of what it took for a girl to become a woman. First the girl must accept passivity, in particular sexual passivity, constructed as an inevitable consequence of the period's notions of female physiology and fantasies about its 'passively penetrated' role in heterosexual intercourse. Second, in order to adjust to her passive role and prepare herself for motherhood, a girl had to be masochistic. This was based on the assumption that she had as much innate aggression as a boy, but must turn it inward and eroticise that choice in order to fulfil her biological function of motherhood. Third, what saved a girl from her own masochistic tendencies (which might otherwise have threatened her ego) was her narcissism, which stepped in and secured her ego by intensifying the girl-woman's love of herself (Badinter, 1981: 268–272). Deutsch also believed that birth was the acme of sexual experience for a woman, to which nothing could compare (Segal, 1994: 127; Mitchell, 1974: 127).

Deutsch's equation of femininity with passivity and masochism is important because it shows up the extent to which the psychoanalytic concept of masochism is shot through with fantasies about female identity. Consequently, using the concept of masochism to analyse women's psychology explicitly or implicitly reintroduces the fantasies of femininity that are embedded in its formation, hence the absence of its use as an analytic tool in this book.

Also problematic is the way in which Deutsch's reading of femininity was incorporated into the Kleinian model of motherhood. As Appignanesi and Forrester point out 'Volume II of [Deutsch's] *The Psychology of Women* is one long paean of praise to the mother, both as privileged first object and as ultimate feminine destiny. It is also the point where Klein and Deutsch are at one' (1993: 440). Indeed, for Klein, as for Deutsch, femininity was essentially maternal (Klein, 1989: 217; Mitchell, 1986: 79–80).

Object relations theorists working through Klein inherit not only the ghost of Deutsch, but also Klein's belief that babies are born with an inherent unconscious knowledge of the existence of the penis as well as the vagina. As sexuality asserts itself, Klein:

more than Freud, argues that biology is destiny. The girl simply 'knows' that she has a vagina and so will assume her natural femininity ... Klein's view of sexual difference as genitally based is finally conservative. She reaffirms a binary relation between masculinity and femininity and insists on the innately heterosexual destiny of each sex. ... Even though it gives the mother more power within the child's phantasy, Klein's work provides no cultural explanation for sexual difference and the difficulty the girl has in establishing her 'femininity'.

(Doane and Hodges, 1992: 12–13)

As Walkerdine points out, this is the point at which Freud's inability to fully resolve his readings of human sexuality is lost. Gone are the complexities of his comments that '[t]he constitution [of the little girl] will not adapt itself to its function [heterosexual femininity] without a struggle (Freud, 1933, p. 117)' (Walkerdine, 1990: 88).

In Klein's work, the 'real' mother is so marginalised that she becomes a figure with barely any agency or subjectivity (Doane and Hodges, 1992: 29), other than that which she expresses in fulfilling her feminine destiny, by becoming a mother. Winnicott takes this a step further. The woman who becomes a mother ' "naturally" denies her own agency: she *desires* to be without subjectivity so that she can be used as a living mirror by the child' (Doane and Hodges, 1992: 29, original italics).

Doane and Hodges expand on this:

Winnicott's description of mothering, which also precisely coincides with his description of womanhood, reduces the sphere of woman's possibilities ... At first glance, motherhood looks like a position of full subjectivity ... But Winnicott's insistence on the fullness of the woman's role as mother requires the redefinition of such issues as freedom, autonomy, and desire. So women are told that their freedom consists in the move from their father's house to their husband's, where they are 'free' to 'arrange and decorate the way [they feel] like doing' ('Their Standards' 87). A woman becomes autonomous, Winnicott tells his mothers, only when she marries, because marriage allows her to feel 'proud' and to 'discover what she is like when she is captain of her own fate'.

(1992: 25)

The realities of women's lives are changing: families are much smaller and most women who are mothers perform the role of mothering only some of the time. Also the number of women having children in Westernised countries is dropping dramatically. For example, the Australian Bureau of Statistics report for 1997 showed that '[o]n 1993 rates, one in four women (27 per cent) will have no children, compared to 9 per cent of women who went through the baby boom (those born in 1936) and 18 per cent of those who went through the great depression (those born in 1909)' (ABS, 1997). These kinds of dramatic changes in the structure and practice of female identity are difficult for object relations, with its implicit assumption that femininity and motherhood are more or less synonymous, to engage with.

Feminist object relations theorists who have tried to respond to these changes run up against the problematic, unanalysed fantasies about motherhood and female identity embedded in object relations. Rozsika Parker points out how Nancy Chodorow's theory of maternally deprived femininity is based exclusively on the loving aspects of the maternal relationship, and that the absence of hate and ambivalence results in an incomplete and unsatisfactory theory (1996: 160). Sayers also points out that the works of Chodorow and Benjamin are problematic from a feminist perspective, since built into the object relations theory at the core of each of their projects is a neglect of social context, which is so central to feminist analysis (1986: 72–78).

Likewise, Jessica Benjamin's *The Bonds of Love* (1988) is haunted by the same object relations ghosts, with the result that women vanish. Lynne Segal provides a description of how this happens. I will quote it at length because of the way in which it describes how object relations narratives render invisible so much that is important in the discussion of women's experience.

> There seem at least three problems with Benjamin's analysis of masochistic fantasy [which is based on *The Story of O*. As a result of these problems Benjamin's work] falls well short of utilizing the potential of psychoanalytic reflection on sexuality (as, it must be admitted, does most contemporary psychoanalytic writing on the topic of heterosexuality). The complexity of the social is ignored, reduced to generalizations about fixed relations of power – as though to be less powerful in society, as mothers so often are, is to be, and to be perceived to be, simply submissive and powerless. The psychic is no longer layered and contradictory, but thought to mirror directly what is seen as the nature of the social – as though to fantasise submission is no different from the experience of actual social subordination. Finally, sexuality is not analysed in her account as a multifaceted but nevertheless distinct and autonomous mental experience, constructed out of the psychic presentations of individual histories of bodily sensation and pleasure. Indeed, when seen by Benjamin as the enjoyment of erotic submission, sexuality is not about bodies and pleasures at all, but the search for subjectivity. Here, women's sexuality can only re-enact their total identification with 'the self-sacrificing mother': 'it is a replication of the maternal attitude itself.' Women's sexual desire, it appears, has not so much been reclaimed by Benjamin, as removed. She ends up with everything to say about the construction of gender identity, but little to offer on women's complex

autoerotic or interpersonal sexual encounters, nor even on women's sexual fantasy.

(1994: 148–149)

Such ghosts are not inherently problematic; they are the very stuff of psychoanalytic process. The problem is that object relations theorists have not accepted as imperative the task of analysing these ghosts and working through the clinical consequences of the splits and fears of which they are the manifestations.[5] A few clinical theorists, such as Rozsika Parker and Adam Phillips, have begun this project, but mainstream object relations is still far from acknowledging the problematic identity and social politics which it is immersed in and actively perpetuates. At the same time, object relations' insight into intrapsychic processes such as splitting and projective identification is invaluable. These insights can, however, be separated out from the wider object relations framework of moral and developmental ideals, and redeployed to support identity projects which do not coincide with the social *status quo*. In Chapter 6 I will return to this discussion of the limitations of object relations, focusing specifically on its narrow and problematic understandings of aggression.

FOUCAULT, LACAN AND FEMINISM

Next, however, I will outline the elements which I draw from anti-humanist approaches and why I have not taken them up as a primary frame of reference either. Foucault's work in particular offers powerful tools for political analysis, and Margrit Shildrick summarises them as follows:

1. Foucault argues that contrary to traditional assumptions, the forms of power that shape lives do not seek to destroy, but to form and maintain, thus perpetuating themselves.
2. Such powers are susceptible to local resistance and redistribution. In the light of this, Shildrick observes that Foucault's tactic of uncovering the archaeology of thought offers the possibility that '... discovering alternative systems of thought profoundly disturbs and deflates the putative inevitability of patriarchal domination'.

(1997: 48)

It is these aspects of Foucauldian thought which I will be drawing on indirectly throughout this project because they open up the possibility of seeing women's aggressive energies as an alternative system which disturbs and deflates traditional constructions of women as inevitably victims of life in general, and men's aggression in particular.

On the other hand, my reading of Foucault is that there is a significant political problem for feminists in his push to reject categories such as female/ male and the identity politics and emancipatory struggles thereof (1980, 1990, 1990a, 1992). This reading coincides with that of Lynne Segal (1994: 187), hence my selective use of his work, and also my choice to access Foucault through feminist thinkers such as Judith Butler and Valerie Walkerdine who have taken Foucault's questions and reworked them so as to serve feminist interests.

Turning to Lacan, Patrick Fuery discusses Lacan's reliance on the notion of the split subject (1995: 12) and his use of the notion of alterity (Otherness) (1995: 13). Given that women's aggressive fantasies and impulses are alienated from much feminist and therapeutic discussion (indeed, they often function as 'Other' to feminine identity), such a model has clear attractions. Lacan's discussions of desire are also useful in terms of how they entwine the formation of the social subject with unresolvable experiences of the Other, thereby opening up the possibility of drawing psychoanalytic thought out from the intrapsychic into an interpsychic and political arena. Similarly, Lacan's engagement with split subjectivity and the unresolvability of desire provides a language for some aspects of experience which are relevant to women's aggressive energies, for example, his notion of *jouissance*. When I take this up in Chapter 4, it will be read in a more politicised, feminist form than is usually the case.

The political problems with Lacan's ideas are, however, such that his work will not serve as a primary resource for this work (Lacan: 1982, 1982a). Again, Segal summarises these problems, arguing that academic feminism's use of Lacan's ideas perpetuates phallocentrism since Lacan 'frees understandings of sexual difference from any biological or sociological reductionism, only to freeze them forever within a universal symbolic order unaffected by either personal biography and bodily encounter, or the specificities of historical and cultural context' (1994: 134). Likewise, Janet Sayers discusses the limitations of post-Lacanian thought, pointing out that it is problematic for feminism because it ultimately deconstructs the category 'woman' and thus dismantles the feminist project itself (1986: 94–95).

An echo of these lines of criticism can be found in Charles Taylor's rejection of the radical deconstructionist position as untenable as a basis of humane, political thought. Taylor also points out that Foucault ultimately shifted position himself, dropping his stance of neutrality towards the end of his life in favour of the aesthetic notion of the self as a work of art (1989: 489). Put simply, I would not be comfortable working exclusively from an anti-humanist perspective as a clinician, and would not seek out a strictly anti-humanist analysis if I were in emotional distress because of the lack of engagement with interior, intrapsychic dynamics which I experience as the accessible and sometimes slightly mutable ebb and flow of my identity. Consequently, I draw selectively on the insights available through these systems of analysis, rather than take them as a primary frame of reference.

AGGRESSION AND ASSERTION

Another body of theory which I have chosen not to use, because of the conservative identity politics embedded in it, is that of assertiveness training. AT, as it is generally known, makes a distinction between 'being assertive', which is seen as good, and 'being aggressive', which is seen as bad. Debbie Cameron points out that the origins of assertiveness training was in behaviour therapy at the end of the 1940s, when it was proposed as a pragmatic, brief intervention alternative to long, drawn-out, understanding-based psychoanalytic therapy. The behaviourists' focus was on 'getting rid of the patient's "dysfunctional" behaviour and substituting something more "appropriate" ' (1994/95: 9).

Cameron points out that assertiveness training aims to help people communicate their 'needs, desires and feelings clearly, directly and honestly (doing it indirectly is "manipulative" and not doing it at all is "passive"), but without infringing other people's right to *their* needs and feelings (which means not being "aggressive")' (1994/95: 9, original italics). The underlying view is that assertiveness is a balanced, healthy position between passivity and aggression.

Clearly, it is valuable for a woman to develop skills that enable her to represent herself honestly and effectively while maintaining the sociopolitical *status quo*, but what is unattainable from within the assertiveness discourse is any kind of critique of the *status quo*. Cameron goes on to draw out some of these problems, pointing out that a 1991 clinical psychology textbook argues that men who batter women can be good candidates for assertiveness training. This text states that it is, however, potentially very risky to recommend assertion to women who are in violent relationships since the result may be to provoke 'further violence'. No analysis of the politics of this position is offered. The author of the textbook '. . . also cites with approval an [assertiveness training] course designed for Puerto Rican women, from which the topic of "saying no" to male partners had been removed' (1994/95: 9). Cameron summarises, arguing that the assertiveness training model is:

> traditionally conceived in the image of 'mainstream societal values', which are white, middle-class, individualistic and male. . . . The common thread running through this sorry history is that AT [Assertiveness Training] aligns itself with the *status quo*. It aims to make people 'better' in the sense of closer to whatever the current ideal is.
>
> (1994/95: 9)

Likewise, Campbell points out that assertiveness training can only help women in the short term before the point where tears and anger overwhelm them (1993: 159). What is also missing from the notion of assertion is the kind of change which engagement with aggression and aggressive energies can offer, in the ways described by Garner. The capacity for deep connection with self and Other which these much more engaged and risky energies bring with them is lost in the desire to keep situations within socially accepted boundaries.

GENDER AND AGGRESSION

I am not suggesting some form of political analysis as a substitute for psychoanalytic psychotherapy, although I do see problems with much psychoanalytic thought when it comes to taking the political nature of subjective experience into account. Anne Campbell's work on gender and aggression illustrates the point. Campbell's research shows that boys learn the 'rules' around aggression from their culture:

> [a boy] must learn whom he can fight, what constitutes an adequate provocation, how to conduct his violence, and when he can reasonably expect condemnation, recognition or glory for his actions. . . .
>
> But what about girls? What explanation of their relative placidity can we offer, if not genetics? Women are not born calm. There is ample evidence that women experience anger as often and as deeply as men. As babies they cry and scream just as much. But they learn different lessons than boys do. Whereas a boy moves away from his mother's condemnatory, expressive view of aggression into a world of men, where its instrumental value is understood, the girl makes no such change. She remains selectively tuned in to a female wavelength, searching for clues to femininity and to aggression. But she finds little to examine. After her mother's early censuring of overt displays of aggression, there is a gaping void. *The most remarkable thing about the socialization of aggression in girls is its absence. Girls do not learn the right way to express aggression; they simply learn not to express it.*
>
> (1993: 20, italics added)

Campbell's research indicates that there are minimal differences between men's and women's internal anger responses: in a typical week, men feel angry between six and seven times, while women feel angry between five and six times (1993: 71). But there are crucial differences both in terms of how men and women experience their own anger, and in terms of how much space they experience themselves as having to 'work' with such feelings.

Campbell writes that women rate their anger as being as intense as men's, but they believe that theirs is out of proportion to the precipitating events (1993: 71–72). Also of note is the observation that for men there appears to be no correlation between intensity of anger and the duration of recovery, while 'for women, the more furious they are, the longer it takes them to get over it' (1993: 71).

What emerges is how women are trained to restrain anger, so that (for example) tears become a viable means of expressing amalgams such as aggression and unbearable frustration, rather than lashing out. Men interviewed in Campbell's study talked of having been trained in a kind of aggression etiquette, with steps and retaliation protocols, based on desires for control of a situation or person (1993: 55–67). On the contrary, women in her study pointed out that feeling aggression and (for example) getting visibly angry felt like a loss of control, and it was read as such by other people (1993: 39–54).

Women customarily experience this loss of control as humiliating, and that humiliation can result in any number of defensive responses. One woman might work hard to ensure that she is never put back in such a humiliating position again. Another might grab onto a rhetoric of power which enables her to 'hit hard' at anyone or any system which poses a potential threat. The problem here is that fear, previous closely related experiences of humiliation, and aggression can harden into tough battle lines very quickly, creating situations which false pride makes it extremely difficult, if not impossible to dismantle. Kathleen Woodward gives an example in her article 'Anger . . . and Anger: From Freud to Feminism', where she discusses the problems of ' "righteous", habit forming anger':

> The paradigm of oppressor-oppressed, once so useful to feminism, is producing serious consequences of its own in terms of generational politics within feminism. With this paradigm in hand, younger women in the academy, for example, analyse their position in relation to older women 'in power' as that of the oppressed . . . Never mind that the general paradigm of oppressor-oppressed is inappropriate in this case. Certainly from this perspective 'anger' senselessly divides women from one another, creating smaller, oppositional groups. This is indeed a serious consequence of the politics of the authority of anger.
>
> (1996: 73–75)

So feminism too is struggling to find new ways of thinking about women's anger and aggression. Perhaps one clue is to consider Anne Campbell's work on women's and men's anger and aggression in which she argues that women experience aggression as a matter of *emotional expression*, while men experience it as a way of getting what they want. In other words, men use it *instrumentally* (1993: 7). In Woodward's example, perhaps the younger women have found a feminist rhetoric which gives them the tools to use their anger instrumentally. The problem is, however, that as Campbell argues, male socialisation creates space for boys to learn whom they can and cannot fight and some sense of retaliation protocol. The women Woodward is writing about are highly unlikely to have had access to these lessons, and consequently are likely to pick the wrong enemy and/or pick a weapon which is too big and use it to hit too hard.

Female socialisation provides little or no training in how to use a 'grey-scale' around aggression and attack or retaliation. The resultant tendency to go over the top in terms of response is well known: when women who are living in domestically violent situations finally snap, they frequently do not retaliate with what the legal system regards as 'appropriate force'. Instead, their response can be quite literally 'overkill', for example stabbing their assailant many times, rather than wounding him once in order to stop his attack. Clearly there is an issue here in terms of the legal system being built around male norms and male socialisation, but there is also an issue for feminism at the level of needing to support women to explore their own 'greyscale' of aggression, for example through working with women's aggressive fantasies.

Furthermore, Campbell's (1993) articulation of traditional differences between men's instrumental expression of aggression and women's expressive use of aggression is important in terms of the shape of this project. Put simply, most of the academic discourses which explore aggression (such as behavioural psychology, ethology, anthropology and primatology) lean towards the exploration of instrumental uses of aggression. As such, their suitability for use when exploring women's experiences of their own aggressive energies is questionable, which is why I rarely cite research from those fields in what follows. Those studies which do explore more expressive uses of aggression still tend to concentrate on their social or evolutionary value, rather than on the potential they offer the individual for psychological growth.

FEMINIST PATCHWORK QUILTING

Earlier, I mentioned that my tactics for gathering these threads and lacks together into an understanding of women's aggressive energies are borrowed from Moira Gatens' image of feminist theory-making as patchwork quilting (1991: 1). If so, the 'backing-cloth' for the patchwork quilt of theory that I am drawing together is undoubtedly post-Jungian, even though I critique Jungian and post-Jungian thought throughout. My loyalty to this and other analytic systems is, however, limited, and I take my measure on this from Elizabeth Grosz's comment that her reading of Deleuze was focused on making his work useful to *her* project, rather than on being faithful to his project (1994: 166). The same is true of my readings of Jung, Freud, Klein, Winnicott, Lacan, Foucault, Bersani, Samuels, Walkerdine, Butler and many others besides.

My post-Jungian backing cloth is also, however, shot through with a thread which comes from Valerie Walkerdine's work in the field of critical psychology. The reason for its inclusion is that without it, it would be too easy to assume (in the way that Segal points out that Benjamin does above) that the gradients in the social construction of identity are static and generate predictable power relations within and between realms of identity. There is, however, another reading, which I draw from Walkerdine's work in critical psychology where the distribution of power and the processes which structure identity are seen as kaleidoscoping, context-dependent interplays.

For example, stroppiness in women is commonly seen as dangerous and negative, while in men it is often seen as an expression of an original and individual mind. Walkerdine's work in critical psychology helps to draw out how (to use an analogy from the card game, bridge) a 'winning hand' can be turned into a 'losing hand' (finessed) by changes in the circumstances around it, and this will be returned to in Chapter 2. Diana Tietjens Meyers lists a range of standard responses to women's expressions of frustration or anger which illustrate how meaning can be reassigned in this way:

> Interpretive conventions furnish three mutually reinforcing strategies for coping with such anomalies. One strategy ascribes a different emotion to the woman. Anger is labelled hysterical rage; humiliation is labelled deference to male prerogatives; indignation is labelled snootiness. The second strategy explains away the emotion by ascribing a defective personality to the individual. Such a woman is insecure, nasty, charmless, humourless, and/or prudish. If all else fails, ascriptions of pathology – 'She's crazy' – are sure to close the discussion.
>
> (1997: 205)

Critical psychology shows that the meaning of what happens is determined by the discourse which is used as a lens through which to view events. Power operates at the level of determining which lenses are more easily available for viewing interactions, and which ones are rendered totally inaccessible. In terms of women's aggressive energies, there are few paradigms through which to view them as potentially meaningful and important and many through which they can be seen as ugly, unacceptable, absurd, or more often, simply irrelevant. Consequently, one of the factors which needs to be monitored when thinking about women's aggressive energies is what social processes and practices are determining the accessibility of an engaged and psychologically creative reading of those energies.

By way of illustration, in Chapter 4 I discuss the experience of one of the women who contributed to this project who was so outraged when a male acquaintance tried to sexually assault her that she shouted at him 'What the fuck do you think you are doing!!' She comments that her use of the word 'fuck' (which was not considered at all appropriate for a grammar school girl in the 1970s) 'shocked his socks off' and averted the assault. In other circumstances, with a different assailant, or coming from a different woman (or even the same woman in a different state of mind) this might well not have worked. But it did, and I am interested in how women *do* access and use their own aggressive energies in order to resist, subvert or undermine presumed 'natural' orders, such as those around gender and power differences.

Another assumption I make in this book is that the individual's desire is for agency as a productive lens through which to view both the psyche and theories about the psyche. Agency has traditionally been thought of as the capacity to act or operate power, and, as with aggression, this interpretation is inflected through traditional models of male experience, moving the emphasis towards 'acting' and away from 'the capacity to act'. Women's aggressive energies open up questions of when and how to act, and when and how to stay with the capacity to act. In terms of this project, therefore, agency needs to be extended to incorporate not just acts but also thoughts and psychosocio moral positions that are available in a given situation. As will emerge, this move reveals a tight linkage between agency, morality, aggression and love.

AGGRESSION AND MORAL IMAGINATION

My final assumption also relates to Samuels' earlier definition of aggressive fantasy. Samuels proposes a link between aggressive fantasy and what he calls moral imagination. He distinguishes between moral imagination and original morality, suggesting that if we get hooked up on the latter:

> our approach to problems that cry out for choice to be made will be 'by the book', correct, stolid and safe, reliable – but missing out on the nuances of the situation. If we are hooked on moral imagination, our one-sidedness will have a different tone: bags of ingenuity and so-called 'flexibility', responsiveness to the uniqueness of the situation – but without any real grounding, conviction, or moral muscle. To make any headway at all when things are tough and complicated, we need [a] blend of certainty and improvisation.
>
> (1989: 196)

Note how we do not move from original morality to moral imagination as a one-way developmental progression: the two states coexist, cooperating and conflicting with each other, demanding creative responses to their tensions. Samuels' discussion of moral processes is related to Jung's emphasis on the clinical significance of splits between the individual's personal ethics and the collective moral code, and the psychological illnesses which can ensue from these splits. The important point here is that aggressive fantasy is closely involved with the development of the moral imagination. Hart's account of his analysand's impulse to push the Sherpa off the cliff, and the kind of growth that arose from engagement with the demands this made on his moral imagination is a case in point.

Analytic explorations of personality damage or narcissistic defences encounter the analysand's experiences of and fantasies about inner and outer Otherness at every turn. With those encounters come questions about aggression, morality and relationship. Indeed Giles Clark suggests that in order to move away from a borderline personality configuration an analysand has to come into being as a moral agent.[6] For some people this represents a potentially unacceptable series of losses and the exploration of those losses, the analysand's capacities to mourn them and, perhaps, make something from them are all very much grist for the analytic mill. Indeed, this is one of the major points of difference between the clinical and theoretical explorations of Jung's work. It is possible to read Jung's work as a body of theory without needing to engage with the links he makes between moral tensions and psychological illness, but it is much harder to maintain that separation if one is using Jung as an internal object in the consulting room.

Clinically, these ideas offer a platform for engagement with material which women of all ages and social groups bring into analysis on a regular basis, although the potential for change expressed in that material is hard to access. Significant elements in the structure of female identity stand in the way, but inroads can sometimes be made. I am not offering help to clinicians about 'what to say' to patients. Nor am I attempting to create an overarching, systematic model of female identity or aggression. Instead, I am trying to offer images, elements of theory and stories which might open doors for clinicians to think about certain elements of women's struggles in a different way.

Chapter 2 explores the voice of women's inner critic, or self-hater, as documented by the first-generation Jungian women. These women described the operation of a woman's inner critic through their own experiences, as well as those of their analysands in a remarkably clear and honest way. Their descriptions are, however, embedded in the traditional Jungian model with its emphasis on the universal and ahistorical dimensions of the archetypal. This model is re-visioned as the chapter progresses, re-framing it in terms of processes of identity formation and identity politics in order to support a more political understanding of the phenomenon of the self-hater. The vehicle used for the re-visioning of archetype is Jung's interest in anima figures such as Salome and Rider Haggard's *She* (Ayesha). These female fantasy characters are explored through the lens of *fin-de-siècle* art, and what emerges is the way in which they functioned as containers of culturally specific, taboo desires. The implications of this run deeper than simply making Salome and Ayesha transient archetypal images of universal and ahistorical archetypal themes. The archetypal becomes instead a function of a given culture's practices of identity formation. In order to illustrate why depth psychological theories need to engage with the issue of identity politics, the chapter finishes with a vignette from the field of critical psychology which illustrates how and why intrapsychic accounts of an individual's psychological circumstances are inadequate.

Chapter 3 takes the theme of women's inner critic or self-hater further, and uses the kinds of resistances I encountered while researching women's aggressive energies as the basis of a research methodology. This meant taking the clinical concept of countertransference and applying it to material collected from 14 women who contributed material to this project. As a research tool, the notion of countertransference was, however, applied more broadly, so that the kinds of collapses and terrors encountered in the research process were used as the basis of understanding the subject being researched, that is, women's aggressive energies and fantasies. The process of articulating the resultant methodology brought with it the setting-out of a psychoanalytic theory of knowledge. The development of this theory raises questions about the ways in which our understandings of femininity and aggression are entwined with a cultural fantasy of the rational, moral social subject, who is tacitly assumed to be male.

Chapter 4 builds on the preceding chapter's more theoretical explorations, but amplifies them through the voices of the women who contributed material to the project around their use of rape fantasies for erotic purposes. This discussion raises questions about the nature of fantasy, the multiple layers and psychological positions which operate in such fantasies, and aggressive energies and fantasies as a form of female *jouissance*. It also raises questions about the violences involved in the formation of female identity, and different notions of agency available in different circumstances.

Chapter 5 looks at how women's aggressive energies reside in their bodies. A group experiment is discussed in which women were invited to explore their own experience of becoming visible to the Other. For many women this produced results which were surprisingly aggressive in their tone, and sometimes explosive. The cultural use of women's embodiment as a marker and container of space in which Others are agents is discussed. Themes such as women's use of clothes, fashion, makeup and the manipulation of appearance as a means of managing aggressive energies are also discussed.

Chapter 6 moves the discussion into the clinical arena, concentrating on the aggressive energies encountered when working with people with severe and chronic eating disorders. What emerges is that the extreme aggressive imagery which can arise either directly from working with people with such disorders or in associated countertransference material can be interpreted meaningfully. This is especially so if the connective *telos* of aggressive fantasy can be born in mind.

Chapter 7 looks at the responses that the women who contributed to the project gave as a result of having read the final draft of it. In effect, this was their response to my having made an interpretation (in the form of the final draft of my text) based on my countertransference reactions to their contributions. The theme of aggression and relationship, and aggression and social responsibility came through strongly in the women's second-round contributions.

Garner's discussion of her own aggressive energies opens up space for these explorations and questions, and in doing so her discussions are a political act. But this is politics at its best – it has a heart and a mind, it is engaging, and it is witty. It is also psychology at its best – open to, and engaged with inner and outer Otherness, full of the desire to learn about what is mentally, physically and emotionally possible for a human being who operates from a specific set of personal equations and in a given set of circumstances. What I want to document here are the ways in which 'ordinary' women struggle to connect to their own aggressive energies in these ways. In order to do so, I need to start by describing the post-Jungian backing cloth that I am using to hold this project together, shot through, as it is, both with critique of Jungian and post-Jungian theory, and with threads from other theories.

Chapter 2

The *telos* of aggression: a post-Jungian perspective

THE SELF-HATER

In this chapter I will outline how self-hatred can be seen as a manifestation of women's aggressive energies, and also how 'the self-hater' can hold the seeds of agency, morality and psychological change. This perspective rests on an unlikely intersection of post-Jungian thought, critical psychology, and, as will emerge in subsequent chapters, feminist philosophy. These bodies of thought might seem like strange bedfellows, but as will become apparent in this and the following chapter, there is an important point of connection.

A patient once described life with her self-hater as: 'living life with one eye watching yourself on closed-circuit TV, accompanied by a ruthlessly attacking commentary from an invisible, nameless critic who has the authority of God.' Donald Kalsched, discussing a clinical vignette which fits this pattern, quotes from the tyrannical inner voices of a depressed middle aged woman: 'you're an asshole . . . you're sick . . . you're stupid, . . . you're psychologically retarded, . . . you should kill yourself' (1998: 98).[1]

Another clear articulator of these phenomena is Doris Lessing who, in 1969, described an interaction between the character Martha Quest and her 'inner critic' or self-hater thus:

> Martha was crying out – sobbing, grovelling; she was being wracked by emotion. Then one of the voices detached itself and came close to her inner ear: it was loud, or it was soft; it was jaunty, or it was intimately jeering, but its abiding quality was an antagonism, a dislike of Martha: and Martha was crying out against it – she needed to apologise, to beg for forgiveness, she needed to please and to buy absolution: she was grovelling on the carpet, weeping, while the voice uttered accusations of hatred.
> (Lessing, 1969: 518–519)[2]

Fourteen women contributed material to this book, and the next chapter describes how those contributions were collected. Sara, one of the contributors, describes her internal attempts to outmanoeuvre her self-hater.

> **Sara:** If someone said something nice to me I would feel so uncomfortable and go to endless trouble to prove them wrong. I wanted people to like me but the game was that you must never tell me that you liked me because I didn't know what to do with that – I didn't know how to be with KNOWING how you felt about me unless it was negative. If you liked me I'd feel I'd conned you and the imaginary horns would grow. If you let me strive I'd be able to be alive/here/breath. I wouldn't ever know how you felt, but it's the not knowing which helps.

Feminist analysis of this kind of material is usually given in terms of it being a psychic embed which occurs as a near inevitable result of women's growing up in a patriarchy. Psychotherapeutic analysis of it is usually in terms of deficiencies in the individual's early environment. In order to develop another perspective which can sit alongside these, I need to assemble certain elements of Jungian and post-Jungian thought and in order to explain the logic behind the selection of these elements, I will tell two stories. The first describes my encounter with how the first-generation Jungian women approached their own self-hater (which they refer to as their inner critic), and the second draws out where their perspective was coming from in Jung's own work. As will become apparent through my telling of these stories, my criteria for selection of which elements of Jungian and post-Jungian thought to use has been through a critique of the identity politics which underlie them, and the clinical implications which flow from those politics.

In 1986 I went into analysis with a Jungian. A number of months into analysis, I decided to read around the process I was in and walked into the wall of Jung's sexism in the form of his essay 'Woman in Europe' (1927). Next I looked to Juliet Mitchell's *Psychoanalysis and Feminism* (1974). Mitchell's work was interesting, but it was, like Jung's work, trying to fit women's experience into a theory which seemed to be organised around a series of agendas which were not centred on the lives and interests of the kind of women I knew. What I was looking for was something which started from the odd fragments of women's lives – the ordinary, messy, uneasy, in-the-world experiences – and tried to make something of that.

For want of any other way forward, I went back to Jung's writings on women's psychology and they continued to infuriate me. Yet flickering behind the specifics of his text was something which caught my attention. I could not put my finger on what it was, but read on through his work, being irritated and arguing all the way. Some years later I came across a quote from Jung's *Visions Seminars* which expressed what I had glimpsed in Jung's text that had kept me reading in spite of myself:

women often improve tremendously when they are allowed to think all
the disagreeable things which they had denied themselves before.

(1998: 1105)

These comments seemed quite different to many of Jung's simpler, culture and
period-bound formulations of his thoughts on women's psychology. His
comment struck me as powerfully accurate, and it set me the task of unpacking
it and trying to understand it personally, as a clinician and as a theoretician.

The first thing I thought about was the number of times I have been in
conversations in which women describe their darker thoughts, and then say
something like 'of course I wouldn't tell my therapist about this stuff . . .
they'd lock me up!' The apparent 'undiscussability' of such thoughts left me
wondering: what *are* the disagreeable thoughts that women deny themselves?
What is the permission that is needed for women to think these thoughts,
and whose is it to give? What possibilities for movement and change can be
accessed? Why is it so hard or frightening to engage with such thoughts?

In particular, I became fascinated by the dark thoughts which form the
basis of that which was referred to as the 'inner critic' by Jung's female
followers. I had an inner critic, and so did my female friends and colleagues.
At last I had found something which spoke directly to my experience of the
world. This inner critic or self-hater repeatedly tells a woman that she is
useless, ugly, stupid, hopeless and so on. In contemporary culture we would
now probably add 'fat' to the list. Clinical work with male patients has indicated to me that men, although they seem to be psychosocially structured in
different ways, have equivalent phenomena. While those phenomena interest
me greatly, they are not the focus of this book.

THE FIRST-GENERATION JUNGIAN WOMEN AND THEIR 'INNER CRITIC'

Among the first generation of Jung's analysands who became his pupils,
Irene Claremont de Castillejo and Marie-Louise von Franz discussed their
experience and work with this inner voice. They refer to it (through Jung's
terminology) as the 'negative animus', which is generally understood as
women's internalised version of a universal 'masculine' principle. Following
an account of a dream of her own, Claremont de Castillejo writes:

I should like to say a little more about the animus that is woman's worst
bugbear. He is the one who tells her she is no good. This voice is particularly dangerous because it only speaks to the woman herself and she is so
cast down by it that, as likely as not, she dare not tell anyone about it and
ask for help.

(1973: 88)

He [the negative animus] will convince her that she is useless, and that her life past, present and future, is utterly devoid of meaning.

(1973: 104)

The technique Claremont de Castillejo advocates for dealing with the negative animus phenomenon is the traditional Jungian one of developing a dialogue with the internal voice: this may mean finding out what it wants, standing up to it, or entering into a relationship with it, however that might work on an individual basis.

Whether or not this proved to be effective as an approach, my interest was caught by these women who had found a way of writing about an aspect of female interiority which felt real and immediate, and also that they chose to use their own psychological material to discuss it. They were not locating the inner critic as a symptom of psychopathology, which arrived in their consulting room as part of their analysand's illness, and which they, from an uncontaminated position, cured. There was no fantasy that they were above or beyond such terrors and struggles. The implication was that such material was to be engaged with, learnt about and learnt from, rather than somehow removed by the right kind of analytic relationship, or avoided by the right kind of childhood.

It still strikes me as a moment of great courage when a woman in analysis realises that she cannot get rid of her inner critic or self-hater by trying harder, being less irritable, being more organised, more generous, less judgemental, or some other variant of not stepping on the cracks in the pavement. The surrender of the fantasy that the inner critic can be removed either by personal effort, or some magical therapeutic equivalent of surgery, is often a painful disappointment. Sometime it feels unbearable and efforts to search for, or work for, an alternative are doubled and redoubled in order to defend against it. But a point is sometimes reached where the fantasy of a final and conclusive triumph and release is slowly relinquished, giving way to a different kind of relief: the relief of starting to accept that one has a self-hater, and that in spite of the pain it causes, deep down in the self-hater there is something which is of great importance. At this level, Claremont de Castillejo is right: the task is to come to know the voice of the self-hater and to learn about the kinds of relationships with it that are useful.

Claremont de Castillejo's views are, however, embedded in an understanding of gender which is in some ways radical, but in many ways deeply conservative through its inheritance of Jung's concept of ahistorical and universal archetypes. As will emerge, it is an important paradox that this very conservativism is what created the ground for the first-generation Jungian women's radical thoughts. This paradox needs to be handled carefully so as not to lose its potential, while freeing it up from its debilitatingly conservative and reactionary elements.

In similar style to Claremont de Castillejo, von Franz provides the following example:

> I remember once I dreamt a murderous burglar came into my bedroom, and I woke up with a cry of fear. I went through what I had thought the evening before. I had had a very peaceful, quiet day which could not account for such a terrible dream. Then I remembered that before going to bed I had thought 'The book I am writing is all nonsense and I must throw it away.'
>
> (1988: 267–268)

von Franz then explores this thought in terms of her own negative animus. She writes:

> I thought that *I* really thought that. Then when I reflected on the dream, I thought, 'No, I don't think that. It thinks that in me and I needn't believe it. I don't think that at all.' Then I could disentangle myself from the negative thought. I didn't accept it.
>
> (1988: 268, original italics)

von Franz offers this as an example of how the attacking 'negative animus' can be transformed simply by bringing it to consciousness. I would suggest that there is a little more going on in this 'magic' than meets the eye.

By definition, a woman's animus is the carrier of her internal 'masculinity' so that von Franz's murderous burglar represents the negative face of that masculinity. In contrast to this, on the opposite page of her book, there is a quotation from her in which she defines the positive animus as 'an innermost instinctive awareness of the inner truth, a basic inner truthfulness which guides the spiritual woman in her individuation, towards becoming her own self' (1988: 267).

Under the Jungian model, somewhere, buried in the shadow of von Franz's negative animus/murderous burglar, must be its opposite: an unconscious positive animus which is her own 'basic inner truthfulness' and a guide towards her own individuation.

I interpret von Franz, as a Jungian, as knowing this, and 'taking the wind out of the sails' of the attacking negative animus by taking back his clarity of purpose, his aggression and determination, creating new amalgams of them for her own purposes. That is what enabled von Franz to dispatch her murderous burglar so effectively: she stole his energy and put it to her own conscious use, knowing that in his energy lay a kernel of truth. Given that von Franz situated the dream as an attack on her book, I would suggest that the aggressive, clear, determined energies which she reclaimed from the murderous burglar were exactly the energies she needed to get on with writing her book with more energy, conviction and clarity.

From a Jungian perspective, von Franz's burglar does not just represent an internal, destructive, envious attack: the aggression embedded in the negative animus must also indicate something which is missing from her conscious attitude. The dream offers the dreamer the missing elements of her conscious attitude – perhaps her day had been a little *too* peaceful? Presenting these elements as a murderous burglar 'ups the ante' and demands that she either takes them into consciousness, or live under their tyranny while they remain unconscious.

I interpret von Franz's dream as implying that in order to write her book, she needed to re-engage with her own murderously intrusive and forceful energies and get her inner burglar to work *with* her, and *for* her, as the basis of her creativity, rather than attack her project. That is how she got her inner critic to go away: she sent him to work for her, rather than against her.

Thus the traditional Jungian framework, with its reliance on profoundly conservative, if not patriarchal fantasies of eternal, universal, foundational, gender archetypes, offered a radical feminist insight. Women's disagreeable thoughts are so heavily self- and society-censored that they are experienced as totally alien to the ego. Consequently, only a psychological perspective that concentrates on trying to engage with that which is ego-alien is likely to see the value that these thoughts offer. This value would be invisible to a psychology which assumes or strives for a normative outcome. The Jungian concentration on that which is experienced as not belonging to the 'I' but which we find within ourselves as 'Not-I within' or inner Otherness is actually perfectly suited to exploring such fantasies as they demand our attention through dreams, fantasies and so on. Indeed, the 'alien' nature of the masculinised 'animus' concept was yet more helpful to women like von Franz in accessing their own disagreeable thoughts since, being masculinised, the animus can be comfortably expected to represent women's aggression, cruelty and hatred.

Through this model material which is generally regarded as outside socially acceptable female identity can be thought about, provided it is regarded as the male 'part' of a woman. Of course this is a limiting construction, not least of all because that which is assigned to 'animus' in this way is usually trivialised as women's bitchiness, moodiness, meanness and so on, but it does provide a point of access to something which is usually off the psychological map. Indeed, Jung's own ambivalence towards his concept of animus is evident. Claire Douglas provides an extensive exploration of Jung's work on the animus and points out that in his entire writings, Jung had only three good things to say about it, and all of them are in sentences of between eight and fourteen words (1990: 63). As an aside: the most muscular of the clinical feminist critiques of Jung's concept of the animus is by Lyn Cowan (1994), but this work has only been published on the internet.

von Franz's dream also resonates with the kinds of fears and dreams of attack (or threat) which seem to be so much a part of many women's experience. Vivienne, another of the women who contributed material to this project, documented such a dream.

> **Vivienne:** I lie in bed. Geoffrey (husband) is away. The twins, Isabel and Julian, are away. I know everything is locked. I have checked every door, many times. I have unlocked and re-locked doors we never open. I notice the bolts are extremely insecure. An intruder would have no trouble with those. We must have them fixed. I have looked in every cupboard. Under every bed. I have already decided *exactly* which lights to leave on, agonising over whether each one would indicate more whether people were home, and up and awake – or, conversely, that *a person* – me – was home alone, and fair game. I know exactly which lights allow an intruder to see in, and which are just out of the line of vision and *maybe* indicate people out of sight and awake. I curse the uncurtained windows and the acres of glass, which make all but my bedroom visible, it seems. Once in bed, my heart seems to pound very loudly, every nerve is activated. In the dark, I can't imagine how I can be in the house alone so often during the daytime, or in the evening, without the slightest anxiety. Now it seems that the chance of surviving a night here without someone malevolent knowing and coming to get me is minute – I know the world is FULL of evil (mostly men, I think) who have uncanny ways of knowing when women are alone in their homes. I try not to think of what I would do, but I think nevertheless that I would lie still as a dog and hope that 'he' would not see me. I marvel in the dark at the vast numbers of women, including many friends of mine, who live alone – who, quite simply, go to bed at night and fall asleep.

While a percentage of this material is attributable to real, external threats, I am suggesting that there is another dimension which has to do with the structure of female identity itself, and that will emerge in the ensuing chapters. Meanwhile, I return to the story of exploring the phenomenon of women's inner critic or self-hater from within the Jungian and post-Jungian tradition.

In the late 1980s, feminist post-Jungians such as Demaris Wehr and Polly Young-Eisendrath attempted to take the kinds of insights offered by the women among the first generation of Jung's students forward in different ways. Unfortunately, however, their commitment to valorising women means that much of the interpretive power of these links around women's aggression and agency were lost, with this being especially true of Young-Eisendrath's earlier work. Wehr's work comes from a non-clinical background but is stronger. Ultimately, however, her commitment to a slightly modified, but still very traditional concept of archetype limits her analysis.

Meanwhile, the tradition of recognising and being interested in women's aggression continues among the apparently more conservative Jungian analysts with Claire Douglas noting that:

> Guggenbuhl-Craig (1977) writes of other 'archetypal images of man-killing aggressivity' which he considers to be unrecognized or pathologised parts of women's nature. He mentions Penthesilea, Clorinda, Britomart, Juturna, Marfisa, Bradamanta, Camilla, Belphoebe, and Radigund as archetypal images of a side of the feminine that has been misinterpreted and therefore designated incorrectly as unfeminine, masculine or androgynous. His point is that they represent *feminine* characteristics. They are aspects of a vigorously aggressive dark feminine side that is culturally prohibited and out of fashion. It is an archetypal power of the dark feminine which seems very hard to metabolise and calls up images of fierce destruction.
>
> (1990: 223, original italics)

As with von Franz's work, I find the traditional Jungian frame of reference from which Douglas is writing problematic (and the reasons for this will be explored shortly). What interests me is, however, that she is pointing to a view through which women's aggression can be seen as non-pathological. Sylvia Brinton Perera takes a similar position:

> [O]ur culture has clearly discouraged women from claiming impersonal feminine potency. The concept is considered monstrous; thus women are encouraged to be docile and to 'relate with Eros' to sadistic paternal animus figures, rather than to claim their own equally sadistic-assertive power.
>
> (1981: 40)

My sense is that Brinton Perera's impersonal feminine potency is a close relative of what Courtin was referring to in Chapter 1 as strong energy. Clinical experience has taught me that spotting this strong energy, in its many disguises and hiding places is actually something of an art form, as is holding it in mind until a woman can bear to be in contact with it herself. Also of note is how Brinton Perera's use of the term 'sadistic' echoes the murderous qualities of the two women's dreams quoted in Chapter 1. These dreams also resonate with Guggenbuhl-Craig's description of an element of women's 'man killing aggressivity'. Thus there seems to be a certain kind of space in the more traditional Jungian world for aspects of women's aggressive, non-*status quo* inner and outer lives which are not widely discussed in other psychological circles, and it was on that basis that I trained as a Jungian analyst.

Throughout the training, however, I fought with Jung's own attitudes to women, and, in particular with the concept of archetype, with its claims to ahistorical and universal status. In order to understand my fight with this concept and create my own reading of the phenomena it gestured towards, I had to explore in more detail the history of my attachment to Jung's work, and my grounds for rejecting large parts of it, while valuing others highly. The next section outlines the story of that process, starting back at the point when I first entered my own analysis and had begun to search for texts which would help me understand the process that I was encountering in myself. As I read my way through the work of Jung and the post-Jungians I repeatedly encountered images of women – mythical, 'archetypal' women – and I became aware that while I was fascinated by these images, I was also profoundly uncomfortable with something about them.

JUNG, RIDER HAGGARD AND ARCHETYPES

This fascination went back to early adolescence when I had seen (on TV) the 1970s' Hammer House of Horror version of H. Rider Haggard's classic *She*. I was hooked. The final scene was what really stayed with me. In order to encourage her mortal lover to step into the fires of immortality (as she had, thousands of years ago), Ayesha – 'She Who Must Be Obeyed', played by Ursula Andress – walks into the flames which gave her eternal youth a second time. What she does not know is that stepping back into the flames reverses the process of immortalisation, and she ages thousands of years in front of the camera.

As she dies, Ayesha collapses forward and turns to dust, a process signified by the wedding-type veil she was wearing to greet her lover's new-found immortality fluttering flat to the ground as her body crumbles. Something about this tale of an all-powerful, immortal and ruthless woman, finally brought low caught me and subsequently I tracked down Rider Haggard's book and read it.

I would now say that as an adolescent watching the film I was looking for images which might help me work out some sort of relationship between being gendered female and questions of love, power, sex, punishment and death. When I started to read Jung a decade or so later, I discovered that he too was a fan of Rider Haggard's work, there being over 40 references to Rider Haggard, *She* and *Ayesha: The Return of She*, as well as *Wisdom's Daughter* in the index of Jung's Collected Works, compared to only one for Conan Doyle (who was Rider Haggard's contemporary almost to the year, and another significant figure in the popular imagination at the time Jung was writing).

I read everything Jung had written about gender, and then I read the studies on Jung's work on gender, especially *Anima as Fate* by Cornelia Brunner (republished in 1986), a text devoted in large part to a Jungian exposition of *She*. Jung wrote the preface to Brunner's work in April 1959 and in it he comments that:

> [f]or Rider Haggard the significant motif of the Anima unfolds in the purest and most naive fashion . . . If Rider Haggard makes use of the modest literary form of the 'yarn,' this does not curtail the content of his statements. He who looks for entertaining literature or artful use of language can easily find something superior. He, however, who seeks understanding and insight will find rich fare in *She*, just because of the simplicity and naivete of the views which lack deliberate psychological implications.
>
> (Brunner, 1986: xii)

What comes through was that Jung and the first generation of his followers took works like *She* as raw examples of the recurrent and universal nature of certain male fantasies about womanhood. In the preface to Brunner's work Jung also cites Rider Haggard's struggle with the 'anima problem' as being in the same tradition as Goethe's *Faust* and Wagner's work.

I would now say that part of my unease with this position can be summarised by applying a Foucauldian line of questioning – if anima images such as Ayesha are read as pointing to some kind of foundational and eternal experience of femininity, whom does this ascription of foundational and eternal status serve? In other words, who benefits – and how – if we take the attributed authority of these images at face value? Furthermore, how has this authority been arrived at? What social practices maintain it? At the same time, my sense was, and still is, that there is something very important embedded in Jung's use of these images – his discussions of gender *do* point beyond themselves to some kind of contextualised experience of the mystery of Otherness, and through that to potential processes of growth and change.

In a similar vein, Susan Rowland (2002) has written persuasively from an academic perspective about dimensions of Jungian and post-Jungian thought which are relevant to feminism. In particular, Rowland focuses on post-modern moves in Jung's work, tracing out how Jung's view of the unconscious is deconstructive, and aligns with post-modern sensibilities. My own findings parallel and support a lot of Rowland's, although, as a clinician, mine come from a different direction and seek a different end. Rowland's approach is appropriate to her task and her important reading of Jung's work stands in its own right. My approach is focused on the clinical implications of the deconstructive moves which she rightly identifies in Jung's work.

In order to create the context for this, some historical background to Jung's ideas needs to be explored. The other reason for working through this is that, as in the discussion of object relations' history given in Chapter 1, there are highly problematic identity politics at operation in Jung's work, which make its broad application to women's aggressive energies inappropriate. As I draw out these identity politics, I will also identify the elements of Jung's work which I see as not only useable but crucially important.

Throughout his writings on the nature of archetypes, Jung made occasional comments to the effect that archetypal, primordial images may alter over time and with context. Mostly, however, his writings point to the concept of archetype as structured around 'eternal–historical' and 'universal–collective' axes (Carrette, 1994: 173–176). Archetypal images, on the other hand, are seen as the context-dependent expressions of the ahistorical archetypes of the collective unconscious.

In contrast to this distinction I take up Marina Warner's argument that myths and fairy stories are political entities. Warner comments (via Roland Barthes' *Mythologies*) that:

> myths are not eternal verities, but historical compounds, which successfully conceal their own contingency, changes and transitoriness so that the story they tell looks as if it cannot be told otherwise, that things always were like that and always shall be. Barthes's study almost amounts to an exposé of myth, as he reveals how it works to conceal political motives and secretly circulate ideology through society.
>
> (Warner, 1994: xiii)

I would suggest that the concept of archetype, like the myths and fairy stories that it is entwined with, is also political and that all symbols, no matter how powerful, or how apparently universal, operate as political devices and are loaded up with meaning by the process of their own culturally based origination. In order to illustrate this, I will take up an imaginal encounter between Jung and a figure he called Salome.

SALOME IN *FIN-DE-SIÈCLE* CULTURE

This encounter took place in one of Jung's experiments with active imagination, and Jung described it in his autobiography, *Memories, Dreams, Reflections* (1977, first published in 1963). As we shall see, Salome turns out to be a close relative to Ayesha in the cultural imagination, and exploring how images of these women were constituted at the time Jung was writing has helped me to understand my discomfort with Jungian discussions of 'archetypal femininity'.

Jung writes:

> I caught sight of two figures, an old man with a white beard and a beautiful young girl . . . The old man explained to me that he was Elijah, and that gave me a shock. But the girl staggered me even more, for she

called herself Salome! She was blind . . . They had a black serpent living with them which displayed an unmistakable fondness for me. I stuck close to Elijah because he seemed the more reasonable of the three, and to have a clear intelligence. Of Salome I was distinctly suspicious.

(Jung, 1977: 205–206)

Soon after this fantasy another figure rose out of the unconscious. He developed out of the Elijah figure. I called him Philemon.

(Jung, 1977: 207)

Jung's own response to his Salome image is given in two paragraphs (Philemon merits 11 paragraphs). She is seen as a parallel to various dancing girls and a young woman whom Simon Magus 'picked up in a brothel', and as an 'anima figure [who] is blind because she does not see the meaning of things. Elijah is the figure of the wise old prophet and represents the factor of intelligence and knowledge; Salome the erotic element. One might say that the two figures are personifications of Logos and Eros' (Jung, 1977: 206).

In order to put Jung's Salome and serpent in their cultural context it is necessary to examine the art of the last two decades of the nineteenth century which shows an extraordinary number of images of women and snakes, the most common mythical contexts being Salammbô, Lilith, Ishtar and Medusa.[3] Of particular interest is the period's imagery of women and serpents. A plethora of images were produced with titles such as Snake Queen(s), The Scene of The Serpent, Egyptian Fantasy and Serpentine Dancers. At a more generic level, images of Sensuality, Sin, Vice, Lust and so on were popular, frequently featuring women moving snakily, caressing or being caressed (usually ecstatically) by snakes, or with snakes forming part of their anatomy: commonly legs, thighs and loins, or hair. These images sit against the backdrop of a general flourishing of artistic works and surprisingly immodest stories in popular magazines about women's 'natural' tendency to rapidly degenerate to a bestial past and engage in intimate relationships with animals generally (snakes in particular), given half a chance.

In terms of a wider bestiality, classical themes were used repeatedly to explore these cultural fantasies of women and their relationships with satyrs, fauns, birds in general (swans with long sinuous necks especially), dogs, gorillas, lions, tigers, and, of course, snakes. A scene in Flaubert's *Salammbô* published in 1862 described a dark ritual entailing an erotic encounter between Salammbô and her serpent partner and fired the imagination of many an artist of the period (Dijkstra, 1986: 306). Rider Haggard's *She* contains numerous descriptions of Ayesha in snake-like terms: she had a 'terrible whisper, which sounded like the hiss of a snake.' (1888: 197); when she undressed, she appeared 'shining and splendid like some glittering snake when she has cast her slough' (1888: 189)'. Furthermore, her physical being

Figure 2.1 Léon Victor Solon, 'Bacchanale' (Dijkstra, 1986: 292)

Figure 2.2 Gabriel Ferrier, 'Salammbô' (Dijkstra 1986: 308)

was 'instinct with a life that was more than life . . . [and possessed] a certain serpent-like grace that was more than human' (1888: 155).

I am not saying that Jung was directly influenced by these works, even though he may have known them, or known of them. My point is simply that Jung worked in a particular cultural context and that certain images were not only commonplace in that world and carried particular significance which has since changed as the culture has changed, but that the images and their meanings were firmly embedded in cultural processes around the definition of gender. By way of illustration, a painter whose works Jung was familiar with and refers to was Franz von Stuck, a German painter who 'was in the habit of repeating his compositions [of beautiful young women with big black serpents] endlessly, as eager new clients demanded more images of evil women to hang on their walls as cautionary emblems' (Dijkstra, 1986: 313). The rise in enthusiasm for these images was part of a series of cultural shifts which had started with the rise of the cult of what Bram Dijkstra calls the 'household nun' – the institutionalised restriction of women's role to the sphere of domesticity, a world far from the cut and thrust of trade. This cultural fantasy inevitably spawned a shadow – fears of women's tyranny, wantonness, madness and sexual licentiousness began to express themselves in the art of the period. Remember, this is also the period of Gustav Klimt's now famous 1901 painting, Salome (or Judith I), in which a glamorous Salome holds the bloody head of John the Baptist.

Fuelled by the rising issues of women's rights and women's suffrage movements from about 1848 onwards, this fear-based vision of womanhood focused on the dangers of what would happen if women slipped the moorings

Figure 2.3 Franz von Stuck, 'Sensuality' (Dijkstra, 1986: 312) Collection Abraham Somer, Los Angeles

of the domestic sanctuary. Additional impetus was added by the early 'scientific' investigations of women, their behaviour, and most dangerous of all, their experience of a sexuality, which was not merely procreative or a submissive response to male desire. The general reaction was that the 'woman

Figure 2.4 Edouard Toudouze, 'Salome Triumphant' (Dijkstra, 1986: 383)

problem' represented a fundamental threat to the fabric of society and was likely, if left uncontained, to result in the demise of civilised existence. It is interesting to note that these fears are echoed in Jung's paper, 'Woman in Europe', which was first published in 1927.

The *fin-de-siècle* vision of woman was split: the fantasy of the domestically-focused angel (variously tubercular or weightless nature-nymph) being undermined by the suspicion that women were the enemy within the walls of society, a fear which echoes Hegel's earlier view of women as the enemy of the Civil Society. A subtext of these works was that women took men's heads: literally (if men didn't keep their wits about them), failing that, figuratively, by making men fall in love with them and become slaves to their whim through their commoditisation of virtue (Dijkstra, 1986: 352–376). Not surprisingly prostitution was rife. Naive and uncritical use of Jung's work on gender imports these psychologically split and splitting fantasies about female sexuality and woman's Otherness in the same way that the *fin-de-siècle* images offer women fantasies of power, while also bringing with them the oppressive politics of their period.

Salome's trajectory during this period is particularly fascinating. The notion that women bring men low and are essentially corrupt and bestial by virtue of their virginity, by virtue of their purity, plays out in Flaubert's *Salome*. Here, the 'virginal Salome is a blind tool of her calculating mother, who had made certain that her daughter would grow up to be an innocent lure in service to her power-hungry parent' (Dijkstra, 1986: 381).

Oscar Wilde's *Salome*, a popular play which was widely discussed after its performance in Paris in 1896 (it was written in French) and London in 1905, pitched:

> sight against sound. Both may be primary senses, but for Wilde, the battle between sight and sound represents the struggle between materialism and idealism, between the feminine and the masculine. Salome, Everywoman, the moon is 'seen,' perceived solely in terms of her physical beauty, her material presence. One *looks* at Salome, at woman who, in turn, as Jokanaan says of Herodias always gives 'herself up unto the lust of her eyes'.
>
> (Dijkstra, 1986: 396, original italics)

In the light of the foregoing texts, which point to the blindingly dangerous nature of Salome's presence, it is not surprising that she is blind in Jung's fantasy. Given the proliferation of *fin-de-siècle* fantasies about women like Salome, it is also not surprising that Jung's analysis of what she represents in his imagination does not extend to the usual Jungian understanding of blindness in myth or fairy story – that loss of external sight is associated with gains in inner-sight.

The point of this discussion is not, however, to prove a causal link between

Jung's fantasies and the images of the period – that is something which can only be conjectured – it is to show that images, myths, stories and so on are part of the process of social change. Doubtlessly they are also vehicles for the avoidance of social change. Jung's Salome seems to fit the pattern pointed out by Warner, above. She looks like an example of an eternal verity, but is, to a significant extent, transitory and contingent although her structure conceals those elements.

More importantly, the archetypal lens through which Jung views his Salome makes it seemingly unnecessary (I would argue impossible) to discuss the importance of the transitory, political or period-specific aspects of the image since the emphasis of the very frame of reference of archetypal thinking is on stability and universal recurrence of imagery. In this way, images of women like Salome and Ayesha are seen as representations of eternal, universal patterns, rather than struggles with Otherness (including the dangerous, disruptive desirability of the Other), which are very much inflected through the position of the individual in history, culture, class and gender. In other words, the way in which the Other is perceived is significantly influenced by the identity of the perceiver.

OTHERNESS AND THE DISSOCIABILITY OF THE PSYCHE

My argument reworks a thread of Jung's (problematic[4]) reading of Kant. Jung's own position can be summarised as *esse in anima* – all that we can know to be real is psyche. In practical terms this means that one's experience of the world is always and already constituted through the lens of one's psyche so that what one experiences is, in significant part, a function of one's (largely unconscious) psychological makeup. I want to take this a step further and suggest that how one sees a particular phenomenon (such as *She*) acts as a lens, not just on how one's psyche is organised (for example around the question of Otherness), but also on how the processes of identity formation work to channel the individual's experience of Otherness (and expressions of that experience) in ways which are intelligible within a given culture at a specific point in time.

I suggest that this was Jung's own core position, even if (at times) he was all too humanly unable to apply his theory to his own process. David Miller speaks of this Jung when he writes:

> if Jung were alive today, would he not have to be a semiotician rather than a symbolist? Would he not be nearer to the French Freudians than to the American Jungians with all their hermeneutic knowledge?
>
> Today. . . . Jungian fundamentalism [is] symbolic. [It has] become a

knowing. But what Jung called symbolic, and recommended for the soul, is not this knowing. It is the paratactic, 'gappy' unknowing that is today called semiotic.

(Miller, 1990: 328)

In order to take up this gappy view of the psyche, it is essential to understand its clinical background and practical application: it is not just a theory, it is how Jung worked with extremely distressed and disturbed people. Gary Hartman comments that Freud was aware of the dissociative split in libido (in other words, its tendency to fragment into seemingly disconnected parts), but saw it as pathological and pathogenic, while Jung saw it as normal and a natural prerequisite for the movement of psychic energy. John Haule points out that Freud chose to stay away from the ideas of the dissociationist movement of the late nineteenth century (with its links to spiritualism), and wanted psychoanalysis to be regarded as a science, with its own independent credibility (Haule, 1992: 247). Jung, on the other hand, was strongly influenced by the dissociationists who:

held that every aggregation of ideas and images possessed, in some measure or other, its *own personality*. The guiding image for this was the phenomenon of multiple personality, for which there was already a hundred-year-old therapeutic tradition, going back to Mesmer, Puységur, Despine, Azaam and the people Janet calls the 'French alienists'.

(Haule, 1992: 239–240, original italics)

In this view there are semi-autonomous fragments within the psyche which, if engaged with (for example through hypnotherapy) appear to have a personality of their own. The ego is seen as just one of these potential personalities (complexes), some of which will be less developed than the ego, and some of which may, in some ways, be more developed. Some complexes are barely recognisable as personality elements, and operate more like clusters of energy, but each had its own feeling tone and characteristics.

The roots of Jung's work in this field can be seen in his investigations of his young cousin Hélène Preiswerk's mediumistic seances. This work formed the basis of Jung's doctoral dissertation in which he theorised that what was occurring in the seances was that Hélène entered a self-induced hypnotic state, in which her psyche would dissociate. In that state, her ego complex, the one she lived in from day-to-day life, stepped back from 'centre stage'. Other complexes would then take its place, seeming to 'speak through' her. These included Ivenes, a much older, much more worldly woman than the 15½-year-old Hélène. Jung suggested that Ivenes was a complex – a cluster of personality elements within Hélène. Jung's view, based on the work of the French dissociationist, Flournoy, was that Hélène's apparently mediumistic gifts were the product of the floodlight of her ego being switched off in her trance state. Without the ego dominating her personality, the lesser lights of Hélène's complexes became clearer.

So while Freud saw dissociation as pathological, the dissociationists saw it as an exaggeration of the normal (Haule, 1992: 247). This difference in perspectives has important implications and Sonu Shamdasani argues that locating Jung as primarily a Freudian thinker who broke away misses the point of much of Jung's work. Shamdasani traces the influence of Janet's work on Jung (through Flournoy) and offers strong evidence that Jung's model was far closer to the French dissociationist tradition than it was to Freud's work (Shamdasani, 1998: 115–126). In Jung's work, the dissociationist heritage gives rise to the theory of complexes, a word whose use originates with Eugene Bleuler (Meir, 1992: 202). Meir observes that '[m]any impressions are obliterated in the moment of perception on account of their incompatibility with the habitual attitude of the conscious mind; this seems to occur automatically and unconsciously' (Meir, 1992: 205). These ego-distonic impressions cluster together to create centres of 'Not-I-ness', or inner Otherness in the psyche (complexes).

The evidence for the existence of psychological complexes comes from Jung's work on the word association test, which he was experimenting with between 1901 and 1904 (Bair 2003: 66) at the Burgholzli Psychiatric Hospital in Zurich. This test comprised reading (in a set order) a list of 100 or more carefully chosen stimulus words to a subject. The time taken for the subject to respond to each word, as well as the word or words with which they replied was noted. Often the test was repeated with the same subject shortly after the first test and any differences in delays or response words were noted. Earlier scientists such as Kraeplin and Sommer had expected these kinds of tests to show up differences in intelligence, but Jung realised that they showed up differences in emotional terrain as the subject's consciousness was moved around their field of interiority by the impacts of the stimulus words (Leys, 1992: 151).

What Jung found was that words whose associations took the subject into unconscious, emotionally charged internal spaces generated delays (whose duration correlated to the intensity of the emotion encountered), non-responses, perseverations, rhymes, self-references and so on. He argued that these interference phenomena occurred when the subject encountered within themselves a feeling-toned 'complex'.

THE 'NOT-I WITHIN'

As Renos Papadopoulous suggests, Jung's life and work can be seen as a 'progression of reformulations of the problematic of the Other' (1992: 421). A consistent thread through these reformulations was, however, Jung's loyalty to two clinical practices from the dissociationist tradition:

First, he tried to recognise and attend to the aspects of the patient's personality which were 'Not-I' and,
Second, he allowed the time necessary for the characteristics and personality of the 'Not-I' to emerge.

(Hartman, internet paper 1994)

This is where Claremont de Castillejo's and von Franz's approach to women's self-hater voice comes from. I take up their approach and assume that the self-hater or inner critic is an element of the 'Not-I' and has a job to do in the woman's psychological economy. From this perspective the analytic task is to take time to get to know the presenting element of the unconscious as well as possible, so that it can show my analysand and myself what job it is doing and why. I also assume that because of the structure of femininity, woman's aggressive energies are one of the key aspects of women's psychic lives that are likely to have been split off and become 'Not-I within'. Working with women's aggressive potential is not, however, just a matter of personal psychopathology: as will emerge later, it is also political and involves unsettling the very categories on which our notions of identity rest.

An example of the 'Not-I within' is the frequently heard dream of a house in which one lives (whether that be in reality, or as a fiction of the dream) having an extra room, or a secret garden. The feeling tone of this extra space can be anything from terrifying or threatening to blissful, but the point is that it indicates that there are psychological spaces which are part of one's inner world, which are not currently accessible. These dreams can be very powerful, leaving one convinced that somehow these extra spaces are really there in the day-to-day world, even though one knows that they are not. Again, this is based on a dissociationist reading of the psyche, viewing it as inherently plural. In this view, the psyche is not knowable in a complete way, but the presenting edge of the unconscious can be explored as it emerges. This is why Jung viewed the psyche as fundamentally gappy and dissociable, but capable of therapeutic engagement if one saw that state of being as healthy and potentially productive. The specific benefit of this model was that, as Richard Noll points out, it allowed for the 'expansion of the personality through greater differentiation' of its functioning. Normal dissociability was also seen as 'an adaptive survival function', but one which 'creates an inevitable instability' (Noll, 1992: 213).

This way of thinking about the 'Not-I', which one finds within oneself, is particularly useful to the clinician since it offers an imaginal embodiment of it, capturing the fleshy compulsiveness of the impulses in question. Everyday examples of this are commonplace, ranging from comments such as 'I don't know what got into me', to the experience of compulsive behaviour, which, by its nature, feels as if it is not under one's control. As will emerge later, the 'Not-I within' can usefully be thought of as including material from different facets of identity formation, and from the experiences which accrue from living a particular identity in its associated context. But for now, I will treat it as a single entity in order to illustrate the basic shape of my theme.

Take compulsive behaviour as an example: a basic, post-Jungian approach to someone presenting for analysis might start from a loose hypothesis that some element of split-off 'Not-I-ness' is being expressed in the compulsive behaviour. The 'Not-I within' which has been split off in this way cannot currently be brought into consciousness and recognised by the ego without the ego being intolerably threatened. A clinician might then hypothesise that although the material which has been split off is unbearable for consciousness, it has an important part to play in the individual's psychological economy, and is therefore making itself very much known through the compulsive behaviour. The clinical task then becomes one of holding an interpersonal, analytic space in which these elements of the psyche might present themselves, along with the tensions between and around them. If this can be facilitated there may be possibilities of engagement with the analysand's psychological structures, including that which is split off from the analysand's sense of 'I', but demands engagement (for example through eating disorder, compulsive behaviour or recurrent relational difficulties). It should be noted, however, that the split-off 'Not-I within' is not exclusively negative material – it is simply that which cannot be engaged with consciously at any given point in time. These ideas will be expanded on in Chapter 6, which discusses clinical work with people with severe and chronic eating disorders.

Clearly the danger of thinking in this way is that the 'Not-I' may become overcharacterised to such a degree that a sense of responsibility for it is undermined, and along with that goes the capacity to feel deeply *and* think critically about the nature of the relationship between the 'I' and the 'Not-I'. I would suggest that this is part of what happens when Jung discusses his images of Salome, and when he cites Rider Haggard's work as an illustration of the validity of his theories. These images *do* offer a glimpse of some form of Otherness, some element of 'Not-I-ness within', which was extremely potent for a lot of individual men's imaginations in the *fin-de-siècle* period. But that does not make for statements about the true, universal and eternal nature of men's fantasies of inner femininity, far less about women's experiences of their 'feminine' selves.[5]

DESIRE AND JUNG'S OWN 'NOT-I WITHIN'

What goes awry when Jung discusses his internal images is that he only partially applies his own theory, with the result that he prefers to engage with the more accessible, less threatening Philemon, a 'wise old man', and turns away from the unsettling Salome. The issue here is that by Jung's own theory, engaging with Salome's unsettling Otherness might bring greater possibilities for growth, since her unsettlingness flags her as a portal to the 'Not-I within'. As an aside, beyond Salome, there is another, even less accessible (and probably therefore even more important) portal to the 'Not-I within' in Jung's fantasy since, as Claire Douglas points out, '[t]he missing human fourth [in the fantasy] is Baucis, Philemon's biblical wife whom Gerhard Wehr traces through Goethe's Faust, to Philemon and Baucis/Baubo, the crone, the old, vulgar, sexual, and potent woman – the human form of the black serpent' (Douglas, 1990: 24).

Again though, there are other moments in Jung's work where he does make the turn to the unfamiliar, the split-off 'Not I within', and Paul Kugler summarises the importance of these moments thus:

> [the] model of self-reflection found in classical psychology and philo-sophical epistemology works from the assumption that self-reflection is a mirror reflection. The subject-imago being objectively reflected upon is symmetrical (identical) to the subject doing the reflecting. This model of reflexivity adopts the logic of physical reflection. When applied to psychology, the process keeps the reflecting subject always caught in the solipsism of ego consciousness.

> Self-reflection in Jungian depth psychology is a process through which the personality turns back on itself in an asymmetrical fashion. This provides a way out of the philosophical solipsism and therapeutic narcis-sism inherent in the humanistic model. *The mirror at work in the Jungian hermeneutic does not reflect the self-same face. Rather it mirrors back the face of the Other.*
>
> (Kugler, 1993, internet paper, italics added)

This is what makes the Jungian view different from most other depth psycho-logical models – this core engagement with Otherness and the assumption that resistance to unitary identity is normal and potentially available for clinical engagement. Inner Otherness is assumed, however, to be more than just Lacanian alienation, and is, instead, taken as a matter of awe, fascin-ation, terror, enlivenment and radical powerlessness.

Thus, if, instead of reading Jung's references to Salome and Ayesha as being images of an eternal and universal male fantasy about inner (and possibly outer) femaleness, we read his fascinations in the way that I am suggesting, they can be seen as attempts to engage with the nature of *desire*, particularly if we read desire as:

> most truly itself when it is most 'other' to social norms, when it trans-gresses the limits and exceeds the 'proper'. The result is a hotchpotch, formed only by its status as the forbidden.
>
> (Cowie, 1993: 134)

This notion of desire fits with the assumption that some of the most powerful cultural processes are those that define which kinds of desires are regarded as legitimate and which are not. In Foucault's terms, what matters is not 'what we want' but 'how we come to desire what we want' and how we come to believe that our desires are somehow natural, individual expressions of our unique identity, rather than the canalisation of the potential to desire along lines which serve cultural interests and practices.

Viewing this through Derrida's argument that a privileging of presence (which he refers to as the metaphysics of presence) underlies Western notions of identity, Patrick Fuery argues that '[t]he metaphysics of presence – that privileging of the centre over its margins and the marginalised – evokes an immediate if problematic connection with desire. Because presence is perceived as a desirable status, all that is positioned as presence becomes desirable'. Fuery goes on to argue that '. . . desires which are not articulated in centres as presences are denied existence' (Fuery, 1995: 46–47).

What this means in practical terms is that the pull of mainstream identity structures – those modelled on a metaphysics of presence – drag Jung to focus on Philemon, even though his own theoretical commitment would take him to focus on the inarticulate centres of desire that are represented by Salome and the serpent. Through this move a potential epiphany is regulated out of existence.

IDENTITY FORMATION, ARCHETYPES AND THE METAPHYSICS OF PRESENCE

In order to imagine what is lost in this way, picture raw human potential – unshaped aliveness – at a point prior to the formation of any system of identity, and prior to the canalisation of desires required for the formation of identity. The processes of identity formation then begin to operate and are reiterated over and over so that patterns arise and parameters form which mark out domains of liveable identity; in other words, something which is recognisable to others who partake of the same identity system. Canalisations and demarcations occur defining which kinds of desires and alivenesses are thinkable and liveable and which are not and thus raw aliveness is channelled into identity. In effect, these processes mark off the collective 'I' from the collective 'Not-I'. They establish what Gayatri Chakravorty Spivak calls the 'I-slots' which define the envelopes of liveable identity (1988). In the case of Western identity, they establish the familiar metaphysics of presence by mapping out the range of recognisable desires, that is, those which centre on presences.

That which is not incorporated into identity in this way (the collective 'Not-I') forms into clusters of energy, experienced by individual psyches as their 'own' complexes, but related to collective clusters of energy which have been excluded from identity (the archetypes of the collective unconscious), as

Jung describes.[6] Viewing the clusters of energy which we think of as arche-types as the gathered-together leftovers from the formation of a system of identity frees them of their 'ever was and ever more shall be so' quality. They remain powerful markers of the edges of sanity (that is, inhabitable, recognis-able identity), but this does not give them foundational status.[7] Quite the opposite – a different system of identity would incorporate different energies into the realm of the inhabitable 'I' and exclude different energies which, in turn, would form quite different archetypal configurations. Thus 'archetypal' becomes a description of the powerful energies associated with that which is marginalised and excluded in the formation of identity, but which continues to haunt and dominate identity, rather than a name for the specific clusters formed by these energies under specific identity systems.

From this perspective, Jung's dissociationist emphasis becomes all the more important – it offers a point of contact with not only the personal, individual experience of the 'Not-I within', but also with that which is ren-dered culturally 'Not-I' (and often projected and idealised or denigrated). This move also makes the political dimensions of the production and main-tenance of the cultural 'I'/'Not-I' boundary accessible to psychoanalytic technique because the individual's experience of their own 'Not-I within' will contain residues of the processes of identity formation. Thus the dis-sociationist perspective offers a point of contact with the inarticulate desires and resistances to identity, which, as Jacqueline Rose suggests, lie at the very heart of psychic life (Rose, 1990: 232) (I will return to this comment by Rose in Chapter 3).[8] In making this connection I am agreeing with Rowland's view of Jung's deconstructive reading of the unconscious, but also moving the theoretical implications of that view into the clinical, interpersonal realm.

As a clinician I am especially interested in these moments of inarticulate desire and resistance to identity and how they are regulated out of existence through our performance of identity, especially gendered identity. I am also interested in what people do with the kinds of canalisations of desire which constitute identity, in other words, how and where individuals (for example) variously resist, work with or capitulate to these canalisations. Likewise I am curious about how people do (or do not) eroticise and make meaning (or fail to make meaning, or refuse to make meaning) out of their conscious and unconscious choices in these domains of identity.

The metaphysics of absence embedded in Jung's work and articulated by Miller and by Kugler (above) focuses on desires not expressed in centres of identity, and (in particular) desires which do not relate to known presences. In her forthcoming book, *Jung as a Writer* (2005), Susan Rowland also articu-lates something of these dynamics by weaving the works of the Russian literary theorist Mikhail Mikhailovich Bakhtin and Jung into a mutually illuminating dialogue.

One of the points which emerges is that Jung's work can usefully be viewed as structured around two competing sets of dynamics: those forces which are centripetal, tending towards order and centralising structures, and those forces which are centrifugal – moving outwards, away from the static, towards the unknown and unstructured. Rowland comments that:

> Bakhtin's paradigm of language and social representation is that it is funnelled through a constant war between centralising energies that aim to standardise meaning and linguistic form, versus centrifugal forces of dispersion and difference as language is embodied in actual social situations.
>
> (Rowland, 2005: chapter 5)

Seen in this way, my interest is in the centrifugal forces in Jung's work (and in those of other psychoanalytic writers). Indeed my interest in Jung could be said to depend largely on the high frequency and intensity of these forces in his work, in contrast to, say, the majority of writing from the object relations tradition, which I read as more aligned around centripetal forces.

As such, Jung's model takes us to the edges of inhabitable identity, certainly beyond the edges of most depth psychology. Again, this is where Jung's 'Not-I within' comes into play clinically: it provides a way of thinking about such inarticulate desires without necessarily having to 'know' them, 'understand' them or gain access to them in ways which would canalise them into mainstream identity, e.g., into the service of the development of the ego. Desires which drive us to these edges cause endless emotional and psychological trouble, even as they save us from death by psychological atrophy.

Had she chosen to read her dream through a more mainstream metaphysics of presence, von Franz would have constructed herself as a victim of the Other's desires, and of an external attack. Instead, she did something else. Between her discussion of the negative animus in her dream and her comment about positive animus on the opposite page, there is a psychological space in which something unstated occurs. I suggest that in this gap von Franz moves towards a reading of her dream which is based on a metaphysics of absence.

My earlier suggestion was that the shadow of von Franz's negative animus contained the kernel of her positive animus, her own highest potential. In order to access that kernel, she would have had to take back into consciousness the split-off, murderous amalgams of aggression which the negative animus represented. She would have then had to redeploy that aggression in different amalgams, and for her own purposes. Conscious awareness of such steps would have been unthinkable for a woman of her period, but that I suggest was what she did unconsciously when she sent her negative animus away with a flea in his ear. My sense is that between her account of negative animus, and its opposite on the facing page, lies a whole story which she could not tell because it revolved around desires which could not be articulated intelligibly within female identity at that time. In this way, her text is being organised by a metaphysics of absence.

Furthermore, von Franz's 'Not-I within'/inner critic/self-hater is not just a matter of her own psychopathology – she, like Claremont de Castillejo sees it as a characteristic of female identity. Taking this up through my rereading of archetype (above), I would suggest that this kind of self-hater is a by-product of the performance of female identity. It is as if the offcuts from the manufacture of femininity tend to cluster together, expressing themselves as this inner voice for so many women. A different structure of female identity would, no doubt, produce different offcuts. As Kugler argues, our dreams reflect not our own face, but the face of the Other – be it the inner Otherness of the residues of identity production, or the outer Otherness, which that system of identity production binds us to.

GENDER AND THE CANALISATION OF DESIRE

These ideas about aggression and its role in women's resistance to the processes which produce identity by relying on a metaphysics of presence link back to my adolescent fascination with the Hammer Horror version of *She*. In hindsight, I would say that I responded to the film as a young woman encountering one of the culture's morality tales. Specifically, the tale dealt with the cultural assumption of the opposition between love and power, especially for women. Ayesha has power – infinite power, by virtue of her immortality. But thousands of years ago, in a fit of jealousy, she killed her lover Kallikrates, and has had to wait for his return. When he is eventually born again, he falls in love with the woman (Ustane) whom Ayesha has sent as bait to draw him to her.[9] Ayesha's jealousy flares again and she has Ustane killed, but only after she has put Kallikrates in a position where he must chose between her and Ustane.

In the film version, the outcome of Kallikrates' choice between these two women is prefigured in a scene where he looks down on a ruined city from a balcony in Ayesha's walled kingdom. He imagines the roar of the crowd at his command as an immortal god, if he takes up Ayesha's offer of bathing in the fires of immortality. So it is no surprise that when confronted with a choice between mortal love and immortal power, Kallikrates chooses the latter. But by aligning himself with Ayesha's power-centred universe, he unwittingly leads to her destruction when she steps into the fires of immortality a second time to help him overcome his fear of the flames. His choice of power over love also leads to Ustane's destruction. When he chooses Ayesha he frees her to kill Ustane as she wanted all along: all that was preventing her from doing so was the fear that Kallikrates was more attached to Ustane's love than he was to her own offer of immortality and unlimited power.

Thus power and love, as they so often are in the Western Romantic tradition, were set in opposition in the film. Watching this as an adolescent, I recall sensing the massive energy and drama in this arrangement, but also feeling something like distaste about how this opposition was being set up and about how I was being manoeuvred in relation to it, although I had no language for it at the time, and have spent some 25 years trying to build one.

I would now say that the power/love opposition which is so tightly sewn into much of the performance of gender in the West was being enacted melodramatically in the film in such a way as to encourage the viewer to eroticise that opposition and various positions in and around it. As I watched with fascination while the machinery of my culture swung into operation on the TV screen I could feel a torsion. I would now say that the torsion arose from my longing to have my desires channelled into this metaphysics of presence, with well-mapped, gender-inflected positions around power, sex and death made available through it, even though my longing for that canalisation nauseated and alarmed me. Not only was I uneasy about my own fascination with the film, I was also profoundly uncomfortable with the way it was trying to canalise my desire (and trying to seduce me into eroticising that canalisation). These positionings were attractive, but too safe, too much a product of a metaphysics of presence which has always felt deadening and deadly to me.

Of course the curious thing about these processes of identity creation is that one *does* feel them as one's own, just as I felt (and still do feel) the fascination with the *She* story as my own fascination. Even though I can now see some of the 'strings' of identity production and how the film tries to manipulate them, I still note my own longing to eroticise those pulls and tugs and surrender to the production of gender. At the same time, I am also still trying to unravel and subvert those tugs and pulls of identity canalisation in my clinical work and in my writing.

To me, Ayesha and Salome's capacity to fascinate are not a function of their being culturally specific images of an eternal, universal, neo-platonic, primordial essence of femininity. Their fascination is a function of their capacity to represent clusters of energies which have been disavowed in order to create and stabilise an inhabitable field of identity. These disavowed ('Othered') energies are like anti-matter to identity – they threaten to destabilise it catastrophically. This, however, makes them highly attractive, since as Bersani observes, only the decentred subject is available to desire (Bersani, 1986: 64–66, 112–113). Learning how to simultaneously disavow these excluded energies and to eroticise them and their disavowal is an important step in learning how to 'do' gender. These political processes of identity production through disavowal, erotic investment and canalisation of desire need to be made the *subject* of depth psychology, not assumed as its frame of reference.

THE COLLAPSE OF ANALYTIC THOUGHT AS A MOMENT OF BREAKTHROUGH

This process of deconstruction of analysis from within analysis is not just an intellectual exercise: it is a visceral, uncomfortable recognition that the very notions of identity that the analytic process offers are not only gross over-simplifications, but also circulate political ideologies. Nina, one of the women who contributed to this project, writes about a period of fluid gender identification in her life in a way which illustrates this. (Nina did not use any capital letters in her contribution – I have chosen to keep the text in its original form.)

> **Nina:** at times when the destabilisation or change is, or has been more active, i have had periods of confusion and pain. the worst was about from 28 to 30 when my gender underwent a radical 'masculinisation' and i seriously thought about having a sex change. fortunately my analysis of the experience helped me see that any desire to fix the body in this way was not the solution, but a miss-interpretation of the experience, (not that i understood what the experience was, but i had a strong opinion about what it was not; . . . not pathological, not 'gender dysphoria') . . . and that what i was experiencing was perhaps the extreme pole of gendered experience that may or may not eventually swing back.

Nina's experience of gender uncertainty[10] indicates that her position in relation to the gendered dimension of social identity has been unsettlingly fluid. But Nina is also clear that this fluidity was experienced in relation to a social construction of gender which pressured her to be more clear about her gender identity than she, at times, felt. Nina continues:

> **Nina:** these categories of man/woman, homo/hetero, masculine/feminine seem to me false and a way of imposing order and stability on a very chaotic area of human experience. my subjective experience of these categories is complex and one that i have never tried to articulate in any detail in language. it is, however, one of the chief concerns of my film and sound/radio work . . . the project of which is to embody a different experience of those categories and insert them in culture as 'text'; i.e. to represent the unrepresented. this is my way of unsettling those rigid fixed categories that don't apply to me and i suspect, most of the human race . . . but who knows?

Nina is saying that the whole classificatory system of gender has broken down for her, not that she is struggling with a sense of her own inner masculinity. Her suggestion is that the categories of identity (gender, ethnicity, class, sexual preference and so on), while not arbitrary, are far from fixed. This is Foucault's point in *Madness and Civilization* (1995) and *The Order of Things* (1973) – that the ways in which these divisions are made and perpetuated in order to attempt to stabilise the chaos of experience are a form of power: power through classification. This power is the most important form of all. It is what constitutes our very notion of identity, and it is at its most successful when we are convinced that we are voluntarily choosing what the identity system would have us choose in order to support its perpetuation.[11] These ideas matter analytically because the chaotic zones which Nina describes (where identity breaks down) offer access to the most important kinds of agency.

In making this move to critique the identity system on offer through the analytic framework, and in taking on board my analysands' questioning of it, I am trying to find ways of supporting myself and my analysands as we work through the wreckage of the grand narratives to see what, if anything, remains liveable. This seems to me to be the task of living with the question of identity in a post-modern world. Through Marike Finlay's work Kugler asks whether psychoanalysis can survive the desemanticisation of discourse (Kugler, 1993, internet): I would suggest that it can, especially if it uses as a point of departure Leo Bersani's insight that we need to celebrate a certain type of failure in Freud's thought.

Bersani argues that 'the psychoanalytical authenticity of Freud's work *depends on* a process of theoretical collapse' (1986: 3, original italics). Here, Bersani is suggesting that what makes psychoanalytic thought important is that it fails in ways which are themselves profoundly telling, not least of all in the repeating and seemingly inevitable nature of those failures. This is the basis of my interest in the point of failure in Jung's work where he turns back towards a metaphysics of presence. von Franz, in her analysis of her dream, makes a different turn, although in many other places her choices are quite different and are structured very much around mainstream knowable centres of desire.

There is, however, an important moment of collapse in analytic thought which occurs when it is confronted with its role in the formation and manufacture of mainstream identity. Object relations, for example, has, I suggest, restricted itself to those realms of the 'Not-I within' which, even though they may feel terrifyingly alien to the individual analysand, remain within the realms of intelligible identity. In other words, object relations can only 'map' inner Othernesses which can be (potentially) assimilated within the individual without demanding that they transgress the boundaries of socially recognisable identity.

In order to illustrate what I mean, I quote a transcript from the work of Valerie Walkerdine which follows an interchange between two four-year-old boys (Sean and Terry), their thirtyish nursery school teacher (Miss Baxter) and a three-year-old girl (Annie). Annie takes a piece of Lego to add to something she is making, and Terry tries to take it from her. She resists and he responds:

Terry: You're a stupid cunt, Annie.

The teacher tells him to stop and Sean tries to mess up another child's construction. The teacher tells him to stop. Then Sean says:

Sean: Get out of it Miss Baxter paxter.
Terry: Get out of it knickers Miss Baxter.
Sean: Get out of it Miss Baxter paxter.
Terry: Get out of it Miss Baxter the knickers paxter knickers, bum.
Sean: Knickers, shit, bum.
Miss B: Sean, that's enough, you're being silly.
Sean: Miss Baxter, knickers, show your knickers.
Terry: Miss Baxter, show your bum off.
(they giggle)
Miss B: I think you're being very silly.
Terry: Shit Miss Baxter, shit Miss Baxter.
Sean: Miss Baxter, show your knickers your bum off.
Sean: Take all your clothes off, your bra off.
Terry: Yeah, and take your bum off, take your wee-wee off, take your clothes, your mouth off.
Sean: Take your teeth out, take your head off, take your hair off, take your bum off. Miss Baxter the paxter knickers taxter.
Miss B: Sean, go and find something else to do please.

(1990: 4)

Walkerdine's critical psychology-based analysis of this transcript identifies numerous levels of power dynamics. The first is that the boys are simply rebelling against an authority figure. Another level is, however, embedded in how they rebel by latching onto the teacher's femaleness. This tactic provides a way of manipulating the 'rules of the game' (that is, the discourse) so that they can get away with an abusive, humiliating attack aimed at reducing their teacher to a silenced, powerless, sex object, much as the initial insult to Annie was intended to do. The cultural assumption that women 'belong' in this position is not always in operation, but there is always a certain gradient around it as a possibility, especially if other circumstances conspire to make it an allowed, or even a favoured interpretation, in a given situation.

Most importantly of all, Walkerdine describes how the liberal humanist discourse of contemporary pedagogy constructs the teacher as a nurturing facilitator of children's learning through self-expressive play. In another essay Walkerdine articulates the pedagogic fantasy which is structuring the classroom space in which Miss Baxter is working:

Let us imagine such a classroom. All has been transformed to make way for 'active leaning', not 'passive regurgitating'. This pedagogic space is filled with groups of tables, not rows of desks. There may be no playtime, since work and play are indistinguishable, and work cards may have replaced textbooks. Children may choose their own timetables. Freedom is imagined. A whole fictional space is created, a fantasy-space in which the ideal nature, the most facilitating environment (rather like a green-house), is created in the classroom. . . . The teacher is no authoritarian father figure, but a bourgeois and nurturant mother . . . whose attach-ment to the children in her care, together with her total presence, ensures their psychic health.

(1990: 23)

These pedagogic fantasies 'naturalise' a kind of power which the boys can then exercise as being above and beyond question – whatever occurs in the name of 'play' is for the 'good' for the child's development (1990: 7), and that, in turn, is the ultimate 'good' in this system. Through these unexamined fantasies about children, teachers and teaching, a mechanism is put in place which the boys simply make use of. This mechanism enables them to 'switch the points' in the power structure so that instead of the prevailing under-standing being one which positions them as having less power (as children with a teacher), they are able to access another reading of the situation in which they, as males, have more power than the females they are dealing with, regardless of age or position. This is seen as right and normal by the teacher herself who, in subsequent discussions, dismisses the incident as 'normal' for the boys' age (1990: 6). Perhaps like Deutsch's fantasy of the good enough mother, she has turned her own aggression inwards and eroticised it, mean-while being saved from her own masochistic, suicidal tendencies by her own narcissism.

Before coming back to the moment of collapse of object relations, a few more points need to be made about Miss Baxter's situation. First, what is muddled up here is that these boys are not just being rude and naughty. Sean and Terry have discovered that they can trump any power relationship that they find themselves in with a woman by using sexualised aggression, and that the nature of the feminine role is such that while a woman stays in role, she has no effective counterdiscourse.

Second, and more dangerously, while she operates within a role (of teacher) which has been formed out of fantasies of feminine nurturance and childhood innocence, Miss Baxter not only has no counterdiscourse, she has no way of thinking critically about the boys' behaviour. For Miss Baxter to see what the boys are doing is to think extremely disagreeable thoughts about aggression-cruelty amalgams, and aggressive-hateful energies which seek to humiliate and torment the Other. She might also need to think about contempt, spitefulness and viciousness. Such thoughts would demand the development of a moral imagination, and perhaps questions about the damage caused by staying within an identity which is based on fantasies of innocence, unconditional acceptance and passivity. Like Hart's analysand in Chapter 1, she might come to see the way in which her role demands that she enacts the violence of passivity. The boys are being bullies and Miss Baxter is teaching Annie that being bullied by boys is normal and acceptable. She is also teaching the boys that these strategies are acceptable and effective for controlling girls and women.

Third, and most important of all, there is a much more disruptive layer of disagreeability to be thought about which lies beyond these particular boys' specific actions. If Miss Baxter were to start to feel the intensity of the boys' attack, and see its impact on them and on other children, let alone herself, she might then find herself realising that her job is premised in the fantasy that she is supposed to provide a benevolent, containing and nurturing space for what is, in reality, unacceptable and unworkable. She might discover that the apparently benevolent, liberal humanist agenda which informs the very fabric of her work role not only fails to serve her interests or those of her colleagues or pupils, but actually treats them as cannon fodder for its own perpetuation and naturalisation.

This third layer of meaning might emerge if Miss Baxter were in analysis. It might appear as apparently unconnected but probably relentlessly distressing symptoms, such as recurrent migraines, insomnia, depression, nightmares, or recurrent relational difficulties or failures. These symptoms could be read through the Jungian dissociationist idiom as expressions of something which is part of Miss Baxter's 'Not-I within' – part of her which finds the current situation intolerable. Such a situation might well contain many feelings of stuckness and desperation for both clinician and analysand. The less discursively mediated aspects of Miss Baxter's response to her work situation, her own disagreeable thoughts, would probably be deeply buried and experienced as very much part of an unacceptable realm of 'Not-I within'.

The object relations contribution to analysing Miss Baxter's situation would be to examine the part being played by her 'inner family' – in other words, the psychological resources which were available to her in babyhood and childhood, how she has internalised them, and how she has subsequently lived out those internalisations as she has interacted with the external world. These resources and her inner experience of them would become apparent in the analytic transference (and countertransference), with the expectation that what would emerge would be patterns of primitive anxieties around the inadequacies of the internalised emotional objects. The analytic task then becomes that of 'holding' these primitive anxieties; in other words, thinking about them and trying to understand them without being forced into action by them. I am not questioning the value of these skills and tactics. My concern is that they can only access part of what might be going on intrapsychically for Miss Baxter.

Object relations shares with the pedagogic discourse a largely unquestioned liberal humanist investment in the fantasy of the bourgeois, nurturing mother. Consequently it is likely to be blind to any struggle Miss Baxter might be having with the feeling that she is working in an environment which depends extensively on subtle practices which normalise her subscription to a fantasy that she, as a teacher (as Walkerdine indicates, a role based on the image of a nurturant mother), will 'naturally' function within an identity which requires the disavowal of her own aggressive energies and the potential for agency embedded in them. For an object relations therapist to support Miss Baxter's deconstruction of the 'truths' which are assumed to underpin her profession would be to start to deconstruct the fantasies about girls, women and mothers that unconsciously underpin object relations. Taking up the invitation which this level of Miss Baxter's experience presents means turning towards Bersani's point that psychoanalytic 'truth' is revealed in the moment when psychoanalytic theory collapses. Miss Baxter's story demands the examination of a level of 'Not-I within' which cannot be interpreted within object relations – a level of 'Not-I within' which, if engaged with, causes the collapse of object relations.

Indeed, the material Miss Baxter's story offers is usually excluded in order to stabilise the intrapsychic field of experience which has become the naturalised domain of object relations.[12] Creation of such domains involves a violence to the fabric of experience, but that too has become naturalised. Intersubjectivist attempts to address this rip only address the easier part of it. They recognise that the intrapsychic is more closely bound up with the interpsychic than has been understood in object relations but, as will become apparent in the next chapter, there is still a failure to take into account the intra- and interpsychic implications of identity politics. Without a way of speaking about these excluded realms, and how their exclusion supports certain systems of identity, there is no way of exploring the obstacles which lie in the way of women's engagement with their own aggressive energies and the potentials they contain.

As an aside, this is also where assertiveness training fails: it has no means of accessing and analysing the politics of Miss Baxter's situation. More importantly, the conservative identity politics at the heart of the assertiveness training discourse means that it has no willingness or desire to engage with these matters.

Traditional Jungian thought cannot access these dimensions properly either. Miss Baxter might one day be capable of thoughts of man-killing aggressivity which would enable her to find a way of challenging her work situation, but that is a very long way away from where she is in Walkerdine's vignette. Meanwhile, a lot of work needs to be done to find ways of thinking about what stands in the way of her accessing such thoughts. Jung's concept of an ahistorical, universal, apolitical, archetypal animus cannot map the necessary intra- and interpsychic connections.

On the other hand, Miss Baxter is up against matters which go beyond the object relations focus on individual psychopathology and sit closer to the Jungian and post-Jungian concerns with the wider patterns in the human condition. As von Franz and Claremont de Castillejo point out, there are certain factors which are part of the very structure of female identity which can stand in the way of women's agency. These structures are usually experienced by the individual woman as personal and private (in the way that Claremont de Castillejo describes the operation of the inner critic as only speaking to a woman when she is alone and vulnerable). Such structures, however, need to be treated as highly specific to the individual woman and also as part of a wider network of structures (such as the role of nursery school teacher) whose trade in identity politics bear down on her. What I am proposing is structurally very similar to the traditional Jungian approach on how to work with a woman's animus problem. The difference is that I am suggesting that the animus is a symptom of the identity politics which are embedded in the performance of gender and that in order to engage with a woman's 'animus problem' much bigger questions about the nature of the performance of gender need to be opened up, rather than naturalised through Jung's fantasy of contrasexuality. This relies on the rereading of archetype proposed earlier, which took it out of the universal, ahistorical realm and placed it firmly in the realm of identity formation and identity politics.

Again, however, the reasons for staying with the Jungian and post-Jungian position in relation to these questions are that: first, the early Jungian women developed a true-to-experience way of talking about the psychological inner life of the performance of gender, even if that language was hamstrung by the ghosts of German Romanticism. Second, through Jung's dissociationist heritage, his model offers a way of accessing the interior, deep impacts and meanings of identity politics as they are lived by an individual. Perhaps it would be more accurate to say 'as they live an individual'. And here's the rub: Jung's notion of archetype actually provided space to give the liberal humanist agenda of object relations the slip: his work is all about engaging with the impersonal forces which live us, rather than trying to normalise and correct developmental problems.

Again, this reading takes its lead from Kugler's earlier comment that '[t]he mirror at work in the Jungian hermeneutic does not reflect the self-same face. Rather it mirrors back the face of the Other' (Kugler, 1993, internet paper). I would add that this face of the Other is not just the face of the mother as it is in object relations, but the faces of the identity politics which offer us a viable, recognisable identity. In this way elements of Jung's deconstructive approach (as Rowland rightly calls it) can be used to turn the insights of the post-structuralist and post-modern thinkers into clinical praxis. In the next chapter, I discuss a step towards that in the form of my own experiments with turning this theoretico-clinical amalgam into a research methodology.

Chapter 3

Identity nightmares and a methodology in the madness

DANGEROUS FEMININITY

In this chapter I take a deeper look at the kinds of difficulties which arise when women try to explore their own aggressive energies. As a vehicle for this, I use the story of my own struggles with aggressive energies in this project and how a research methodology developed out of those struggles. Threaded through that story are, however, discussions relating to how fantasies about femininity and female (non)-aggression have been woven into the fabric of Western notions of identity and interiority. What emerges is that the cultural invisibility of women's aggressive energies is embedded in the foundation of the Western notion of reason (and through that, identity), so that the exploration of women's aggressive fantasies and energies stirs up associations with madness, and through madness, death. A comment from Isla, one of the women who contributed material to this book, provides a point of departure.

> **Isla:** There is this fear of having my hair cut off (I often fear this in cinemas where I'm sitting in front of someone else).

Similarly, I once heard a woman say that she never wore long, dangly earrings for fear that someone might grab them and rip the earring hooks through her earlobes. In the wider scheme of violence in the world, these threats are comparatively trivial, but they need to be seen in the context in which women describe them – as significant, recurring threads of the fabric of their thoughts and actions. Such comments could easily be dismissed as the neurotic anxieties of an individual woman, but one of the points of this book is to amass a collection of such imagery, assembling it in such a way as to indicate that, although each expression of it is individual and contextualised, such imagery goes beyond individual experience. These fears about comparatively trivial damage to one's external appearance are actually the conscious edge of an extensive, unconscious network of actions and avoidances which are an attempt to manage a pervasive sense of inner and outer threat.

From a traditional feminist perspective these images could be read as expressing the extent to which women's safety is already compromised by prejudicial social fantasies about the female body. Catherine Waldby argues that in the cultural imagination, sexual penetration of a woman's body without her consent does not really count as 'damage' because the boundaries of women's bodies are assumed to be somehow fluid and vague, in contrast with the firmer boundaries ascribed to the male body. For men, Waldby points out, the use of violence as a defence against another man's unwanted sexual overtures is largely considered justified, a situation which:

> points towards an economy of sexual violence in which even the momentary possibility of penetration, the very fantasy of penetration [of the male body] counts as an absolute violation. Clearly if such overtures counted as violence against women, and women felt free to retaliate, the streets would be littered with battered men.

(1995: 269)

Waldby's articulation of this traditional feminist position is witty and revealing, but there is another approach to women's sense of threat which I will pursue. I suggest that part of the sense of threat can arise from the structure of femininity itself. Another comment from Isla touches on this.

Isla: Sometimes groups of women scare me. I feel that they are sharing some secret and I'm not in on it. Often I feel like the anti-woman. I try to be everything that a woman isn't (supposedly). In fact I'd like to be a man. I'd like that freedom, confidence and sense of strength that I think men have. I'm not talking about a sex-change but I don't like the attitude that 'women behave this way' and 'women do this'. I want to be 'not a woman' so I can do everything I want. I often feel suddenly trapped or scared and I think it's my 'femaleness' that makes me feel this way.

In particular, I am interested in Isla's sense of the entrapping or frightening nature of her own femaleness. Again, this could be a comment on the social vulnerability associated with being female, or it could refer to something inherent in the structure of femininity.

Alarming torsions in the concept of femininity become apparent when considering the forms taken by idealised expressions of it. Classical ballet with its waif-like princesses and delicate maidens is made possible through a training which creates a tough, numb, will-based, brutalised embodiment

(Kirkland, 1986). The ultimate image of gentle feminine vulnerability is a product of vicious regimentation, and the toughest ambition. Likewise, it needs to be remembered that Aphrodite, goddess of feminine beauty, was born of an act of immense violence:

> When, at the instigation of his mother, Gaea, the audacious Cronus had castrated his father, Uranus, he cast the severed genitals into the sea. They floated on the surface of the waters, producing a white foam from which rose Aphrodite.

> . . . everything about her was pure charm and harmony. . . . Aphrodite exuded an aura of seduction. To the perfection of her figure and the purity of her features she added the grace which attracted and conquered.
> (Guirand, 1987: 130–131)[1]

At this level of the cultural imagination, it is as if femininity's roots in (dis-avowed) extreme violence enhance its power, as though it were a triumph over the abject. Given that the abject is what is thrown down or out because of how it 'disturbs identity, system, order' intolerably (Kristeva, 1982: 4), the question arises of what happens to such disturbances. They cannot be thrown out of human experience, out of the collective space of the human psyche, since the realm of the abject is forever with us by virtue of our very human-ness – we *are* the very disturbance which is so intolerable, and that disturb-ance, that excluded Otherness inevitably haunts us as subjects. In this way the violence and aggression which are coded as 'Other' to femininity become terrifyingly familiar inner ghosts for an individual woman as she struggles to live her interpretation of gendered identity.

AN IDENTITY NIGHTMARE

Doris, one of the women who contributed material, amplifies this notion of a disturbing threat embedded in femaleness through a dream and her own analysis of it.

Doris: I was in a graveyard and an unknown psychopath had just shot all of my friends and was pursuing me (or a representation of me – as in whenever I watch horror movies I always identify with the pursued and terrorised, not the pursuer). He (this was assumed, the sex and iden-tity of the psychopaths are hidden behind dark glasses, a fright wig and a raincoat – psychopaths in my dreams are always men except for the time Meryl Streep was terrorising me) appeared out of nowhere, pointed a gun and fired. However the gun didn't go off, his arm blew off instead. This turned out to be a fake arm as he was playing with me before the final blow. He laughingly drew a machete with his real arm and sliced my head in two – taking off most of my face. I was still alive so he chopped it off at the neck and I was dead. This dream was different to most psychopath dreams I have in that firstly there was no blood or thick yellow coagulant substances – my head was made of clay – it sliced like plasticine. Secondly – I was killed. Usually I'm just tortured and wake up in a sweat, screaming, crying etc. Often I am in a situation where I too have a weapon with a kill or be killed choice – the weapon always turns out to be faulty – blunt, not loaded etc., and it's no matter anyway because the psychopath is always unkillable. As always, aside from many other interpretations that could be put on this dream, there's a very obvious voice speaking to me with a macabre sense of humour.

Doris' dream could be viewed through Donald Kalsched's (1996) model of archetypal defences of the self; in other words it could be seen as a response to personal trauma, and an attempt to protect and salvage something of a core self in the face of that. To do so would be to opt, in the way of object relations (as discussed in the previous chapter), to only explore the 'Not-I within' which could be assimilated into the conscious psyche while Doris retains a mainstream, socially recognisable identity structure. While this is valid, and frequently necessary as an initial clinical position, I want to introduce a possibility which lies beyond these tactics.

Pursuing this possibility entails regarding Doris' psychopath as an extreme example of the operation of the self-hater, an ultra-extreme version of the fear of a stranger cutting one's hair off, or ripping one's earrings down through one's earlobes. While these images entail less psychopathic, sadistic attacks, they do seem to be on the same continuum of images of attacks perpetrated by strangers who do what they do simply because they want to do it, and can get away with it. In other words, they want to harm, to deface another human being, with the extreme version being the desire to do this as a slow, murderous form of torture. From this perspective, Doris' psychopath dream might be an illustration of the self-hater operating completely without restraint.

While discussing her struggles with the performance of gender, Doris refers back to her dream.

Doris: I sometimes think it would be much easier if I was convinced that the struggle I have around this is because I am a man in a woman's body. In which case I would be saying the gender roles are acceptable. I would be just wanting to adopt the ones appropriate to a different body.

As it is, the struggle I experience is that I have some concept of equality – I treat you this way, you treat me the same way back. This is all very well in theory, but as a biological woman in the real world I get paid less. I have to struggle harder for jobs if I don't want to work in accepted female roles. I have to be wary walking about alone at night.

These it would seem are the psychopaths I fight off in my dreams – not some struggle with my essential male/female sides. The fact is that I can remake myself any way I want but still have to live in a world that doesn't recognise my position in any material way, and probably sees it as aberrant.

Thus Doris makes it clear that she does not regard her psychopath dream as simply an attack from an inner masculinity, nor does she see it as the result of personal trauma. Her attacker is the lived experience of gendered identity itself, and she links the psychopath's attack to her struggle with the exercise of agency. Doris sees her assailant as an internalisation of the impersonal, external process of gender production. I suggest that Doris' dream can be read as expressing how that danger is experienced in an individual woman's inner world.

RESISTANCE TO IDENTITY AS THE BASIS OF A METHODOLOGY

As I set about reflecting on dreams like Doris' and images like Isla's and what kind of methodology I might use to engage with them, I noticed that my responses were in the form of vague senses of discomfort which vaporised or turned to stone when I tried to express them. Usually, if I pushed past this, my own self-hater would cut in, telling me that the whole project was a waste of time, and that even if it was not, I was not capable of doing it anyway. So I had better give up now. Something seemed to be attacking my sense of agency.

Initially this reaction seemed specific and personal. Then I reread von Franz's discussion of her dream. I began to see my own struggles through the lens of that dream, and also through the struggles which the women contributors described themselves as having encountered while responding to my request that they document some of their aggressive fantasies.

Ella: I was just not getting down to this – cups of tea, snacks, tidying up, staring aimlessly through the window – anything but. I decided to deal with it a paragraph at a time, but what could I say that could be of

> any use? I'll let you down, or horror, my material will be so unoriginal and boring it's fit only for trash.
>
> **Dolores:** This has taken me a while to do because, although I had gut reactions, it took me a long time to work out what they were and to be able to articulate them.
>
> **Helena:** Where to begin? The first thoughts I have on setting out on this inner exploration are of exhaustion. Just thinking about it makes me feel too tired. Not so much the thinking as the process of transferring the thoughts, impressions, memories, ideas down onto a piece of paper.

Articulating aggressive fantasies seemed to take women participants into areas of internal resistance, and this paralleled the resistance I encountered in myself around the project. I began to wonder if these resistances were connected to Jacqueline Rose's suggestion that:

> [f]eminism's affinity with psychoanalysis rests above all ... with [the] recognition that there is a resistance to identity which lies at the very heart of psychic life'.
>
> (Rose, 1990: 232)[2]

It is this psychoanalytic notion of resistance to identity as the lively, necessary and healthy heart of psychic life, which I find missing from object relations, and which I see as the mark of its unacceptable, normalising agenda.

Viewed in the light of Rose's comment, however, my reactions, like those of the women participants, might be saying something about how women resist female identity and the part played in that resistance by aggressive fantasies and energies. On that basis I began to suspect that I might be able to use my own resistances as a countertransference-type of instrument through which to develop an understanding of the material women were giving to me. The tactic of developing hypotheses based on countertransference reactions is what analysts are trained to do in relation to their analysands' unconscious structures, and I began to experiment with adopting this analytic position in relation to the whole issue of women's aggressive energies, and my relationships with the women participating in my research.

Towards the end of this project, I came across a use of countertransference which parallels aspects of this experiment. In order to teach psychiatric trainees in a large mental hospital the psychoanalytic stance of having an experience and being able to think about it at the same time, R.D. Hinshelwood (2002) interwove the practice of psychoanalytic infant observation with Isabel Menzies' (1959) classic study of a general hospital's nursing service as a social defence system (Hinshelwood, 2002: 163). Psychoanalytic infant observation entails spending time with a mother and baby each week from soon after the baby's birth with the aim of exposing the trainee analyst to the kinds of primitive anxieties which attend the early stages of life for both the baby and those around her or him. While this practice is fraught with problems (Austin, 2003), it does help trainees to learn to examine the feelings that are induced in them by a situation, reflect on those feelings, and use them as a basis for developing a speculative understanding of the unconscious dynamics present.

Menzies wrote an object relations based study of a hospital nursing service, drawing out how its structure and operation were being driven by primitive psychological defences, rather than by any of the conscious goals it claimed for itself. Hinshelwood put this idea together with the infant observation practice and used the result as the basis of teaching psychiatric trainees to think about the unconscious torsions which were driving the hospital psychiatric system they worked in. In order to do this, trainees were taught to observe the interplay between the psychiatric service and its patients and were supervised in the use of their own experience as an observer to develop countertransference-based hypotheses about underlying anxieties and defences in the psychiatric system (Hinshelwood, 2002: 164).

In the same way, I have tried to observe my own countertransference reactions to the material women gave me and use those reactions as the basis of hypotheses about the unconscious patterns embedded in women's aggressive fantasies. The post-Jungian perspective which I am using means, however, that I am not only interested in unconscious anxieties, but also in the unconscious *telos* or purposive direction of those anxieties and the patterns of energy and fantasies they produce.[3] At the same time the critical psychology perspective which I am also using raises questions about the cultural fantasies of gender and identity which shape that *telos* and the psychological accessibility of women's aggressive energies.

EMBODIED COUNTERTRANSFERENCE: A SOURCE OF HYPOTHESES ABOUT THE OTHER'S INNER WORLD

Staying, for the moment, with the question of using countertransference as the basis of a research methodology, Samuels describes the analyst's experience of embodied countertransference as follows:

> Suppose, after a session with a particular patient, I feel depressed (this may be a single occurrence or part of a series). Now I may know from my own reading of myself that I am not actually depressed and certainly not seriously depressed. I may conclude that the depressed state I am in is a result of my close contact with this particular patient. It may be that the

patient is feeling depressed right now and that neither of us is aware of it. In this instance, my depression is a reflection of his or her depression. I call this (my depression) 'reflective countertransference'. In time I may be able to make use of this knowledge.

But there is another possibility, my experience of becoming a depressed person may stem from the presence and operation of such a person in the patient's psyche. The patient may have experienced a parent as depressed, and my reaction precisely embodies the patient's emotionally experienced parent. I have also become part of the patient's inner world. I emphasise inner world because I am not attempting any kind of factual reconstruction that would discover a depressed parent. Indeed, the depressed parent may himself or herself be symbolic of a depressive theme active in the patient's psyche rather than literal or causative of anything (parent as symbolic image). This entire state of affairs I have come to call 'embodied countertransference,' and I distinguish it from reflective countertransference. Sometimes, there is no person, and what is embodied is a theme that is active in the patient's psyche.

(2000: 411)

Samuels makes the post-Jungian assumption that the unconscious material which the analysand is struggling with is physically and psychologically infectious, and its effects need to be noted by the analyst. These effects can then be used as the basis of hypotheses which are offered back to the analysand in the form of countertransference-based interpretations. The analysand's responses about the usefulness of the interpretation may or may not be verbal. Indeed, the most powerful responses are often unconscious ones such as whether the analysand stays with the subject matter being interpreted, or links to an apparently different subject off the back of the analyst's interpretation. These kinds of lateral links can reveal the 'energetic' structure of the unconscious – the interpretation triggers an unconscious link for the analysand so that instead of their next comment being made from a logically related, conscious place, it comes instead from a place that is closely linked to it at an unconscious level. Mapping unconscious connections in this way can draw out something about the 'real' structures which make the decisions in a person's life, the level at which they are being 'run' by their unconscious structures, around which logic and rationally are being 'bent' in order to serve an unconscious imperative.

Other changes which can indicate the structure of unconscious links in response to an interpretation include changes in the emotional tone or temperature in the room, the spontaneous emergence of imagery, bodily sensations for either (or both) analyst and analysand and so on. These changes can be subtle or drastic, fast or slow, immediate, or delayed, but if the analyst and analysand can come to be open to these kinds of to-and-fro processes in the interpersonal space, patterns and themes eventually start to emerge. My personal image for this is that it is like the childhood experiment of placing a magnet under a sheet of paper and sprinkling iron fillings onto the paper. The magnet charges the filings and they fall into a pattern which indicates the lines of magnetic force around the poles of the magnet. The to-and-fro of the analytic interaction, if danced lightly and carefully enough and with enough mindfulness around unconscious communications, eventually reveals something of the shape and texture of the analysand's emerging unconscious landscape.

IMAGES OF THE UNCONSCIOUS AS AN EXPERIENTIAL LANDSCAPE

A key aspect of this kind of psychoanalytically informed practice is that it involves turning up, session after session, to open up this kind of space in which the inner Otherness of the analysand might slowly make its presence felt. This inner Otherness is usually unclear, always changing and mostly fragmentary in nature. Yet it may be glimpsed from time to time as its capacity to shape the analytic interaction is felt. Imagine the space which the analyst and analysand form by working together as a landscape, but with the analyst and analysand exploring this landscape together blindfolded and with diminished hearing ability. You can pick up muffled sounds, and distinguish between their tones, and the odd word or part of a sentence gets through, but that is about all. The analyst has two advantages: first, their training analysis should have provided them with the opportunity of exploring their own emergent unconscious landscape (with all the dangers associated with that) with their own analyst. Second, they will have had previous experiences of slowly coming to know parts of other psychic landscapes with other analysands and having seen this (sometimes) enables the analysand to live their lives a little differently as a result. Of course, both of these 'advantages' can easily turn into the liability of presumed understanding based on previous experience. Nonetheless, the psychic landscape remains a shifting, strange thing, with the analytic attitude being that one can try to learn to think and feel as fully as possible around whatever facet of it is being presented at a given point in time.

In addition to being a development of the reading of Jung's work on inner Otherness outlined in the preceding chapter, my use of these images of psyche as landscape relies on Butler's interpretation of a remark by Walter Benjamin, who suggests that melancholia tries to reverse or suspend time producing 'landscapes' as its signature effect (Butler, 1997: 174). Thus, Butler argues, '[o]ne might profitably read the Freudian topography that melancholy occasions as precisely such a spatialised landscape of the mind' (Butler, 1997: 174). Elsewhere, Butler remarks that '[w]hat Freud here calls the "character of the ego" appears to be the sedimentation of objects loved and lost, the archaeological remainder, as it were, of unresolved grief' (1997: 133).

Joining this idea of a Freudian topography to the notion of the 'Not-I within' embedded in Jung's work (see Chapter 2) offers the image of an unconscious psychic landscape which the analyst and analysand encounter through meeting regularly. My own sense is that, as Benjamin's reading of Freud implies, this landscape is significantly formed by patterns of losses, lacks and defeats, and what (if anything) has become of them or been made from them as they have settled out to form the individual's inner landscape. Again, Jung's clinical focus on developing ways of coming to know the analysand's experience of the 'Not-I within' provides tools and attitudes which are especially suited for exploring the emergent landscape of the psyche.[4]

The sustained holding of a space, which seeks to receive and interpret (articulate) the analysand's unconscious communications in this way, is psychoactive. In such a space the Otherness within the analysand starts to appear through forgotten appointments, late arrivals, the analysand not being able to get access to the analyst's rooms at the appointed time for some reason or another, dreams, rapid changes in the 'emotional temperature' during an analytic session (which do not correlate to the conscious content of the conversation), abrupt changes in lines of thinking, a sense of no-go zones where thinking falls apart, one or other party suddenly feeling sleepy or any other of the myriad of expressions of transference and countertransference. Analytic training gives trainees a chance to calibrate and explore their ability to pick up these kinds of clues and cues and think and feel their way around them, reflecting on their potential meaning in the light of the analysand's conscious communications.

COUNTERTRANSFERENCE AS A THEORETICAL RESEARCH TOOL

Moving such an approach into my research entailed regarding my own images of broken-up states, nausea, fear or madness in relation to the material women contributed as core information about the unconscious landscapes of women's aggressive energies. This meant consciously refusing to fall into the obvious position which was to regard these states as a distraction that I needed to push through in order to get on with some 'real' research. Like von Franz's interpretation of her burglar dream, the intrusive, alarming Other turned out to contain the seeds of what was needed for the project to progress. This Other was a source of agency, rather than its undoing, although it was a very different kind of agency to the more usual will and rationality-based varieties which underlie traditional research methodologies.

Slowly, I came to identify with von Franz's burglar more and more, imagining that I was trying to break into the stuck elements of depth psychological theorising of women's experience. I wanted to get women's aggression, physicality and agency back into bodies of theory which have been largely stabilised by their exclusion or distortion. My initial attempts were angry and attacking, shot through with fear and frustration. As outlined in Chapter 2, depth psychology, and especially object relations contains and unconsciously perpetuates a conservative, and at times reactionary, identity politics, and it took me a long time to find elements of theory which I could use to jemmy open a window on this.

A powerful crowbar came in the form of the work of Leo Bersani, which I also referred to in Chapter 2. In *The Freudian Body: Psychoanalysis and Art*, Bersani (1986) argues that the nature of the psychoanalytic project is that it is about the unconscious, and that the unconscious is something which cannot be pinned down. Bersani suggests that the brilliance of Freud's work is that even as he attempted to document the unconscious, it broke through and unravelled the dominant narrative of his text through his footnotes. In this way the operation of the unconscious is evident in Freud's work – he was not just writing about it, it was present and undercutting his conscious argument. Bersani takes this further, arguing that the nature of the psyche is such that it inevitably subverts any account of itself. He writes that '[p]sychoanalysis is an unprecedented attempt to give a theoretical account of precisely those forces which obstruct, undermine, play havoc with theoretical accounts themselves' (1986: 4). My aim was to try to note some of the forces which obstructed, undermined my project and played havoc with its development and use my observations of those forces as the basis for developing theory. No doubt, even as I have done so, yet more unconscious dynamics will be undoing those efforts, in their turn, especially, I suspect, around my use of the image of psyche as a landscape.

This approach led to my interest in Derrida's critique of the metaphysics of presence, which I touched on at the end of Chapter 2. In line with the idea of there being a metaphysics of absence, Bersani seems to be pointing to psychoanalysis as an attempt to express that which cannot be completely expressed, yet must be expressed in some way, even if we are never quite sure of why or how to do it. From this perspective, the 'real' focus of psychoanalysis is to attend to disruptive, inarticulate desires and fascinations. Consequently, Bersani's point is that it may be more useful to look at the relationships between parts of a text, rather than the content of a text in order to glimpse the workings of the unconscious.

My own and other women's attempts to think about our own aggressive energies generated painful confusion and contradiction. Accordingly, through this reading of Bersani and Derrida, I have tried to let the project form around and gesture towards a contradictory and irreconcilable metaphysics of absence which seems to fit better with women's aggressive energies. In order to develop these tactics I chose elements of theory, be they from Jung or elsewhere, which supported this sense that things can be learnt from unconscious processes, but that those unconscious processes can never be 'known'. This may present difficulties for readers with a more traditional academic training, but, as a state of affairs, it should be familiar to clinicians. With this context established, I now outline how I collected material from the women who participated in this project, developing, as I go, a position about the nature of knowledge (an epistemology).

CONVERSATIONS ABOUT WOMEN'S DISAGREEABLE THOUGHTS

The first version of this project was a doctoral thesis, which I subsequently completely rewrote as this book. While writing the PhD I discovered that mention of my interest in women's aggressive energies in non-clinical conversations with friends, acquaintances and strangers quickly and easily elicited vignettes about the pleasures and terrors of 'women's disagreeable thoughts'. These arose in response to a number of images of my own which I had developed to illustrate the kinds of material I was trying to think about. When I had a sense that a particular woman was interested in my work, I asked her if she would be willing to write down some of her responses which had emerged in our discussions. If she said yes, I provided a document containing some illustrations of the kinds of material which seemed to belong under the umbrella of women's aggressive fantasies. Usually within a few days, sometimes a few weeks, the woman either contacted me and asked to meet so that she could give me her contribution, or she posted or emailed it to me. Had I not included these vignettes and used them privately as the basis of my own thinking, this book would read as one woman's ideas, when in fact it is the result of the thoughts and experiences of many women and men. The relationship between aggressive fantasy and morality (see previous chapter) made it important that I traced and attributed as many contributions as possible and made the project's collaborative quality clear.

On the other hand, inclusion of these vignettes creates significant methodological and epistemological problems. Starting with the methodological ones: I knew all the women who made these contributions personally, and I accepted contributions where I could find them, rather than setting up a rigorous selection procedure to locate participants who were not known to me. In order for knowledge to count as acceptable in the social sciences, there has been a pressure to imitate the physical sciences and create researcher-independent, reproducible, experimentally gathered evidence in support of theoretical hypotheses. In reply to this Fonow and Cook point out (through Joan Acker's 1991 work) that it is important that feminists document the 'difficulties and rewards of piercing the methodological dictum of non-involvement with one's subjects. One of these benefits is the higher quality of information possible as a result of mutual disclosure' (1991: 10) and Stanley and Wise argue that the vulnerability necessary for this kind of engagement can be used in disciplined, scholarly and rigorous ways (1983: 197). Thus my decision to use the vignettes women gave me was on the basis that they offered a more intimate perspective on women's lived experience of their aggressive energies. Above all, because the contributions grew out of normal conversations, they illustrate women talking about their everyday inner lives in a way which more closely resembles normal interaction, rather than reflecting how women would talk to a researcher who they knew to be running a more formal or structured data collection process.

While participants came from a variety of Euro-Australian and European cultures, classes, backgrounds, lifestyles, levels of education, ages, parental statuses and sexual orientations, I make no claim to reflect social diversity. What is presented is a situated, partial view, offered in the hope that it will sit alongside other situated, partial views, which collectively acknowledge differences between women, and produce a diverse range of strong voices from the margins of normal women's experience of their own gendered identity.[5]

The main difficulty which arose from my knowing all the contributors was that it made it impossible to give basic demographic information about each participant in order to situate them socially. From a feminist perspective this kind of information is essential in order to draw out differences between women's situations and how these differences affect their experience of the world. The problem was, however, that some of the contributors were acquainted with each other, and if they were to participate in the project confidentially, I could not provide this kind of outline of their lives in my discussion of their contribution. Consequently, there is a danger that I have assumed a relationship between aggressive fantasies and female identity while ignoring differences of (for example) class, ethnicity, education, choice of sexual object, relationship status, age, and whether or not the woman had children.

When I sent the near final draft of the PhD project back out to the women participants for them to review and comment on my interpretation of their material, I specifically asked them to be critical of these kinds of generalisations and any way in which I had failed to express the specifics of their individual experience. One woman questioned an oversimplistic link I had made between class and women's experience of their own aggressive energies, and another two women (independently) explained how I had missed connections between their contributions and their ethnic backgrounds. These women's feedback was worked into the final copy of the PhD (and into the book version of this project) but without identifying the source of the changes in order to continue to protect the anonymity of the contributor.

While working in this way does not fit with the social sciences' models of data collection, it does fit with the feminist research emphasis on creativity, spontaneity and improvisation in the selection of both topic and method. Fonow and Cook suggest that 'this includes the tendency to use already-given situations both as the focus of investigation and as a means of collecting data' (1991: 11).

Sending copies of the PhD version of the project out to the women contributors elicited further contributions, amplifying and focusing certain elements of their initial contribution. In effect, these second-round contributions were their further thoughts and experiences of their aggressive energies voiced in response to having read what I had made of their and other women's initial contributions. These second-round contributions largely comprised the final chapter of the PhD. Actually, I had no idea how to write the final chapter until this material came back and I realised that the last chapter should be dominated by the participants' responses to my interpretation of their initial contributions.

The whole project was then completely rewritten as a book, and again, the women who contributed were asked to either check the sections where their contributions were used, or reread the whole project (if, by some miracle, they were still interested). Again, their concerns were addressed in the final text. The book rewrite was built around the one consistent complaint which came back in the second-round feedback, which was that the language used in the PhD was too academic, and obscured my arguments. The perception was that feminist post-structuralist and deconstructionist theory was too far away from the experiences that women had contributed to really do them justice. Dolores put it as '. . . I want to know more about what *you* think'. Out of these comments came my decision to rewrite the project as a series of stories of explorations and processes, and to use words like 'discourse', 'subjectivity' and 'subjectivation' as little as possible. Within the structure I am proposing, the participant's criticism could be seen as a parallel to an analysand rejecting a clumsily expressed interpretation, but being more able to make use of the same interpretation if couched in plain English.

What the contributors also fed back in the second round of interaction was a strong focus on relational struggles with aggressive fantasies and impulses, the difficulties and fears associated with those struggles, and concerns about the relationship between their own aggression, morality and ethics. These themes coincided significantly with the theme of the relational *telos* and moral imagination embedded in aggressive fantasy, which I had focused on in my 'interpretation' (that is, near final draft of the text).

In summary, something about my initial interests had stirred up conversations with women out of which they had documented vignettes. These vignettes could be seen as snapshots of their own conscious and unconscious engagements with their own aggressive energies. I went away and put ideas together around those vignettes, exploring them through my own countertransference, and offered the resultant draft text back as an interpretation. To my surprise, a significant percentage of the initial participants wanted to engage further, taking up my interpretation as part of the process of telling me about how they had been exploring their own aggressive energies in the interim.

Originally fourteen women made contributions to the project, of whom two died during the span of the project. Of the resultant twelve women, seven made a contribution at this second stage, and five did not. Of the five who did not contribute, three had had either first or subsequent children, and did not have time to read a 90,000-word document beyond checking the sections where I had used their material. One was in a major life transition, and felt she could not contribute (beyond basic checking) for the same reason. The other woman was also willing to check how I had used her contribution but indicated that she felt that my use of feminist academic language had taken my interests in a different direction to hers, leaving her with no energy to contribute further. This was one of the signals which led me to rewrite the project as a book using the bare minimum of technical language, as a way of trying to keep the focus on the women's contributions and the story of the project as much as possible.

Reflecting on the three women who did not contribute because they had had children, perhaps the consideration of aggressive energies and fantasies is a child-free woman's privilege. On the other hand, Parker's (1996) work on maternal ambivalence would imply that women with children have immense struggles with social (and psychoanalytic) fantasies about maternal responses, in particular the expectation that a woman who is mothering is somehow detached from her own aggressive and sexual energies.

Perhaps the women who did not offer back second-round contributions did not resonate with my interpretations of their first-round material and used their domestic circumstances as a polite excuse to withdraw. Of those who did not offer back second-round contributions, one wrote back saying that she regretted not being able to respond more fully. She also wrote that our previous connection around my research had been important to her and that she hoped that her contribution to it might help make a difference to her young daughter's experience of life.

Perhaps the degree of initial interest these women expressed in their own aggressive energies and the high degree of energy they put into reading my interpretation of their initial contributions and responding to that interpretation is a social aberration, a mark of my social subculture. Given the changing profile of the amalgams of women's aggressive energies and their impact on society, from female suicide bombers to the untapped anger women bring into my consulting room, this seems unlikely.

The other main methodological issue with my approach to data collection was how to choose which material to include, and how to use it. Importantly, the material women contributed frequently moved off at tangents from the original material I had supplied to illustrate my areas of interest. Often a number of women took up a similar theme which had nothing to do with my original ideas, demanding that I rethink the nature of the project and expand my notion of women's aggression. These expansions also meant that I had to reconsider the relationship between women's contributions and the bodies of theory I was familiar with, since the material women offered could not be addressed adequately within those theories. Linking this back to the final section of Chapter 2, the material women contributed took me to places where analytic theory collapsed and I realised that, rather than just being a nuisance, this said something important about women's aggressive energies.

LEARNING FROM A COLLAPSING PROJECT

Early drafts of this project were summaries of theory scattered through a text which was dominated by the voices of the women contributors, as I tried to 'catch up' with them, and lost myself in their voices. The next drafts were theory-dominated, with the contributors' voices almost missing, while I tried to develop a suitable thinking structure for reflecting on my countertransference reactions to their material. Eventually I broke both kinds of drafts down into clusters of ideas and women's contributions, rearranged them, and sewed the project back together in a totally different shape, trying to use the women's contributions to both illustrate theory and push beyond it, and use theory to amplify and deepen the themes women had raised. This breaking-up and resewing process was repeated many times.

What drove me to keep breaking the project up and rearranging it was that, again and again, the collages I made collapsed as theory failed to help me express what I could see and feel countertransferentially in response to the women's contributions. Likewise, as patterns began to appear in the women's contributions, they too would collapse when explored in the light of theory. A third kind of collapse also emerged at the points where my countertransference reactions became chaotic.

These collapses happened over and over again, leaving me hopping between elements of theory, women's experiences and my own countertransferences. As each of these failed in turn, I began to notice that there were patterns in the types of collapse. I realised that the interesting patterns in women's experiences evaporated when I tried to restrict myself to viewing them through a limited number of theoretical lenses. Theory often collapsed when I demanded that it account for the complexity of women's lives, rather than cut their lives up in order to fit the theory, pathologising them as I went. And my countertransference reactions became chaotic when I refused to acknowledge the importance of these two previous kinds of collapses and let my choices of theory and arrangements of the women's material be guided by those patterns of collapse.

Such an approach demanded highly 'unfeminine', physical, aggressive, repeated attacks on my own and other people's work. The anxieties associated with that were extremely informative. Part of what made this breaking-up of bodies of theory and recombining them around clusters of marginalised experiences possible was Samuels' introduction to *The Cambridge Companion to Jung* (1997). There, Samuels breaks the Jungian edifice down into a number of principles and relates them to contemporary intellectual and clinical endeavours, providing a model for using aspects of Jung's work without having to adopt his whole model as a framework for thinking.

Each iteration of breaking the project down and rewriting it taught me something about how hard it is to consciously harness women's aggressive energies – both my own and those of the women contributors. In effect, I kept rewriting until I could achieve a line of 'best fit' through the material women had given me and the elements of theory which seemed to amplify them in enlivening ways. What also became evident was that, as with my own struggles, women's contributions often contained contradictory and plural responses, underlining the need to assume that any reading I might make is only one of many possible readings.

THE NATURE OF KNOWLEDGE AND THE QUESTION OF THE AUTHOR'S VOICE

While rewriting this chapter for the book version of the project, I had a series of 'wake-in-fright' dreams about being burgled, and reflected on the terror of these dreams, realising that I was in danger of overidentifying with von Franz's murderous burglar and the thrill of breaking in/breaking up and entering closed realms of theory. My unconscious was reintroducing what had become marginalised in consciousness – by identifying more with the burglar, the victim position had become 'Not-I within' for me. I reflected on how the bodies of theory which I experienced as offensively closed were actually 'home' to someone else, and that I was duty-bound to take up the moral imagination demanded by my own aggressive fantasy and respond to that in some way. That response came as the decision to position myself into the narrative of my work, as opposed to using the academic fantasy of objectivity and neutrality, which would have been much better for covering the tracks of my own aggressive energies, allowing me to break and enter bodies of theory with impunity.

This question of the position of the author's voice also links back to my earlier point that collecting contributions from women raised epistemological questions, the main one being: can the methodology which I have outlined be considered as generating any form of knowledge? I argue that it can, and furthermore, exploring the kind of knowledge which it can offer also reveals how traditional notions of rationality rely on the marginalisation and invisibility of women's aggressive energies. This has important clinical implications – a woman who unsettles these socially sanctioned splits can be profoundly disturbing to herself and those around her because of the way in which she is unsettling our collective fantasies about identity and our defences around those fantasies.

But before developing that argument, I want to explore further the question of what counts as knowledge. Elizabeth Grosz summarises the problem thus:

> Knowledge [in the traditional, representational view] is considered *perspectiveless*. If it represents a particular point of view, this point of view is accessible to anybody, insofar as they are suitably trained. This process of 'suitable training,' rather than the regularity of the objects investigated, helps produce the regularity and repeatability of results, which is a necessary criterion for objectivity.
>
> (1995: 28, original italics)

Grosz's critique of the representational view of knowledge is important, but it leaves her with a problem, which is that recognition of the powerful, non-rational nature of the unconscious creates a crisis for rationality (Taneseni, 1999: 224–225). My methodology is an attempt to outmanoeuvre this crisis based on Alessandra Tanesini's comment that our understanding of knowledge needs to take into account the non-rational unconscious, the consequence of which is that '[t]he significance of meanings and desires cannot simply be read off by the subject who has them' (1999: 228). In other words, rationality alone does not account for phenomena, such as our making choices (sometimes repeatedly), which do not serve our own best interests.[6] Taking up the idea that there are powerful, non-rational forces involved in how we view the world and how we experience ourselves unsettles the presumed supremacy of rationality. But as every analyst knows, it is possible to relinquish a habitual overattachment to rationality and move to a psychological position which draws more creatively from a combination of rational and non-rational energies.

While the kind of knowledge which becomes available through an analytic training does fall foul of Grosz' criticism (it is accessible to anyone with a 'suitable training') it can never claim to be complete or perspectiveless because of the nature of the unconscious which, as Bersani describes it, obstructs, undermines and plays havoc with any attempts to create a theoretical account of itself (1986: 4).

On the other hand, this psychoanalytically inflected reading of knowledge needs a counterpart in order to stop it becoming trapped in an intrapsychic model which can offer no account of the kinds of dynamics outlined in the Miss Baxter vignette discussed in Chapter 1. And this is where the rest of Tanesini's observation about the nature of knowledge comes in when she writes that '[also] . . . rationality and justification cannot be found within the subject. Instead, we must understand them in terms of practices' (1999: 228).

So my suggestion is that in order to engage with women's aggressive energies, we need a notion of knowledge which expands in two directions. First, it outgrows the traditional, academic representational theory of knowledge in favour of a clinical, psychoanalytic view which values and trusts the counterrationality of the unconscious as a valid generator of structures, processes, desires and meanings. I say counterrationality (as in countertransference, or counterweight) not to imply an opposition to rationality, but to indicate that the unconscious is not without a rationality of its own. It is simply different to conscious rationality, and has to be engaged with on its own terms.

Second, the proposed understanding of knowledge simultaneously grows in what appears to be the opposite direction, which is to include the notion that knowledge is a series of social practices. These social practices, over time, come to be mistaken as generating 'truth' in the way that Grosz describes when she refers to training processes, which are assumed to create an objective, 'perspectiveless' understanding. Psychoanalytic perspectives and trainings are social practices in this sense, generating knowledges which seek to establish themselves as disembodied truths. Consequently, I am suggesting that psychoanalytic insight can be used to expand our understanding of knowledge, but only if it is simultaneously critiqued and examined in terms of whose interests it serves, and how. It is also crucial to monitor the way in which, even as they are used, psychoanalytic perspectives obscure the processes which convert a massing together of social practices into something which is thought to be 'truth'.[7]

KNOWLEDGE AS A PRODUCT OF A BODILY DESIRE TO LIVE AND CONQUER

Grosz develops this idea of knowledge as an active entity and offers a description which speaks to the physical, aggressive nature of knowledge-making. Her description fits with Garner's observations about her mind coming together for the first time ever while fencing, discussed in Chapter 1. Grosz writes:

> Knowledges are a product of a bodily drive to live and conquer. They misrecognise themselves as interior, merely ideas, thoughts, and concepts, forgetting or repressing their own corporeal genealogies and processes of production. They are products of bodily impulses and forces that have mistaken themselves for products of mind.
>
> (1995: 37)

This description of knowledge production brings out the physicality, the struggle and the aggression involved in developing ways of seeing, which the psychoanalytic traditions have been loath to acknowledge in their own bodily drives to live and conquer – in other words, their own needs, fears and longings.

Consequently my selection of elements of theory has been on the basis of those driven by the bodily desire to (paradoxically) explore the places where embodiment, identity and desire collapse, wiping out theory with them, and in doing so, reveal something about the operation of the unconscious and the psyche. The elements of Jung, Freud, object relations, feminism and critical psychology which I draw together all gesture towards these places, either directly or indirectly.

Again, the basis for this selection was that these were the places which women's aggressive fantasies seemed to be trying to reach: this seemed to be their *telos*, and my hunch was that engaging with and learning from that *telos* might evolve into a different notion of agency. Hence also my concentration on using my own countertransferential feelings of deep disturbance and distress around the project as the basis of trying to understand something about that *telos*, or direction. Grosz's view of knowledge as a product of the bodily desire to live and conquer also determined my choice to make the background to my authorial choices available to the reader. The aim was to make more visible than is usual the *telos* of my own processes of knowledge production, so that readers can then make their own decisions about how much of what I say is congruent with the *telos* of their own need to make knowledge out of their own desires to live and conquer.

CHOOSING TO LET UNCONSCIOUS PROCESSES STRUCTURE THE RESEARCH

Choosing this model of knowledge necessitates stepping outside of academic understandings: the academic tradition has been built on a notion of rationality which relies on the logical, conscious mind, and is expected to be entirely accountable within those terms. The clinical, psychoanalytic world is one which assumes that the unconscious has a rationality too, but that it is different from conscious rationality. At times these two rationalities may be quite similar, and at other times they may be at loggerheads, causing considerable discomfort and, occasionally, madness. From a clinician's point of view, it is these jams which matter most, not the areas where conscious rationality exercises unchallenged authority. This was what Jung realised when he suggested that the results of the word association test pointed to differences between people's unconscious landscapes, rather than differences in intelligence, as many of his colleagues assumed (see Chapter 2 for further details).

So in order to engage with the unconscious material around women's aggressive energies, rather than just discuss what was consciously available, I had to let unconscious processes shape the project. In other words, I had to make the clinical assumption that I could not determine my method in advance, but needed to assume that there was something to encounter through women's aggressive energies, and that that encounter would shape my thinking and feeling and 'teach' me how to research it as I went along.

Again, this is what psychoanalytically informed clinicians do all the time. This is not to say that I have abandoned the notion of rationality altogether, as Luce Irigaray does, in favour of trying to develop a feminine symbolic.[8] Instead I am proposing a notion of working from the space in the tensions between conscious rationality and unconscious counterrationality.

This epistemological position also offered a way of working through the demands which engaging with women's aggressive fantasies made on my moral imagination by providing an ethical position in relation to the Other; in this case, the women who participated in the project. That ethical stance was one of engaging as fully as possible with other people's accounts of their own experience, and being prepared to work with the unconscious processes that such engagement created. It meant being 'infected' by the struggles of the participants and using that infection as a source of information for my own psychological and theoretical researches, as well as offering the results of those processes back to participants for comment or amplification. As such, it operated under the feminist requirement that the researcher and the subjects of her research be on the same critical plane: my responses were as much up for examination by the women who participated in the project as theirs were by me.[9]

This approach is an extension of the feminist commitment to working with the 'negative effects' of research, which Fonow and Cook describe as a willingness to 'address what happens when the research act evokes negative reactions for the investigator and her subjects' (1991: 10). I suggest that there is a position beyond this, such that 'negative' effects (for both the researcher and her subjects) are seen as essential information about the unconscious dimensions of a project, which can and should be used to access deeper levels of engagement with experiences and ideas for both the researcher and her subjects.

Above all, Grosz's view of knowledge fits with Bersani's comments that the authenticity of psychoanalysis depends on its own theoretical collapse. Psychoanalysis, as a system of thought, *must* mistake its own bodily impulses and forces for the products of mind, and then rely on the resultant theoretical apparatus too heavily. Fortunately, this inevitably collapses in the way Bersani identifies in Freud's *Civilization and its Discontents*, hence my choice to turn the examination of these moments of collapse and defeat into the basis of my methodology, through the countertransference responses they provoked in me.

THE VIOLENCE OF IDENTITY

Reading these ideas back through Doris' psychopath dream, the starting point becomes her observation that the psychopaths are the social practices which define and police her limits as a woman. This is where her bodily desires to get on with her life on full and equal terms run up against the sickening, socially normalised constraints which thread through the performance of gendered identity. Doris' dream offers a window into a realm where identity politics are experienced as meaningful psychological 'objects'.

If Doris were in analysis, talking with her about how she has internalised the identity politics which create the I-slot which she lives in would not be a dry, unpsychological, politically correct discussion about rights and empowerment. Her psyche has already offered powerful imagery for talking about her experience of identity politics. Doris' experiences of being formed into a socially recognisable identity are associated with isolation (all her friends have been killed), death (she is in a graveyard), and the kind of terror associated with being tortured by a monstrous psychopath. These components alone provide a rich palette for depicting how she has internalised the production of herself as an intelligible, gendered, social entity. In this way the levels of helplessness, terror and desperation which attend the kinds of splits and disavowals necessary for the creation and maintenance of social identity become the stuff of analytic sessions.

I need to make it clear that when I refer to identity, I do not simply mean the manufacture of a social self, mask or persona. In the same way that I argued in the preceding chapter that the archetypal could be thought of as clustered together offcuts from the processes which mark out what constitutes socially recognisable identity and what does not, this level of identity production is about marking out what is 'sane' and what is 'mad', what is inhabitable and what is not. Susan Stryker illustrates such a moment of identity formation when she describes the 'nonconsensual gendering' at the birth of her daughter.

> A gendering violence is the founding condition of human subjectivity; having a gender is the tribal tattoo that makes one's personhood cognizable. I stood for a moment between the pains of two violations, the mark of gender and the unlivability of its absence.
>
> (Scheman quoting Stryker, 1997: 140)

Stryker's point is crucial: the precondition of being intelligible as a person is to be gendered. It is part of what defines the 'I-slots' that we make our lives in. I suggest that this is the level of identity formation which Doris' dream points to. Here, a series of violences are being negotiated – failure to embrace the violence of gendering creates another, equally unliveable predicament which Grosz terms the violence of presumed sameness (1994: 208). Coming to have what Stryker calls a cognisable personhood involves numerous such marking processes, gender being one which is particularly powerful, but curiously unresolvable. I take it that Walkerdine is pointing to these tensions when she writes that 'we can explore the constitution of femininity and masculinity as not *fixed* or *appropriated*, but *struggled over* in a complex relational dynamic (1990: 105, original italics).

Butler adds another strand to this way of understanding gender as a process or series of negotiations when she argues that gay is to straight not as copy is to original, but as copy is to copy (1990: 31). The point being made is that the 'gender story' has now been performed so many times that it looks 'natural', making it impossible to tease out which elements of gender are actually based on physiological differences, and which are a matter of socialisation. From this perspective, the important question is: if gender is an uncomfortable, unstable, negotiation between the violences of separation and the violences of lack of differentiation, what spaces do the genders have to engage with these identity violences?

Campbell's work (discussed in Chapter 2) suggests that an important difference between male and female socialisation is that male socialisation includes a training in the use of instrumental aggression. While many individual men may have limited, uneasy access to these processes, there is at least a cultural assumption that masculinity is in some way associated with an engagement with aggression and its amalgams. It is assumed socially that working out a relationship between frustration, aggression and desire is involved in the development of male agency. This, in turn, provides men with at least some kind of framework, albeit limited, contradictory and gappy, for trying to access the foundational violences of identity.

For women, the situation is much less clear hence, perhaps, Jung's observation about women getting better in therapy when they were encouraged to think the disagreeable thoughts they had previously denied themselves. Perhaps thinking these thoughts *is* a point of access to the foundational violences of identity which, if engaged with, open up a kind of raw, lively aggression of the kind that Samuels describes when he writes that '[a]ggressive fantasy promotes a vital style of consciousness' (1989: 208). In other words, perhaps access to these foundational violences, albeit limited, indirect and in the form of 'disagreeable thoughts', opens up possibilities of aggressive imagination, and through that, agency. Aggressive energy, as Garner illustrates in Chapter 1, can be experimented with in different amalgams and circumstances to produce breakthroughs at the level of identity.

These breakthroughs exist in relation to the processes which confer identity. Butler, in rather technical language, describes these processes as follows:

> Called by an injurious name, I come into social being, and because I have a certain inevitable attachment to my existence, because a certain narcissism takes hold of any term that confers existence, I am led to embrace the terms that injure me because they constitute me socially . . . only by occupying – being occupied by – that injurious term can I resist and oppose it, recasting the power that constitutes me as the power I oppose. . . .

If, then, we understand certain kinds of interpellations to confer identity, those injurious interpellations will constitute identity through injury.
This is not the same as saying that such an identity will remain always
and forever rooted in its injury as long as it remains an identity, but
it does imply that the possibilities of resignification will rework and
unsettle the passionate attachment to subjection without which subject
formation – and re-formation – cannot succeed.

(1997: 104–105)

Butler is arguing that the violence of becoming a recognisable, socially
formed person (a social subject) is part of what makes human existence
possible; there is no alternative to this, no 'natural' or 'uncomplicated' state
of freedom. It is not the case that with 'good enough' loving parents, or the
right genes, we would be saved the pains of subjection. Circumstances may
moderate, intensify, or refocus these pains, but the fabric of subjecthood is
inevitably, unhealably and unavoidably shot through with the hallmarks of
loss and violence which attend its formation. These processes number among
them the losses, lacks, defeats and moments of abject helplessness which, in
an earlier image, I suggested can be thought of as forming the basis of
something akin to an inner, psychic landscape. It is these hallmarks of the
processes of identity formation which I believe are currently beyond the reach
of object relations, but within the reach of a post-Jungian approach. The
resultant blind spots are the psychological landscapes of difference, loss
and lack created through the identity positions associated with class, gender,
colour, sexual orientation and so on.[10]

For Butler, there can be degrees of choice about how to respond to the
injurious terms which call us into recognisable being, but the degrees are
small, and chiefly comprise resistances and subversions. Translating this into
clinical concerns concentrates the analytic engagement on the exploration of
the small possibilities of agency which may come to light through the exploration of how one is lived (consciously and unconsciously) by those injurious
terms.

BEING GUILTY OF THE CRIME OF IDENTITY FORMATION

Ella contributed a dream which illustrates these kinds of inner struggles with
the processes of identity production.

Ella: I'm like my father – nasty to the people close by, in this case
Fitzgerald, whom I've been looking forward to seeing, but as soon as I
hear the balcony door open, a barrage of unpleasantness leaps into my

mouth. I snap (just like my father) if he doesn't immediately understand my oblique comments. I am presently developing strategies to deal with this even if I can't quite understand it as I don't think it's reasonable to join Amnesty and treat your partner like dirt. I have noticed that if I go forward towards him, look at him, smile, and then move on to do something else, things improve. It must be a relief to him not having me hovering and waiting for him to sort out my life! It's as though I've got to 'live myself' differently through this one – it can't be sorted out by talking because I just get clever and try to tie him in knots. I had a dream about waiting to be hanged for a murder I didn't commit. I wanted to send a message to Fitzgerald to let him know he hadn't been living with a killer, but was worried that the knowledge of my being unjustly executed would be even more destructive. The day after I had the dream I saw for the first time that my attitude towards suicide was more like execution. It wasn't 'goodbye cruel world I've had enough', more like 'you don't deserve to be here – hop it'. I'm not sure why I had to tell Fitzgerald – maybe because when I've asked him about the bad times with me and how he stayed (when he did stay . . .) he talks about there being another part of me which he can sense, through which some kind of light shines.

In the first instance, Ella's death sentence could be read simply as an internal punishment for her own murderousness towards Fitzgerald, as expressed in her nastiness towards him. A more subtle variation would be to suggest that Ella's struggles with the moment when her partner comes home could be seen as her longing for some form of powerful connection with him (indicated by her comment about her hovering and waiting for him to sort her life out for her), and being anxious and ambivalent about the intensity of the aggression and desire caught up in her longing (indicated by her nastiness towards him). In a different context, these energies could turn into the kind of moment of learning Garner described in Chapter 1 when fencing with her sister, a moment when an aggressive tussle revealed a deep love and closeness. Ella's aggressive energies, however, could not be channelled into connective amalgams. Instead they flipped over into an attack, perhaps as a result of Ella being frightened by their intensity and the sense of vulnerability which can attend that. In some ways, Ella's decision to 'live herself differently' could be seen as an attempt to interrupt the habitual formation of the 'catty', 'nagging' amalgams which women's aggression tends to form, for want of other socially recognised amalgams.

Another interpretation focuses on what it is like to be Ella living with a murderous aspect of the 'Not-I within' which could demand her suicide at any point. Her survival depends on trying to manage a self-hater which could simply announce that she 'doesn't deserve to be alive' in a hanging-judge way.

Not surprisingly, she is edgy about drawing close to Fitzgerald. She may long for closeness and a feeling of safety and comfort, but the closeness which offers that might reveal that there is something murderous in her, which she struggles to contain. This echoes Claremont de Castillejo's description of the 'negative animus' from Chapter 2.

> I should like to say a little more about the animus that is woman's worst bugbear. He is the one who tells her she is no good. This voice is particularly dangerous because it only speaks to the woman herself and she is so cast down by it that, as likely as not, she dare not tell anyone about it and ask for help.
>
> (1973: 88)

> He [the negative animus] will convince her that she is useless, and that her life past, present and future, is utterly devoid of meaning.
>
> (1973: 104)

From this perspective, Ella's attack on Fitzgerald could be seen as a humiliating externalisation of what is going on inside her all the time, but especially when she is alone. Ella is stuck between the knowledge that she is *both* a hanging judge (since the self-hater is part of her) *and* its victim. The obvious choice is to identify solely with the victim position, but Ella cannot sustain that split, and starts her contribution by talking about her struggles with the nasty, attacking, mean aspects of herself. As Campbell's comments imply, this kind of material is profoundly difficult for women to engage with in themselves because of the way in which femininity has traditionally been associated with non-aggression.

Beyond this lies another level of interpretation which discusses why it is so hard for Ella to get any psychological leverage around her nastiness to her partner. At this level, Ella's dream could be read as exploring the experience of having murdered inner possibilities (as part of the process of her own identity formation) and being judged as responsible for those murders. Such murders may not have been committed knowingly, their having been part of the scramble to find a cognisable personhood, as Stryker puts it (above). Yet at some level Ella is responsible for them: they were her possibilities, and she is the beneficiary of the recognisable identity which their deaths make possible.

Viewed in this way, the dream pulls together the 'I' which coincides with Ella's consciousness, and two aspects of her 'Not-I within'. The first of these is that which has been cut off or murdered in the production of her identity, and the second is a part which witnesses those destructions and holds the 'I' which benefits from those murders responsible.

This 'I' which Ella lives from must fight to stabilise its existence by disavowing the murders which sustain its own stability. The idea that Fitzgerald might see this is intolerable. Yet no doubt he does see and feel something of it when Ella is nasty to him. This is the problem which women face when they try to access their own aggressive energies. At a deep level, the performance of femininity is based on a disavowal of its own violences and aggressive fights to maintain an identity based on a fantasy of non-aggression. The I-slots which are available within recognisable femininity are contingent on this disavowal, hence Ella's comment that if she tries to talk her pattern of behaviour through with Fitzgerald, it does not work: she gets clever and tries to tie him in knots. Defences cut in to protect her own disavowal, and fight to protect that disavowal almost independently of her.

In this third interpretation what emerges is the way in which the disavowal of the violence of identity formation can create schisms and intrapsychic conflicts. For women, access to those violences and engagements with the splits and defences which surround them is made all the harder by the structure of femininity. Donna Haraway offers an image which depicts something of the violence of identity formation when she questions the processes which enable us to claim a perspective:

> Vision is *always* a question of the power to see – and perhaps of the violence implicit in our visualizing practices. With whose blood were my eyes crafted? These points also apply to testimony from the position of 'oneself.' We are not immediately present to ourselves. Self-knowledge requires a semiotic-material technology to link meanings and bodies.
>
> (1997: 287–288, original italics)

Ella's dream could be read as elements of her 'Not-I within' posing a question to the 'I' from which she lives. That question is based on Haraway's (above), but restated in the second person: 'with whose blood were your eyes crafted?'.

Haraway is suggesting that our knowledge of the world and of ourselves is only possible through complex, deeply embedded, socially normalised fantasies about how the inner and outer worlds relate to each other. Again, these normalised fantasies are accessible to psychoanalytic critique, but lie beyond the reach of traditional object relations because they are so deeply embedded in its development goals of the stage of concern or depressive position.

For example, Miss Baxter (in Chapter 2) views the behaviour of Sean and Terry through the eyes of the liberal humanist pedagogic discourse which determines what it is to be a good nursery school teacher. The eyes through which she views the interaction have been formed at her own expense, placing her in a position where she is blinded to the damage being done to her and to Annie, and to the boys by letting them get away with unacceptable behaviour. The personal costs involved in the creation and maintenance of this perspective are also rendered invisible through the way in which the perspective reifies and naturalises the fantasy of the benevolent, unconditionally accepting teacher, and the child who will learn 'naturally' if left to play in an uncritical, unfailingly facilitating environment. So successful is this naturalisation that it seems blasphemous to question it. In Haraway's language, the fantasies through which the individual experiences their relationship with the inner and outer worlds (the semiotic-material technology which links meanings with bodies) are soaked in past and present violent power struggles about who gets to claim authority for their own perspective. No perspective, no matter how pacifist, alienated or downtrodden escapes the violence of its own formation, and this may be the point of Ella's dream. As she sees herself through the eyes of the identity position which she experiences as 'I', she is presented with the violence which attends the formation of that identity position. These violences are outside the cultural mind. They are buried in the underpinnings and disavowed splits which make the formation and maintenance of the cultural mind possible.

Attempting to access the internalised violences of identity formation entails a woman dismantling the I-slot which gives her recognisable identity. Stirring up such energies starts to unravel identity in terrifying ways, with the threat of madness or death as the ultimate outcome and punishment for doing so. In Chapter 5 I will discuss some of the images which occur when women transgress these boundaries and encounter the energies which police them. Meanwhile, I want to explore further the role which the disavowal of women's aggressive energies plays in stabilising the concept of rationality.

AGGRESSIVE ENERGIES AND WOMEN'S MADNESSES

Women often accompanied their contribution to this project with a comment or note that they would not be offended if I found their 'ravings' unusable. As with Bersani's reading of Freud's *Civilization and its Discontents* (Bersani, 1986), these footnote-style communications carried the unconscious story which could not be told directly in the body of their contributions. A tone of madness was, however, also indirectly present through the structure of some of the contributions: both Ella's and Doris' dreams refer to the threat of being killed, and of being powerless to stop it. Doris' murder is at the hands of a madman, and Ella's impending death has a Kafkaesque madness to it. One woman, Vivienne, did, however, respond to the invitation to explore her own aggressive energies with an explicit account of her fears of a descent into madness.

> **Vivienne:** I am sitting in the house, which is knee deep in everyone's stuff. Isabel's teenage girl chaos – combs, notes, hair accoutrements, homework, lolly papers. Clothes dropped on the ground. Julian's HSC books, papers, artwork, music, pencils, and more books and papers. All piled everywhere. Dry washing waiting to be folded – all over the table

where we are hoping to eat. Everyone's afternoon tea mess. Dust and cat's fur as far as the eye can see. Shopping – bought, but not put away. Cats on the bench meowing. Furniture covers all over the place – and covered with the above mentioned. And all this in just a day, or maybe two, of feeling 'stuff the housework'. My head fuzzy, I float around above the ground moving things around, starting in one area and then noticing something just over there and moving there. Nothing happening. Cotton wool in head. Can't think how to attack this. Hearing friends say, 'housework isn't important, it's a waste of time, I'm going to forget about it for a few days.' It sounds OK, and yet I notice their homes are always fine, just fine. They don't seem to deteriorate like mine. I seem to never stop, and never get anywhere much. And if I do stop, just for a moment, or a day or two, I'm sure it will swallow me and I'll never emerge. I remember the woman, described by a friend, who had 'given up, let it go', and who ended up having a nervous breakdown in a house full of shit – faeces, cat pee, washing and stuff and filth up to the ceiling. She had just not been able to keep quite abreast of the manifesting chaos, and, ever so slowly, it had enveloped her. The fear is of not doing quite as much ordering as the disordering that is an organic process in my place, leading to an inevitable 'entombment' or burying in stuff.

Shildrick offers insight into Vivienne's vignette when she suggests that the cultural fantasies which are threaded through the female body are such that it remains forever in a state of 'pre-resolution', so that its boundaries can never be secured. Instead 'the female body can never finally answer to the discursive requirements of femininity but remains caught in an endless cycle of bodily fetishisation that marks a failure of control' (1997: 56).

In this way, Vivienne's comments can be read as the exhaustion and feeling of being overwhelmed by the prospect of yet another iteration of the endless cycle of failure to control her female body/house-as-body, as its boundaries disintegrate. Vivienne also implies that the threat of deterioration applies to her capacity to think and maintain sanity. Note, however, the way in which Vivienne is positioning boundaried, sane identity: it is something she has to fight to maintain; it is not a given. Instead, it is constantly disintegrating under the law of entropy, threatening to dump her into the abject humiliation of becoming the Other: one of those who have given up, let go.

This image of Vivienne's raises questions about the way in which the concept of femininity has been entwined with fantasies of an anchored, safe space which serves the interests of others, and this will also be returned to in Chapter 5. At this stage, however, I want to pursue the question of the relationship between women's aggressive energies, the threat of impending collapse of order and boundaries, and the concept of reason.

FEMININITY AND UNREASON: DEFYING THE LAW OF ENTROPY

Vivienne writes that she can't think how to 'attack' the housework, implying that the holding of the boundary between order and chaos requires certain amalgams of aggression which are not available to her at that moment. An aggressive stance is required to resist the threat of collapse into disorder and madness. I suggest that this is one of the ways in which women's aggressive energies are rendered invisible through being diverted from the outer world into the task of policing the boundaries between order and disorder, sanity and madness. In Shildrick's language, aggressive energy is absorbed by the task of trying to answer to the discursive requirements of femininity; in other words, to secure the boundaries of an identity position which, by definition, remains forever in a state of pre-resolution.

This state of pre-resolution is created and maintained by many factors. The one which interests me is the way in which femininity has been repositioned repeatedly in the cultural process of defining the nature of reason, and who has most 'natural' access to it (Lloyd 1993). These repositionings have the effect of associating femininity with the unsafe, incomplete and unstable realms of non-reason.

As Foucault suggests in *Madness and Civilization* (1995), in order for reason to exist as an entity, there has to be a separation between reason and unreason. Genevieve Lloyd traces how the development of reason as a human characteristic has been associated with the capacity to draw away from that which was regarded as feminine. She also points out how the content of what is excluded and signified as feminine in this way has changed repeatedly over time. Consequently, the conceptual category of femininity is not stable – it reflects that which needs to be cleared away to enable the conceptual entwining of masculinity and reason which, in turn, has always represented the current version of desirable subjectivity. As Lloyd points out '[a]n exclusion or transcending of the feminine is built into past ideals of Reason as the sovereign human character trait. And correlatively, . . . the content of femininity has been partly formed by such processes of exclusion' (1993: 37).[11]

Through this, Vivienne's contribution can be read as describing how the performance of female identity involves the channelling of aggressive energies into a self- and other-policing role which is designed to keep at bay something which is experienced as threateningly non-rational and chaotic. Seen in this way, Vivienne's struggle becomes an exhausting attempt to round up and corral the madnesses and messes which have to be cleared away to make space for a rationality which transcends and excludes that which has been signified feminine. For Vivienne to perform femininity 'well' she must take into her own body (and its representations, including her house) responsibility for the maddening task of rolling back the law of entropy on a daily basis. Failure to do so would unravel identity and with it, the fantasy of rationality which demands a transcendent triumph over physical reality. Ultimately this fantasy of rationality demands an absurd and unsustainable daily resistance to bodily entropy and death.

Success at holding back the law of entropy would also, however, bring with it a form of death. Butler comments that this 'mastery' which, in the Freudian model, is conceived of as being sought by the ego, is identified with the death drive so that '. . . life, in a Nietzschean sense, would break apart that mastery, initiating a lived mode of becoming that contests the stasis and defensive status of the ego' (Butler, 1997: 194). If we succeed in achieving coherent identity, we die: desirous aliveness is only possible when we are decentred – outside our own coherence. This is a point of immense and unresolvable tension in identity. It is intolerable, and cannot be lived, yet it cannot be avoided, because it is what lives us. Throughout history philosophers have, in their different languages, struggled with it, either consciously in their work or unconsciously in the defensive structurings of their work.

Charles Taylor's work on the history of the self argues that the late sixteenth and early seventeenth centuries saw the advent of a neo-Stoicism which focused on the '. . . ability to take an instrumental stance to one's given properties, desires, inclinations, tendencies, habits of thought and feeling, so that they can be worked on, doing away with some and strengthening others, until one meets the desired specifications' (1989: 159–160). Taylor also suggests that Descartes' picture of the disengaged subject articulates an understanding of agency which is most congenial to this movement (1989: 159–160). Inextricably bound to the Cartesian notion of reason as it is, this model of agency is shaped by the need to defend against the abject within: it provides a sense of control since who I am can be 'worked on'.

THE IMAGE OF DEATH BEHIND THE MADNESS

In Foucault's terms, this is a move which serves the need to establish distance between reason and unreason (Cooper, 1995: xi) and reduce anxiety about inner Otherness and abjection. Foucault provides a crucial insight into the terrors that our shifting notions of rationality and madness attempt to manage:

> Up to the second half of the fifteenth century, or even a little beyond, the theme of death reigns alone. The end of man, the end of time bear the face of pestilence and war. . . . Then in the last years of the century this enormous uneasiness turns on itself; the mockery of madness replaces death and its solemnity. From the discovery of that necessity which inevitably reduces man to nothing, we have shifted to the scornful contemplation of that nothing which is existence itself. Fear in the face of the

absolute limit of death turns inward in a continuous irony; man disarms it in advance, making it an object of derision by giving it an everyday, tamed form, by constantly renewing it in the spectacle of life, by scattering it throughout the vices, the difficulties, and the absurdities of all men. . . . Madness is the *déjà-là* of death. . . . But when the madman laughs, he already laughs with the laugh of death; the lunatic, anticipating the macabre, has disarmed it. . . .

The substitution of the theme of madness for that of death does not mark a break, but rather a torsion within the same anxiety.

(1995: 15–16)

Thus, rationality becomes not just a means of managing the fear of madness, but also implied within that, the fear of death. Structured into Cartesian rationality is an attempt to manage that torsion of anxiety by transcending the mortal body in the name of 'freedom'. But as Butler points out, we *are* our attachments to these anxieties, these injurious and limiting terms (1997: 104–105), so that freedom from mortality and limitation is always an illusion.

Consequently, the madnesses which a woman feels when she explores her own aggressive energies and fantasies is the result of the way those energies necessarily take her outside the realms of rational identity, and onto the slag-heap of madnesses which is the by-product of that rational identity. To some extent, this is likely to be true for both women and men but, as argued before, male socialisation does at least contain some notion that there is a potentially useful relationship between aggressive energies and agency, while female socialisation contains no such notion. So when women explore the edges of themselves where identity breaks down and aggressive energies start to unleash, the fear is that this is the edge of madness. Hence, perhaps, the way in which Doris' dream expresses her aggressive energies, bent back against her, in a terrifying, psychotic, sociopathic world. By being located in the realm of that which is radically Other to coherent, rational, moral agency, women's aggressive energies have become entwined with experiences of madness, death and terror.

Doris' dream confronts the madman's laughter, the *déjà-là* of death as it exists within her unconscious through the inheritance of the splits and defences which underlie Western identity. Her interpretation of her dream is that the psychopath represents the culture's practices around gender, and those practices are one of the places where the culture's anxious enforcement of identity is at its most ruthless. The problem is that, as Butler's work suggests, while it is right and necessary to fight social inequality in the outer world, the ruthlessness of those inequalities runs through the identity structure that we internalise and make our own. Ella's struggle has similar characteristics: what is one to do with the violences of identity which offer one inhabitable personhood, while resisting them and being terrified of them?

Again, Ella's dream can be read as asking Haraway's question of 'with whose blood were my eyes crafted?'

MADNESS, DEATH AND THE MORAL IMAGINATION

Such questions provide windows into the precariousness and vulnerability of identity, and the extent to which it is violently fought for, and barely maintained in a state of aggressive tussle with those forces of inner and outer life which would undo it. These awarenesses are important: by making visible the violences of identity, they call moral imagination into being, and offer a deep awareness of the Otherness of the Other: given that we all partake of the violences of identity, how are we to treat each other? Can the injuries and violences of identity be thought about and experienced in such a way as to enable the aggressions embedded in them to be freed up and reused in other amalgams of emotions?

David Cooper's Introduction to Foucault's *Madness and Civilization* provides a clue:

> We chose to conjure up this disease [of madness] in order to evade a certain moment of our own experience – the moment of disturbance, of penetrating vision into the depths of ourselves, that we prefer to externalise into others. Others are elected to live out of the chaos that we refuse to confront in ourselves. By this means we escape a certain anxiety, but only at a price that is as immense as it is unrecognised.
>
> (Cooper, 1995: viii)

On first glance, Cooper's comments could read as though they belong to the object relations discourse. Cooper is, however, making a much bigger point: the inner Otherness that he is gesturing towards is not just the individual's phantasy/unconscious fantasy of an emotional object; it is the Otherness of the structure of identity itself. His point is that the formation of 'sane identity' involves a kind of culturally endorsed (enforced?) splitting, and that can never be resolved, only displaced. Again, this is not a matter of individual psychopathology – it is the damage and disturbance which inescapably attends inhabitable, socially recognisable identity positions. Aggressive energies and fantasies offer women access to these layers of self-experience: the sense of madness associated with these energies is, if viewed in a different light, a moment of potentially penetrating vision into ourselves, and through that, the Otherness of identity formation. Our unconscious, habitual trafficking in identity positions would have us elect the (inner and outer) others who would live out our inner chaos, but as we do so, we pay an immense price. In the case of women's aggressive fantasies we lose a whole source of information about ourselves and the world. Living with, and working out how to make use of that information is not easy because doing so positions a woman outside of traditional notions of recognisable female identity. On the other hand, the willingness to take one's extremely disagreeable thoughts seriously worked well for von Franz, and could, I suggest, make quite a difference to Miss Baxter.

Ella and Jane contributed examples of the kinds of thoughts in question. Both also make the link between the kind of thinking which happens around women's aggressive energies, the edges of inhabitable identity, 'madness' and death.

> **Ella:** My sensory disturbances happen when I'm tired. I often jump because I think there's something or someone (or even just a flash of light) just behind me and always on the right side (where the committee hangs out perhaps???). Also I can't make sense of visual images – the TV is incomprehensible; photographs are likewise. Sometimes the whole room seems to 'shrug'. Death's around too.[12]

When tired, Ella's capacity to manage the socially sanctioned splits involved in female identity starts to break down. As this happens, her internalisations of this split become more 'visible' than is usual: her external perceptual field breaks up, leaving a clearer sense of her inner landscape, including a sense of some sort of presence in the region which she has previously identified as the 'home' of her self-hating committee. (Ella's descriptions of this committee will be returned to in Chapter 5). These domains of inner Otherness could be telling the story of how Ella has internalised the processes of gendering, where and how those processes, and the losses and violences which they entail, have been laid down inside her psychosomatic envelope to form the landscape of interiority which she inhabits. If these 'mad' phenomena are taken seriously, they offer a language through which Ella's experience of herself and the world can be taken up.

For example, if Ella were in analysis and, one session, reported a lot of activity in her imaginal field just behind her, on the right side, and made the link between that area and the home of her self-hating committee, I would wonder about a number of possible avenues of exploration. First, I would try to get as clear as I could about my own countertransference to Ella in the moment when she described the phenomena. If, as Ella described the position of the committee in her perceptual field, I felt (let us say) a sense of dread, I would try to recall other occasions when I had felt this dread around Ella. I would be interested in what had happened in the sessions that preceded and followed those sessions. If Ella had been late, or forgot the session that followed, I would speculate that this was possibly associated in some way with the dread I had felt (and I would wonder if Ella had also felt it consciously or unconsciously). Likewise, if I had made an interpretation in the preceding session which I had sensed that Ella had rejected, I would wonder about a link between this and the increase in her self-hater's activity. Perhaps Ella dreaded and was afraid of her own need to reject something I had offered her, and the anxiety associated with that precipitated an attack by her self-hater. Certainly I would start to wonder what it was that was dreadful about her unconscious landscape, what thoughts and possibilities it closed off in her life, and how. Any interpretations I might make along these lines would be intended to amplify (in Jung's classical sense)[13] Ella's material. In essence, I would assume that we were in the presence of highly charged, largely unconscious material which, as it came a little closer to consciousness than usual, created perceptual phenomena for Ella and also countertransference experiences in me (see Samuels' comments on embodied countertransference, above). The analyst–analysand task is to come to know these effects slowly, carefully and over time, seeing what kinds of thoughts and feelings are associated with them, what thoughts and feelings they make impossible, and generally how they shape the analysand's experience of, and interaction with, the world.

Above all, I would be working from the hunch that Ella had experienced a strong reaction to her own critical thoughts about me or some other aspect of her world, and a self-hater attack had ensued. For Ella to take her own critical thoughts seriously, examine the world for evidence to support her reading, and make up her own mind about which parts of the world (including our analytic relationship) she wanted to take in and which parts she wanted to either spit out, vomit up, or shit out would be to step outside of traditional female identity. Femininity has long been associated with acceptance and containment, structured along the lines of Miss Baxter's nursery school teacher role. For Ella to come to trust her own judgement, she would need to trust her own aggressively desirous and aggressively rejecting reactions to the world. At times, the violence of these reactions can be shocking for a woman, especially given that female identity is structured around a socially sanctioned, if not enforced, splitting-off of the violences of identity formation. Again, this is where I suggest that the post-Jungian feminism that I am proposing can move beyond object relations. For a woman to think such disagreeable thoughts involves unsettling the disavowals and splits which are naturalised as the performance of femininity, and could provoke powerful censure in the form of vicious attack from her self-hating committee. In this way, the intensity of the self-hater committee's activity could be used like a Geiger counter whose pulses become more frequent in proximity to something radioactive. The radioactive substance in this case is Ella's disavowed critical or disagreeable thoughts which are dangerous to the stabilization of her performance of female identity.[14]

I would also wonder if Ella's initial rejecting reaction had been to some element of identity politics embedded in the conceptual tools underlying a preceding interpretation I had made. Ella might be unconsciously picking up the ruthless desires to live and conquer which are embedded in all theories, including psychoanalytic ones. These theories, which I, as an analyst, would be using to support my thinking and feeling about my experience of Ella's presence and communications, might carry in them desires and agendas which work directly against Ella's best interests, especially if she is black, gay or working class. Again, the heightened activity of her self-hater committee might be a read out that she is in the presence of something which supposes itself to be benevolent (and which I might have slipped into colluding with) when, in fact, it is destructive to her.

This is one of the many ways in which the self-hater can feed back important information about a person's relationship to the outside world. If the information which is caught up in the activity of the self-hater is taken seriously over a long enough period, it can be used to build hypotheses about the world which can be tested repeatedly on the world. In this way, the self-hater can eventually be calibrated as an unconscious tool for gathering information about oneself and the world, although this process of exploration and calibration can be hard for consciousness to bear. This is especially so for women as it involves seeing a great deal more darkness within oneself and the world around one, and having to make active choices in response to that. Although such a departure from the illusion of passive, receptive identity (being a 'nice girl' or a 'good woman') can be terrifying, it is also the basis of agency. Radioactive substances can be used to create bombs, generate power or transform whole branches of medicine. The question is: how responsible is the person who is making the choices, and how well can they hold the creative tensions between basic morality and moral imagination? To me, the value of object relations-based clinical skills is that they offer ways of sitting with, and thinking about, intolerable levels of anxiety and frustration. The capacity to sit with these psychological states must be taken as an end in itself in the analytic moment. But it must also, on reflection, be seen as carrying identity politics which, if unanalysed, are likely to be destructive to the analysand. Object relations perspectives can support analysands in developing crucial skills for inhabiting and making meaningful the I-slot through which they find themselves called into identity. Because of its failure to reflect on its own socio-political heritage, object relations cannot, at this point in time, support the analysand when they need to deconstruct the conditions of their own identity. This turn is not the privilege of the few: in my experience, working with patients who need to deconstruct the analytic project, even as they make use of it, actually widens the range of people who can take on analytic therapy and make something from it. This double-focus tactic offers analysands the possibility of examining the costs associated with the Western identity which the analytic space helps them to make meaningful.

Specifically, it allows them to look at, and take responsibility for, the inner and outer costs associated with that identity, so that analysis does not turn into a narcissistic endeavour. It becomes, instead, a vehicle for taking up responsibility for, and in, the world. This position is based on the Jungian sensibility that 'we are in psyche', rather than 'psyche is in us'. Seen in this way, the strange ghosts of the psyche which we encounter through our dreams and fantasies do not offer information about 'who we are'. Instead, as Kugler suggests, they show us the Otherness which is folded into our being. As we come to know ourselves as folds in a wider realm of the fabric of being, that Otherness expresses itself through the processes of identity formation. Maybe Ella's willingness to tussle in this way with her own amalgams of aggression and with the violences and ethical responsibilities entailed in having a recognisable identity are among the parts of her through which light shines for her partner.

THE IMPORTANCE OF BEING BEASTLY

Jane described phenomena which illustrate this as well as offering a different angle on some of the themes in Ella's comments.

> **Jane:** Sometimes my outcasts visit me when I try to become too narrow. Driving along the road, I see Death standing at the Bus Stop along with the 8.15 commuters. Or I'm tired and the furniture starts to move and pull faces at me. People's faces distort when I look at them. Sometimes they become animals, sometimes other people I have known or characters from fiction. This is the stuff I'm very careful about talking about in therapy. Sometimes though this tiredness stuff acts like an early warning about what the person I am dealing with is REALLY like – I mean, what they are like when they are in a tight spot. I'm amazed at how often their 'animal face' in my imagination turns out to have been telling me something important. It still alarms me though. Sometimes what I see is terrifying.

Jane's outcasts might be read as that which is 'Not-I within' – that which she has to cast out in order to create a space in which recognisable identity can be performed. Illustrating Butler's comments (above), she regards the visits from her outcasts as a mark that she has achieved too much mastery, become too narrow, is living within her I-slot too well. Interestingly, Jane links this explicitly to an image of death. But she also indicates that in these places where coherent identity and rationality start to break down, she has access to other sources of information. People's faces morph into animals, or fictional characters, and she gets insight into levels of their psychological structure which her rational, day-to-day self finds deeply threatening.

The use of animal faces provides an interesting vocabulary for Jane's unconscious to convey information. The animal world could be read as an imaginal realm in which there is no guilt associated with reading the Other as a threat, an object of desire (as food, or for sex), or as demanding that one fight for survival. I wonder what animals Terry and Sean would become if Miss Baxter's could trust the places where her identity breaks up, freeing her imagination to explore how she is experiencing their behaviour. I wonder too what would happen if she could think about what kinds of animals she and Annie look like for Terry and Sean.

These penetrating, terrifying insights into the other come when Jane's conscious identity is breaking down. I would suggest that at this point she, like Ella, does not have the energy to sustain the splits and disavowals required to perform femininity 'properly', and blind herself to her own unsentimental perceptions and reactions to the world. The darknesses which become visible in such moments offer an invitation to come to know more about oneself and the world. Through them come the possibilities of fighting as Garner says in Chapter 1 'not in the ordinary wretched way of the worst of my personal life – desperate, ragged, emotional [but] with formal control and purpose' (2001: 175). In the next chapter I will explore this longing, starting with a vignette from Vivienne.

Chapter 4

Transgressing rational identity

AGGRESSIVE ENERGIES, AGENCY AND LOVE

In this chapter, I take up the theme of the relational possibilities embedded in women's aggressive energies. The main vehicle for this exploration is the apparently anti-relational phenomenon of women's erotic rape fantasies. On close tracking, the connective *telos* of aggressive fantasy emerges through the ways in which such fantasies bring one unavoidably up against the Otherness of the Other. So the point of this chapter is to take an apparently masochistic and, according to some views, pathological element of ordinary women's interiority and explore it so as to bring out the enlivening, relational possibilities of agency which reside within such fantasies This exploration leads into a discussion of the terror of helplessness which necessarily attends agency.

As described in the preceding chapter, part of my research methodology was to give near final draft copies of this project back to the women who had made contributions to the initial text so that they could respond to my interpretation of their contributions. One of the women, Vivienne, responded with the following story, pointing out the important role of amalgams of aggressive energies in the formation of her marriage. I use her vignette here, rather than in the final chapter (where it logically belongs) because it goes to the heart of this chapter's discussion of aggressive energies in love and agency.

> **Vivienne:** Some time during our 'courtship', when Geoffrey and I had been going out regularly for a considerable amount of time, I began to have the feeling that he had lost enthusiasm for our relationship. One night, as he was about to leave, I found the courage to ask him about it. I actually asked him whether he really still cared about me, or whether he needed someone to accompany him socially. Or something like that. I assumed he would assure me about his continuing affection (– why else really would he have continued the relationship). However, this was not

to be. He looked uncomfortable, but replied that what I had feared was true – he said, quite simply, that I was filling a need for him. I felt as if I was cracking into a hundred pieces, but managed to stay together long enough to ask him to leave – which he did, very quickly – before the messy combination of shock, rage, humiliation and loss overflowed as I integrated his simple admission. Somewhere in the mess, though, I registered that he had given me an honest answer to my question. Much later, together after a long break, planning marriage, and later still, married to Geoff, I was to assign to this quality of unambivalent honesty a greater value. Somehow I could trust someone who was willing to express such an unpalatable truth.

Before marriage I had come to know Geoff in a particular way. We had found deep resonances between us of a particular combination of spiritual, altruistic dreams and hopes. It was as if I was privy to an inner potential in him which was invisible to the casual observer. And I understood that it was a reciprocal experience. He seemed to allow me to open up to him my own most deeply felt wishes and hopes. This was our primary intimacy, from which developed a trusting physical intimacy. Unusually, even for that time – 30 years ago – we lived more or less separately until marriage. Upon marriage, the experience changed – mystifyingly, sharply. I found myself thrown into a world where Geoff's primary focus was (apparently always had been, had I been able to see it) the lived outer reality of a male camaraderie which completely overshadowed the commitment to home, relationship and shared dream.

For me it was like watching a black movie – his world, unfolding, regardless of me, except as a filler of gaps. Friday night – his night – drinking, gambling, till all hours; Saturday – his day – at the races – drinking, gambling, beginning around 10 a.m. (just up) with the always too loud radio 'form guide'. (Of course, I was invited to go. . .); Saturday night – dinner (my bit of his weekend) – with the racing crowd of course. Sunday – his recreation – golf. No place for me there. Sunday evening, together, if you could call it that – I and some remaining scrap of him, asleep in front of telly. Monday to Friday – work in the city for both of us – and some good times shared. The theatre. An opera. Meals together. And occasional unannounced breaches even of these islands of normalcy.

Attempted conversations. Promises. Recriminations. Occasional apologies. My attempts to discuss what felt to me like a betrayal of our previous intimacy, were repudiated on the grounds that 'it always turns into an argument'. And we couldn't have that. I felt emptier and lonelier as the months passed. Once only I locked him out . . . he leant on the bell until I was forced to answer and admit him. Nothing worked. I experienced incredible impotence and mounting rage.

Then one night, 18 months into the marriage, something changed in me. Impotent rage coalesced into a penetrating focus. If this is life with Geoff, then I'm out of it. Over some hours I observed this idea – tossing it, turning it, challenging it, digesting the possibilities, feeling the fear of it, until I felt absolutely clear. I realised I did, after all, have some power in this situation. I steeled myself to face the consequences, whichever way he responded – and I had absolutely no way of knowing, and allowed my feelings of disappointment and betrayal to flow into a letter which basically set out why I was leaving and what would have to change if I were to reconsider life together. If he even cared. It was very clear, and I felt very strong. I did not know the outcome, but trusted I could manage, whichever way the cards fell. I left no contact number, and went to stay with a friend.

Suffice it to say, 30 years later, we are still together. Geoff refers to 'the letter' each year, on our anniversary. Apparently, that letter gave him the necessary strength to do what he wanted to do anyway, which was to reconnect with that part of him that I had known first, and disconnect from some pretty unhealthy people and practices. He was able to acknowledge them as such. Marriage is not perfect, but we muddle onwards, with a level of mutual respect for each other's differences and individual needs, together with a number of shared visions – some manifesting or manifested – and interests which I guess are the 'glue' of the relationship.

Vivienne's story illustrates Robina Courtin's comments (see Chapter 1) which outlined the Buddhist task of learning to distinguish between the negative, neurotic, I-based uses of energy, and other potential uses of it. Courtin lists the characteristics of negative use of energy as 'it comes from a huge sense of I, it comes from fear, it's narrow, it's a sense of separateness, and it wants to harm' (Courtin, interviewed by Rachel Kohn: 2003). She contrasts this with what she calls 'strong energy', which can manifest as anger or, if brought into an amalgam with different energies, compassion.

The aspects of aggression which interest me fit closely with Courtin's definition of strong energy. While trying to sort out her relationship with Geoff, Vivienne accesses this energy and, like Garner when she is fencing, she brings it into an amalgam of compassion, generosity and commitment to relationship. She gets into a fight with Geoff, but she is not fighting *against* him: she is inviting him to *fight with her*, for the relationship, knowing that if she does not fight there will be no relationship, even if the marriage lasts for 60 years.

Vivienne conducts her fight 'cleanly', with her fears having been explored and then largely put to one side. She writes of impotent rage coalescing into a penetrating force, an image which parallels Garner's discovery that while fencing in 30° heat and high humidity, something coalesced inside her that could think strategically. Vivienne's tossing, turning, challenging and digesting of the possibility of leaving Geoff echo a fencer's manoeuvres, and she writes of 'steeling herself' to face the consequences of her decision. What comes across is her capacity to focus her aggressive energies and cut free from the destructive momentum in the relationship. Through this, Geoff is also able to cut free from his old habits and associations.

This amalgam of aggression, compassion, generosity and commitment to relationship is the subject of this chapter. Here, I am interested in the relational role of aggression and how that connects to the preceding discussions about aggression and agency. This is especially important for women, who often experience relationship and aggression in terms of either/or, rather than both. But again, the problem for women is that their aggressive energies are so often experienced as an inner Otherness, with the structure of female identity working against their being able to learn from that Otherness.

Part of what enables Vivienne's stand to work is that she is not coming from a small, fear-dominated, blaming, or vengeful place. She does not blame Geoff for her disappointment, or demonise him. She arrives at a place of clarity about his limitations and makes her own decisions in relation to what she sees. This combination of razor-sharp, unsentimental clarity of vision combined with compassion can be seen as a distillation of what lies at the heart of aggressive fantasy: Vivienne writes that prior to bringing things to a head, she felt 'incredible impotence and mounting rage' and what she does with this rage can be read in the light of Samuels' comments, quoted in Chapter 1, that:

> aggressive fantasy may want to make contact, get in touch, relate. . . . Aggressive fantasy forces an individual to consider the conduct of personal relations. When one fantasises an aggressive response to one's desires on the part of the other, one is learning something about that other as a being with a different but similar existence to one's own. Without aggressive fantasy, there would simply be no cause for concern about other people and so aggressive fantasy points beyond ruthlessness to discover the reality and mystery of persons. 'It is only when intense aggressiveness exists between two individuals that love can arise.'
>
> (1989: 208–209, quoting Storr)

As impotent rage coalesced into a penetrating focus, Vivienne realised that she had some power in the situation – she had the power to say no to this relational structure and leave. There are two important points in this. First, this kind of agency is born amidst strong emotions, often places where there is a sense of hopelessness, defeat and appalling stuckness or impotence: the place where irresistible force meets immovable object (I will return to this, towards the end of this chapter). Second, Vivienne's response to this is not to argue any more, but to write to Geoff saying what the situation looks like from her point of view, how she is responding, and why. She holds on to her own experience, while also giving him room to make his own choices, and this can be read as her beginning to explore the reliability of his previously demonstrated honesty, even though it was painful when first encountered.

It is as if Vivienne boiled her rage down to a sharp point where it could be used to cut away the layers of rationalisation for both parties, exposing the unpalatable truth, and opening that up as solid ground from which decisions could be made. This trusting, respectful, but demanding and determined move is love in the sense that Samuels describes above. Once this level of vulnerability and honesty had been achieved, Geoff was able to move on in his own life, cutting free from his own destructive habits and sorting out his real priorities. This is what Garner seems to be gesturing towards too (see Chapter 1) – the sense that if aggressive energies can be boiled down, focused and explored, significant changes can occur, provided that the longings for connection and learning which dwell within the aggressive energies can be kept in mind.

Aggression is not anti-relationship; it is the very stuff of relationship. Again, Garner describes this at the end of the first bout of fencing with her sister:

> It was glorious. We both burst out laughing. We only stopped because she didn't have a glove: I almost struck her hand and she flinched back. We lowered the blades. She pulled off her mask. Her eyes were bright, but I saw with a shock how gentle her face was, how feminine, under the cloud of hair.
>
> (2001: 174)

As Samuels argues, certain amalgams of aggressive energies can act as the gateway to the reality and mystery of persons. The underlying similarity between Vivienne's situation and Garner's is that they are both able to trust that the Other knows the 'rules'. Their respective Others will fight hard either to win, or to look after their own needs (or defend their own fears), but that fight will be fair. The interactions are not being shaped by malice or resentment: Vivienne is not afraid that Geoff will harm her (physically or otherwise) in retaliation, and Garner is not afraid that her sister will use the fencing match to level an old score. In both cases, the possibility of drawing together the amalgam of aggressive energy, compassion and relational commitment which offers the breakthrough depends on trust and, specifically, a lack of fear. Presumably reaching such a place had been part of Courtin's Buddhist training, but in Vivienne's case, the clue we get is illustrated below.

> **Vivienne:** Much later, together after a long break, planning marriage, and later still, married to Geoff, I was to assign to this quality of unambivalent honesty a greater value. Somehow I could trust someone who was willing to express such an unpalatable truth.

Vivienne's enlivening, relational use of her own aggression is based on her choice to trust Geoff's earlier display of honesty, and to risk testing out whether mutual honesty could form the basis of their relationship.

REFUSING TO SLIP INTO ROLE

In many situations, however, mutual honesty is not even a remote possibility. I now move to the opposite end of the spectrum to illustrate very different relational facets of women's aggressive energies. The following anecdote comes from a radio interview with Robina Courtin, the radical Buddhist nun (whom I also quoted in Chapter 1. At the end of the interview, a friend describes an incident from Robina's life:

> So the story was she was hitching along and these two Americans came along in a big car and she said 'Look, I've got to get to Geneva to catch this train', and they said, 'No worries, we'll get you there'. Great. And then they start, they go down the side track, down into the marshes and she thought Oh no, here we go, trouble.
>
> So they pulled up and sort of said you know, 'We're going to rape you', and she said 'OK, you're going to rape me, but we're going to do it my way. 'First', she said, 'you come first. Now come on. Get out of the way, let me get into the back seat, for God's sake!' And she gets in there: 'Just let me get undressed!' and she pulls her knickers off and she says 'Right you, come 'ere, come on! Come on!' and she was like 'Come on, get it over with! What's wrong with you? Can't you do it?' And as he was doing it, she said 'What would your mother think of you if she could see you like this? What would your mother think?' And she wouldn't let the other one watch.
>
> She said 'You, get out of the way! One at a time! I'll run this my way, it's my rape, I'm going to have it my way!' and she shouted and abused him the whole way, and when they'd finished, she said 'Now, get behind the wheel you two, get me to that train!' and they drove, they were scared little boys; they'd turned from these ferocious sexual giants to these scared little boys.
>
> (Courtin, interviewed by Rachel Kohn, 2003)

When I heard this I thought, I wonder what the world would be like if every woman could do that?

In some ways the physical sexual attack on Courtin parallels the verbal sexual attack made by the boys in Miss Baxter's class (see Chapter 2). But Courtin has such a firm grasp of the amalgams which aggressive energies can form that she does not let fear of someone else's aggression/power/cruelty or hate amalgam take away her own agency. And she holds onto her own agency not by being assertive, but by being aggressive – by shaming and humiliating her attackers in the most effective ways she can. She stays with her own aggression/agency/sense of separateness as an inviolable self-amalgam and simply will not countenance the men's attempts to override her own aggression and fierce holding of her boundaries. While this is clearly a matter of great courage and also of Courtin's Buddhist training, it is not the sole reserve of Buddhist nuns. It lies on a continuum with the courage to say 'I will not put up with this behaviour from you'.

Dolores offered the following vignette in the second round of contributions to this research, and again, I use it here (instead of in the final chapter where, strictly speaking, it belongs) as it illustrates the point exactly.

Dolores: I recalled a little vignette that happened to me when I was in my late teens, still at school and which I have always thought was quite funny. A chap gave me a lift home but drove into an isolated area and stopped in the middle of a field and lunged at me. I said, 'what the fuck do you think you are doing?' and he sat back in shock (in those days nice girls didn't swear) and said 'What did you say?'. Ha Ha! he was going to jump me but had his socks shocked off because I said fuck!!!! I always thought it was funny mainly because I was never really scared; he wasn't threatening, just doing what he thought a man's gotta do (and that tells us something too!)

The point here is that Dolores is not afraid of her attacker – she simply saw him as trying his luck and needing the verbal equivalent of a slap across the face to bring him to his senses. She accesses her aggression and is able to use it to break up the gender role set piece which would otherwise unfold. It is as if Dolores's aggressive refusal of the cultural associations around the 1970s, grammar school femininity (and the way in which they become entwined in the bodies and minds of individual women) does the job of slapping her assailant out of simply performing the 'man's gotta do . . .' script.

BEING THE ANTI-WOMAN

I am interested in these moments where women resist the identity or position which the performance of gender pushes them towards. Again, crucial to this is Jacqueline Rose's suggestion in her paper 'Femininity and Its Discontents' that

> [f]eminism's affinity with psychoanalysis rests above all ... with [the] recognition that there is a resistance to identity which lies at the very heart of psychic life.
>
> (1990: 232)

Isla discusses the pressures on her to perform her gender 'properly'. She also describes her transgressive tactics for resisting identity in the face of those pressures.

Isla: I always feel that as women we've only got one thing: intelligence, beauty, talent, compassion and caring or maybe scintillating wit. In a way you can chose (in the perfect dreamworld) but really you can only chose which one you go with. Sometimes the choice is obvious (i.e. I'm no Venus but I'm shit hot at Maths, ergo I'm smart. Sometimes you get a choice between two that are neck and neck) – but remember, you can only have one. I feel that society wants women to be 'one' thing. No shades, no complexities. Certainly no opposites. Unless you're movie star gorgeous: then you can be clever, talented and charismatic. In fact its not quite so cruel but the underlying rule is that if you're not beautiful (in a 'model' sense) then you'd better play by the rules, don't play above yourself. There is so much emphasis on exterior beauty that I often try to go completely the other way: be unattractive, rude, aggressive and masculine just to annoy people. To be the anti-woman is quite satisfying.

Evidently, women do refuse or subvert the performance of their gender. Isla is very clear about the rules of that performance and especially about the power to bend the rules which beauty brings. This theme of resistance to identity and its connection to women's sense of agency and use of their own aggressive energies comes up again in Rose's paper, 'Femininity and Its Discontents', where she writes that:

> psychoanalysis [is] one of the few places in our culture where it is recognized as more than a fact of individual pathology that most women do not painlessly slip into their roles as women, if indeed they do at all.
>
> (1990: 232)

The painful encounters where women do not slip into role which Rose is pointing to coincide with the preceding chapter's argument that aggressive energies take women to the edges of, and beyond, their identities, often in disturbing ways. Rose's notion of resistance to identity overlaps with Jung's model of an inner Otherness which cannot be assimilated into consciousness and is the source of desire and the potential to connect. Along similar lines Butler comments that '[p]erhaps only by risking the *incoherence* of identity is connection possible, a political point that correlates with Leo Bersani's insight that only the decentered subject is available to desire' (1997: 149, original italics). My point is that for women, aggressive fantasies often express an inner Otherness, a place where they refuse to slip into role, and this provides a point through which to explore further this chapter's theme of women's agency as an amalgam of aggressive energies, compassion and relational commitment.

Walkerdine's work on how women's desires are shaped so that they function in the interests of others, (i.e., for a society dominated by male interests) rather than in their own interests, illustrates how female desire is shaped so as to work against the formation of this amalgam. One of her projects has been to look at the narrative structures offered for the management of desire (and any other strong feelings) in magazines aimed at early adolescent girls. From her analysis Walkerdine concludes that:

> if we want to understand the production of girls as subjects and the production of alternatives for girls, we must pay attention to desire and fantasy. It is no good resorting to a rationalist account which consists simply of changing images and attitudes.
>
> (1990: 104)

Again, we are moving beyond the notion of assertiveness training.

PRODUCING ALTERNATIVES FOR GIRLS

Walkerdine points out the dangers of simple 'feminist' appropriation of images in fairy stories and the like as an attempted solution to the question of producing alternatives, arguing that:

> What we need to ask here is how such texts operate at the level of fantasy. For some girls they might well provide the vehicle for an alternative vision, while for others they might, by stressing the one as an alternative to the other, feed or fuel a resistance *to* the feminist alternative.
>
> We could ask, therefore, what exactly fiction, along with other cultural practices, produces for girls. And in examining current practices we can begin to explore the constitution of femininity and masculinity as not

fixed or *appropriated*, but *struggled over* in a complex relational dynamic. The question of alternative fictions for girls might then engage with the relational dynamic. How might other kinds of fantasies be produced which deal differently with desires and conflicts?

(1990: 104–105, original italics)

Doris wrote about the quandary of being left to make sense of her own gender position using fiction aimed at adolescent girls.

Doris: It's not just that I will be judged by whether I have tits or a cock – not that I am just an ungendered body. It's that all those books I read when I was a kid where the girl breaks her back or her legs in her journey to womanhood don't have endings. Or that those things may happen to girls – but I was somehow not implicated. I often find myself in that space – the sudden realisation that I am a woman and the negative connotations that 'tomboy' has. All that being empowered by the essence of your gender just never held any water for me.

Doris' comments imply that her tomboy stance offered her a form of gender neutrality, allowing her to give the slip to the kinds of desire-forming stories that Walkerdine discusses. It is as if Doris tried to avoid having her back (spirit?) broken by the processes which teach girls how to perform their gender role. She was also aware, however, that it is a strategy with limited effectiveness, and that she was working on the margins of a cultural identity structure which takes no prisoners.

My argument is that women's aggressive fantasies offer access to the processes which shape female desire. They also offer points where these processes of shaping can be subverted. Later, this will lead to an exploration of women's use of rape fantasies as erotic toys, but for now the key point is that girls are taught how to be girls not by being fed simple narratives or role models, but through complex cultural processes which operate at the level of structuring their desires. One way of understanding our attachment to such processes is through Lacan's notion that as babies our subjectivity is a matter of polymorphous desire moving off in all directions. Segal summarises Lacan's view of development, saying that 'the infant's jubilant, but still illusory, sense of unity [is] gained through the appropriation of its reflection in the mirror [of the mother's unifying gaze]' (1994: 131). From this state, the processes of maturation are primarily structured around the management of alienation which inevitably attends the acquisition of language-based subjecthood, bringing with it the symbolic order and phallic law. Walkerdine's discussion of how girls are trained to be girls tracks these processes of coming to be a subject through engagement with social discourse and how that shapes desire.

In her studies on pedagogics, Walkerdine looks at how girls are taught to behave in classrooms and the purposes this training serves. She points out that for a classroom to operate in a calm, orderly and smooth way, it is useful to have a number of 'helpful' children in the class. Yet in private interviews:

> many female teachers openly despised the very qualities of helpfulness and careful, neat work which at the same time they constantly demanded from their pupils, often holding up the work books of such girls as examples, or reprimanding the boys for not behaving like the 'responsible' girls. Yet they would simultaneously present such characteristics in the girls as a problem. Furthermore, it was common for female teachers to dislike intensely the girls who displayed them. They would describe them as 'boring', 'wet', and 'wishy-washy'. Such girls had no 'spark', 'fire', or 'brilliance'. Yet it is such girls who had become these teachers. When describing themselves as children or making reference to girls who reminded them of themselves, it was precisely such qualities that they discussed.
>
> (1990: 75)

These female teachers are split off from their own experience of spark and brilliance. Consequently, they cannot tolerate these qualities in the girls they teach. Transgressive, demanding behaviour generally associated with such qualities is admired when it occurs in boys, but not when it occurs in girls. Such behaviour in girls is 'unfeminine' and, at best, regrettable. At worst it becomes directly threatening and must be stopped by constructing it as inextricably linked with unfeminine, unacceptable traits – Walkerdine cites an example of a girl who is regarded by a (male) teacher as ' "interested in ideas and abstract problems", "a great problem-solver, natural talent". She is "constantly trying out ideas"; this makes her "lazy, selfish" ' (1990: 78).

The demanding, greedy, selfish qualities of such talents in girls are intolerable for these teachers, male and female alike. Girls are supposed to be feminine; that is part of what makes them girls: it is a circular definition. Yet to stay within role is to despise oneself, and to despise others who do the same.

The pleasures of breaking up ideas, smashing through systems of thought, cracking the bones of someone else's work are not 'seemly' for a good girl. Wrestling a solution from a stubborn and lumpish problem is not acceptable. Things are even worse if the solution is clever or nimble: somehow that implies dubious moral fibre if the protagonist is female. Walkerdine's studies of pedagogics are in accord with this, and she raises the point that girls' anger is dealt with in different ways, depending on where in the construction of female identity a girl sits: good girls' anger is met in very different ways to that of bad girls (1990: 102).

Returning to Walkerdine's question of how to produce alternatives for girls in light of the above, I would suggest that such a project runs up against the levels of experience Lacan referred to as *jouissance*. Fuery reads *jouissance* as the agency of transgressive desire, basing this on Freud's notion that pleasure needs to be managed. I read this the other way around: for women, *jouissance*, or transgressive desire, can contain the raw material of agency.

FEMININE JOUISSANCE

Adequate management of pleasure does not, however, placate desire; indeed pleasure marks the boundaries of the management of desire, and the inevitability of insatiability. Fuery writes that for Lacan, it is pleasure that sets the limits on *jouissance* so that by definition, the very nature of '*jouissance* is transgression, and (perhaps even more strikingly) that transgression is *jouissance*' (1995: 31). In this way *jouissance* is necessarily 'a paradox because it contains within all its senses of extreme pleasure and enjoyment a negativity that stems from the transgression of moral structures' (1995: 32).

Lacan, as the originator of the term *jouissance*, argued that female *jouissance* may be unknowable, and a number of French feminists, such as Irigaray and Kristeva, have engaged with this within post-Lacanian terms, theorising feminine *jouissance* as interwoven with female physicality, or with motherhood. Other feminists have, however, questioned these strategies, suggesting that they rely on foundationalist readings of female physicality. Gamman and Makinen argue that French feminists have failed to look for a 'yet unsymbolised . . . signifier that would allow girls access to desire and to the symbolic code' (1994: 107–108). Hence my choice is to reread *jouissance* through Fuery's work in order to offer ways of thinking about women's transgressions of moral structures and the pleasures and terrors associated with those transgressions. Running this back through the self-hater material discussed in the preceding two chapters, it can be argued that while the inner critic phenomenon can be seen as a fantasy attempt to bring the experience of being the object of Foucault's Panopticon 'gaze' under control, the perspective which emerges from the above synopses of Lacan's model offers a different insight. From this point of view, such fantasies might become women's attempts to *have a taboo fantasy about being seen*, being the object of fascination, and of being looked at with desire. If the subject of the fantasy is somehow taboo, the transgressive impulse at the core of the fantasy has to be converted into something painful, something which prevents fulfilment. (This theme of women's struggles with visibility and space will be returned to in the next chapter.)

Such a pattern of tensions would also seem to fit with the masturbatory (and indeed, unconsummative) fantasy of beauty and desirability offered by women's magazines: a narrow (to the point of fetishised), fictional account of desirability and beauty is offered which is almost universally unobtainable, and from any sane point of view, actually undesirable. With this toy, women can play endlessly with the edges of the potentially transgressive fantasy of being desirable, and suffer mightily for it in the form of disappointment, sense of inadequacy and failure.

A second level of pain is also available to assuage the guilt of this taboo fantasy in the form of tormenting ourselves with the desire to consume what we cannot afford, in the belief that it will bring some orgasmic satisfaction and a world where we too can experience ourselves as the objects of the Other's all-consuming desire. As with *jouissance*, the suffering and the satisfaction are inextricably threaded together.

Thus if feminist discourse is to provide alternative notions of subjectivity for girls, it needs to engage with the neurotic illusion of enjoyment, the nature of its forbiddenness and the transgressive impulses it invokes. Further to the argument in Chapter 1, I am not suggesting that women are essentially masochistic and deserve the advertising industry as some sort of cruel playmate. Indeed Walkerdine's researches into the narrative structures of cartoon stories in adolescent girls' magazines explore how an advertising-receptive female subjectivity is formed. In these stories (taken from mid-1980s' magazines), girls' desire and ambition are only tolerable when held on behalf of others, or in the role of supporting others. One of the most commonly recurring themes was of the immensely high moral value placed on girls showing superhuman tolerance for cruelty, discomfort and attack: being 'good' will win through. And what will be won is a paradoxical and impossible prize, a secret sense of goodness at the core of one's being which will be evident to some judging, God-like figure, while unknown to the people one deals with in life, lest it makes them uncomfortable, or feel inadequate. Walkerdine's point is that these stories are an example *par excellence* of how female adolescent desire can be canalised along socially acceptable lines.

In the light of this analysis, the ease with which the entwined relationship between desire and suffering can be exploited becomes clear. A point of disruption is available if women become more familiar with their transgressive desires – especially those which the processes of subjection encourage women to canalise into sitting ducks for the advertising industry. Therein, I would argue, lies a possible response to Walkerdine's question of how we might begin to think about alternative subjectivities for girls.

Necessarily, this takes us beyond the realms of the politically correct, for that is where the transgressive goes. David Miller points out through the work of Barthes and Kristeva that pleasure (*plaisir*) contents, fills, grants euphoria, does not break with culture, is linked to what is comfortable, and is connective, while *jouissance* imposes a state of loss, discomforts, unsettles assumptions, and leaves nothing the same (1990: 326). In the light of this, we could say that what Walkerdine's schoolgirls are offered by their female teachers is a fantasy of *plaisir*, if they learn their roles well and excel within their narrow definition.

What is not allowed is the *jouissance* of rigorous engagement with anything, ideas in particular. Clearly excluded is the kind of engagement that means that nothing is left the same, that those things which had been assumed to be true may get knocked to bits. The taboo for these girls is aggression, most clearly visible here as the kind of aggression which accompanies spirit and brilliance.

Actually, the situation is a little more complex: the *plaisir* offered as a reward to those who behave themselves is not quite what it seems. It is not possible to be good enough, thoughtful enough, responsible enough to claim euphoria or safety through the 'feminine' role. But, here we find ourselves back at the possibility of *jouissance*: the satisfaction derived from the symptom, and the suffering derived from satisfaction. The pursuit of a secret sense of goodness offers endless possibilities for torturing oneself and others, whether with an eating disorder, a self-hating internal critic, or whatever. Thus perhaps *plaisir* is subverted into something which glimpses *jouissance*. The problem is that this is a *jouissance* which cannot be recognised as such: it is structured so that it must operate as a perverse passion, accessing the thrill of destruction in a compulsively repetitious way. It can never run its course.

For Lacan, the pleasure that is women's *jouissance* lies in what goes beyond the phallic fantasy of totalisation on the part of the male (i.e., lies beyond his fantasy of 'the' woman) (Flower MacCannell, 1992: 187). Let us speculate then, that the unsymbolised signifier that would allow girls access to desire and the symbolic code lies in the realm of what is outside of the social definition of 'the' woman, where impulses towards selfishness, greed and above all, aggression can be mobilised. If this is so, the realm of aggressive fantasy could provide a vehicle for girls and women to develop an increased sense of agency, one of the core interests of the feminist movement. Perhaps this is what Isla is pointing to when she writes of the satisfaction of being 'the anti-woman'.

HAVING A SEX WHICH MUST BE SATISFIED

Putting these ideas together provides a basis from which to explore a profoundly unsettling and recurrent theme in female sexuality, which is the erotic rape fantasy. It is too easy to write such fantasies off as masochism. I suggest that the aggressive energies in them are complex and offer insights not only into the processes that produce gendered identity, but also into how women subvert those processes, finding pockets of *jouissance*.

So what form do ordinary 'good' women's and girls' resistances to identity take? How does the *jouissance* of resisting identity through aggressive fantasy appear? Doris offers a clue as illustrated below.

> **Doris:** Sexually, when I fantasise either during sex or masturbating I am always a man, and perpetrating some kind of rape, sexual harassment at work, seduction of innocence, incest etc. The thing that disturbs me about this is not the content, but that I choose to be a man because of another myth about men I was brought up on. Imagining I am a man I can be an aggressor, I can have a sex that must be satisfied and one that is visually apparent. However as a sexual partner I lean strongly towards the feminine/bottom/receiver – the fantasy is about being able to orgasm quickly – another male myth – that men always orgasm. So I use the myth as a sexual aid. Even though I am a lesbian. Interestingly, it is the emotional side of sex that draws me primarily to women – men are fine as sex objects and I can love them – but I feel no fascination for them.

Taking the rapist position in sexual fantasies gives Doris access to a psychological space where she can explore a combination of aggression and being ruthlessly selfish and demanding, the exact opposite of the girls in Walkerdine's 1980s' magazines. She has a sex which is visually apparent and must be satisfied. It also gives her an entrée into the gender script position that says men orgasm quickly, and every time. In this way she can outmanoeuvre the scripts about women and sex which are woven into her body as a woman, and have an urgent, demanding, sure-hit sexual experience, without the weight of responsibility for satisfying the Other. This is a fantasy about being radically and aggressively unfair, greedy, selfish and indifferent to the point of cruelty.

Relating this back to Vivienne's vignette at the start of this chapter, the capacity to trust the Other's honesty can provide a basis for using aggression relationally. But, at the same time, aggressive fantasy can enable a woman to explore the shadows of human nature, opening up a number of possibilities. First, through coming to know something about these darknesses in herself and others, a woman can develop a sense of trust in her own judgement – who of the people around her is honest enough to work through the relational struggles in the way Geoff did, and who is not? Second, these darknesses provide access to how one has internalised the injurious terms which have called one into being, and how one has eroticised those terms and is unconsciously lived by them.

This paradoxical shift to a sense of greater solidity and integrity through explorations of one's own and the Other's darknesses is illustrated by Brinton Perera, a Jungian analyst from the classical school. She expresses this move through her account of the Sumerian myth of the goddess Inanna, a story which contains a Medusa-like goddess (Ereshkigal), whose rage and hideousness can be 'survived' if encountered in the right way. In fact, the encounter is not only 'survived', it leaves Inanna, the woman who actively seeks out an encounter with this (inner?) Other monstrous woman knowing:

the abysmal reality: that all changes and life demand sacrifice. That is exactly the knowledge that patriarchal morality and the father's eternally maiden daughters have fled from, wanting to do things right in order to avoid the pain of bearing their own renewal, their own separate being and uniqueness. Inanna comes up loathsome and claiming her right to survive. She is not a beautiful maid, daughter of the fathers, but ugly, selfish, ruthless, willing to be very negative, willing not to care.

(Brinton Perera, 1981: 78)

A third possibility is that through erotic rape fantasies a woman can explore the paradoxes of her own being. Doris is a lesbian, but she is clear that her use of men as sex aids in her fantasies is how she appropriates the cultural fantasies about sexual experience and gender, and turns them to her advantage. This reveals a fourth possibility – that encountering the kinds of limitations and taboos structured into gender and cultural fantasies about sexuality immediately invites the transgression of those limitations. As Cowie argued in Chapter 2, desire is:

> most truly itself when it is most 'other' to social norms, when it transgresses the limits and exceeds the 'proper'. The result is a hotchpotch, formed only by its status as the forbidden.
>
> (Cowie, 1993: 134)

Again, the realm of tension between oneself, one's desires and the desirable/repulsive Otherness of the Other quickly surfaces when aggressive fantasies are explored. What also emerges is, however, that the aggression in these fantasies relates to the development of morality, compassion and concern while also supporting the development of agency. I imagine that this is what von Franz realised (in very different language) about her dream of a murderous burglar breaking into her bedroom: that in order to be original and creative in her writing, she was going to have to find her 'inner murderous burglar' and use those energies to be demanding, selfish, greedy and ruthless. In other words, she was going to have to occupy the space which Walkerdine's female pupil occupied when her interest in ideas and abstract problems and her talent as a natural problem-solver got her labelled lazy and selfish by her male teacher.

This moment of intensely demanding, aggressive lunging for something is also a call for an able and generous fencing partner, in the way of Garner's story (see Chapter 1). This is the partner to whom one is grateful, and who one loves intensely for the honesty and cleanness of their fight.

Again, I am taking a post-Jungian, dissociationist-influenced position of reading the 'Not-I within' as expressing something of what has been exiled from consciousness, but which needs to be engaged with by consciousness for growth to occur. Specifically, I am suggesting that the 'Not-I', or inner

Otherness, of women's aggressive fantasies needs to be engaged with in order for conscious agency to expand.

But prior to exploring these connections further, I need to say a little about how I am using the concept of fantasy. What will emerge is that, as Samuels' comments in Chapter 1 imply, one of the elements of inner Otherness in aggressive fantasy is morality, although the traditional opposition between femininity and aggression makes access to this hazardous for women.

At the simplest level, fantasy allows a woman to explore the allure of difference. One of Loretta Loach's interviewees expresses this while explaining why she is a fan of the pornographic magazine *Colour Climax*. She says 'it's like going to a restaurant ... you want something a little bit more unusual than you'd cook yourself' (1993: 268). Segal expands on this notion of fantasy as a 'break out' moment in the following way:

> Ideology is precisely what most fantasy does *not* express: hence, the well-known incidence of fantasies of powerlessness from leading patriarchs, fantasies of sexual domination by black men (or women) from white racists, and rape fantasies from feminists. Such fantasies do not express ideological wobbles in political outlook, but rather have an authentic, autonomous psychic existence of some considerable complexity.
>
> (1993: 71, original italics)

Segal's view fits with the dissociationist-based model being offered here: desire is only possible in the decentred realms of inner Otherness, where strange and contradictory longings collide. Taking up the politically incorrect nature of fantasy, Elizabeth Cowie discusses the writings of a woman who describes herself as a dyke, but whose rape fantasy is of being 'repeatedly and ritually fucked by three policemen' and likes it. She resists: '[b]ut I'm a lesbian, her public persona objected. This doesn't have anything to do with that, the wiser voice replied' (1993: 142). Rosa, one of the women who contributed material to this project discussed similar themes.

Rosa: I suppose the other side [of being a woman] is [that] I have seen the odd football team on the oval where I walk the dog and thought it would be pretty nice and affirming to be pack-raped one by one without me having to agree or not. I'm also repulsed by the thought but quite honestly Rhett Butler carrying Scarlet up the stairs against her will does excite me. Yet there are times when I've been pinned down on my back in bed with the man I love – in jest – when my rage has been triggered and all I want to do is kill! I think most of my fear around being a woman is to do with humiliation. This will be brought on quickly by wearing sexual clothing.

Rosa is clear – her pack-rape fantasy enables her to express and explore something which is otherwise at odds with the rest of her personality and 'real' desires – in other words, it is not a desire that she would want fulfilled. Hence Cowie's comment that 'accepting the reality of women's fantasies of rape in no way implies accepting rape as a social practice, as if it were a real "answering" to those fantasies' (1993: 148).

For both Rosa and Doris, fantasy renders available a kind of *jouissante* sexuality which the social construction of femininity makes it undesirable or difficult to access otherwise, be it the sexuality of being overwhelmed, or a sexuality which is selfish, urgent and orgasms quickly and easily every time. Rosa's comments also imply that in fantasy, she can be aroused by something which she would otherwise find repulsive. Somehow the nature of fantasy is that it not only copes with these kinds of tensions, but thrives on them, a point which takes us back to Chapter 2, in which Jung's fascination with Rider Haggard's *She* was considered as a period-specific expression of the power of desire for that which is Other to social norms, transgressing and exceeding the proper (Cowie, 1993: 134). Cowie develops her model of fantasy further, suggesting that it is a:

> kind of palimpsest, a layering of multiple positions in a specified relation of oppositions. This may involve wishes and positions which, logically, cancel each other out – the wish to have something and not to have it, or the wish to be punished for one's wish. Fantasy is therefore not only the realm of pleasurable wishes but also a domain of anxiety: fear of punishment by others for one's forbidden wishes. The fantasy of rape may also constitute a fantasy of punishment in which the sexual aggression of the other is a punishment for sexual desire.
>
> (1993: 145–146)

Thus fantasy can be seen as exploring and eroticising the inner landscape, and especially the kinds of torsions, violences and losses which, in the preceding chapter, were seen as the hallmarks of the production of (gendered) identity. Such a reading relies on a hybrid of Walter Benjamin's remarks that melancholia tries to reverse or suspend time, producing 'landscapes' as its signature effect (Butler, 1997: 174), and Bersani's reading of Freud, which emphasises that 'all comparatively intense affective processes, including even terrifying ones [spill over into] sexuality . . . It may well be that nothing of considerable importance can occur in the organism without contributing some component to the excitation of the sexual instinct' (1986: 37–38). In other words, our inner landscapes are significantly formed by the workings of melancholia around the losses which are entailed in coming into socially recognisable being, as well as those which arise in our individual lives. The intensity of these losses cannot but be eroticised, so that the violence of identity formation itself must be eroticised, partly as the cultural fetish of gender,[1] but also in the workings of gender. And this, I suggest, was part of my adolescent struggle with the Hammer Horror 1970s' film of Rider Haggard's *She*, discussed in Chapter 2. The film encouraged me to eroticise these losses and, through that, to slip into performing my gender role. This simultaneously fascinated and repulsed me.

Again, the positioning of female identity as most alien to these foundational violences (for example, through myths such as Aphrodite's birth, touched on in Chapter 3) makes it all the more likely that women's erotic lives will be entwined with attempts to explore the losses and violences of the formation of the social subject. In particular, erotic energies are likely to focus on the formation of the cultural fantasy of female identity, with its emphasis on the processes of disavowing the violences of its own formation.

Fantasy is an extremely complex theatre of the mind and body in which positions, dynamics and states of being, past and present, can be explored and used to move around within the field of interiority. It is absolutely *not* an expression of what one really wants, but dare not ask for. This contradicts Andrea Dworkin's view of female sexuality where, in a presumed non-aggressive and non-transgressive 'natural state', rape fantasies are thought to be 'concentration camp pornography' which make the mistake of playing into the social notion of the suffering woman (Williams, 1989: 217). This is too simplistic and Williams argues that:

> Sadomasochistic fantasy for and by women does not necessarily mean the increased domination of sadists; more likely it means a further exploration of the role of power in pleasure. It is precisely this conjunction that traditional (sexually 'good') women have been taught to ignore in themselves. Sadomasochistic fantasy offers one important way in which groups and individuals whose desires patriarchy has not recognised as legitimate can explore the mysterious conjunction of power and pleasure in intersubjective sexual relations.
>
> (1989: 217–218)

Williams' comments bring out two important themes, the first of which is that women's aggressive sexual fantasies can provide access to multiple positions with a tableau, as well as the tensions and dynamics within each position, an idea amplified by Nina.

Nina: that which is not satisfied at the actual level is satisfied at the hallucinatory or fantasy level. rarely do i have woman to woman sexual fantasy, unless i am attracted to someone that i choose not to act on. occasionally i will have male to male fantasy, but mostly my fantasies are heterosexual. my position in these fantasies is fluid, vacillating between the man and the woman. at the point of orgasm it is almost impossible to differentiate between the fantasy positions so it's like i'm coming for both of them. occasionally i will be clearly differentiated as one or the other and my orgasm will be attached to theirs.

i sometimes have fantasies about the sullying of innocence or pedagogical, instructive sex. power seems to be the arousal factor here, again i swap between positions. some of my sexual fantasies are about force or violent sex, rarely rape.

Nina's second paragraph draws attention to the second important theme in Williams' comments, which is that women's aggressive (in her terms, sadomasochistic) sexual fantasies can provide access to the mysterious roles of power and pleasure in sexual relationships (and, I would add, all relationships).

RAPING THE RAPIST

And here we start to reconnect to the idea that the *telos* of aggressive fantasy is an encounter with the Otherness of the Other. Through that, a sense of separateness can develop which offers an awareness of basic morality and the development of moral imagination and compassion. These pleasures and dangers of power are important in the operation of femininity, as Adele illustrates below.

Adele: The times when my rage and viciousness are closest to the surface have been when I am trying to exert my will over a child or an animal, they have resisted my control and I've become frustrated and angry. I know then that I am quite capable of cruelty and I resent being the kind, gentle, nurturing woman. I thank God I have no children to act this rage out on in the secrecy of our home.

Adele's comments focus on her struggles with the insistent nature of her own will, the wilful Otherness of the Other, and, in other moments, an awareness of the Other's vulnerability. This is a complex intersection: vulnerability can serve many uses of power, as well as acting as the brakes on power.

An image of von Franz's illustrates this. She describes how a woman can use her own vulnerability in the way that a Mafia thug might grab a small girl and hold her up as a human shield (von Franz, 1988: 243), while pointing a gun at someone else. Here inner vulnerability is being turned into a commodity and exploited in order to access power. Likewise, the vulnerability of the Other can be used to similar effect. I once heard a psychiatrist colleague, Jill

Welbourne, speak of a patient who had a history of dating the kind of men who, pretty much by simply walking into a bar, could spark a fight which they would quickly become involved in. A little while into therapy, this patient acquired a new boyfriend who was a haemophiliac, for whom such fighting was potentially life-threatening. The patient's previous two boyfriends had also been known to 'get rough with her', and she tried to provoke her new boyfriend to do the same, but again, this was out of the question. Shortly after starting to go out with her new boyfriend, the patient's life began to fall apart. It was as if she had been using her previous boyfriends to vent energies which her new boyfriend could not relieve her of, and she was left not knowing how to live her life while taking responsibility for those energies.

Isla takes up this theme of exploitation, but in the realm of fantasy, through which she discovers that the Other is truly Other.

> **Isla:** Of course the big difference to real rape is that I chose the rapist (unfortunately so many 'rape' fantasy men turn out to be gay in real life, so that's disappointing) and he only does what I want. In a way, I'm raping him.

Isla starts by playing with the victim position in an erotic rape fantasy, but then she reverses it, exploring the fact that in her fantasy she is using the Other. What appears to be an exploration of being humiliated and used turns out to be about being the exploiter, the rapist. But note the order of Isla's comments. *She* chooses the rapist in her fantasy: *she* decides whom she wants to use and why, and then she runs into the fact that so many of the men she chooses are gay. In reality she would not be to *their* taste. Even as Isla makes use of these men (rapes them) in her fantasies, she encounters something of their Otherness. She is forced to consider the nature of difference, even as she moves to exploit it for her own pleasure, in line with Samuels' comment that '[w]hen one fantasises an aggressive response to one's desires on the part of the other, one is learning something about that other as a being with a different but similar existence to one's own' (1989: 209).

This double awareness of difference and similarity, and the desires and terrors it precipitates, is the basis of morality. Mandy Merck offers an understanding of this:

> We confront [the law of our morals] at the peril of our own undoing, for it is powered by nothing less than the self-aggression which Freud discovered at the root of our conscience and our bliss. Suffice it to say, our morals are as difficult to come to terms with as our pleasures, because they *are* our pleasures.
>
> (1993: 262, original italics)

At this point, I want to emphasise Merck's second sentence: that our morals *are* our pleasures. Doris, Rosa, Nina and Isla's sexual fantasies all, in their quite different ways, explore moral taboos, and through them, a place where the anxieties of conscience and the bliss of *jouissance* coincide. If the cultural fantasy of female identity and sexuality is that it is relational, nurturing and supportive, it is almost inevitable that a domain of female *jouissance* will exist around the exact opposite kind of sex, and that this domain will be the subject of fantasy. It is also through this shadowy realm that the possibility of relationship and learning about the Otherness of the Other is most likely to be presented.

Mary, another of the contributors, explored similar ground, but in a way which responds to Segal's question about whether a woman can have a sexually aggressive fantasy without putting herself in the male position (Segal, 1994: 239).

Mary: In one of my favourite fantasies, I'm unfathomably rich. I have a private castle, or chateau in Europe somewhere with loads of servants. My interest in life is a kind of breeding project so I go around the world attending professional gatherings, fucking my way through the men who are at the top of their field. Doesn't matter if it's sport, art or astrophysics. Each round is intended to get me pregnant. I want the sperm from the best and I get it. Nine months later the baby is handed over to the servants to raise and I go off and find the next group of unwitting donors to get working on. The important thing is that the men don't know what I am up to. They don't know that they father children on these opportunistic fucks. Only I know who I fucked and I'm playing a kind of roulette with that: which of the 10 or 12 men at a particular gathering was the actual biological father of this baby? I don't know and I want the pleasure of never knowing. I'm so rich that I can be outside the rules that demand that I know or care, I also relish the pleasure of watching (from a distance) a dozen or so babies grow up as mixtures of me and the top of a given field. It's a kind of stealing from the men really. Sometimes the fantasy has a variant, which is that as I fuck these men, I drain them of their life-time supply of sex. A kind of sex-vampire. I'm their mind-blowing ultimate fuck but their last one.

Part of Mary's pleasure is in being outside the rules which demand that she perform her role as a woman intelligibly and behave in a nurturant, responsible, relational manner. Her comments resonate with Isla's earlier thoughts about how women are supposed to only be one thing, unless they are movie-star gorgeous. Mary is adding another option, imagining that being stupendously rich might also place her outside of the rules of identity and, thus, conventional morality. The thrill on offer is not just breaking the social rules, but of being able to defy the rules which set the parameters of female identity, without being destroyed.

EROTIC DESTRUCTION

The final variation in Mary's fantasy is one of destruction towards the Other, laying waste to their sex, as it were. Drawing out the *telos* of Mary's fantasy we might say that she is exploring the ruthless, selfish, demanding and controlling aspects of creativity, and fantasising about an uninterrupted, omnipotent binge. In the first part of Mary's fantasy there are no partners to be negotiated with, no parental responsibilities to be worried about – perhaps this is the female equivalent of sowing (and then walking away from) one's wild oats. If so, it would seem to be an exploration of the pleasures of rejecting notions of responsibility and relationship, and the erotics of slipping out of those roles. Isla also wrote of this kind of slipping out of role in terms of exercising a creativity which has traditionally been a male preserve.

> **Isla:** When I paint I feel omnipotent. I think it's the closest I'll ever come to the 'God' or a higher being. Or, maybe it's what men feel like. It's a thrill and even more so because I rush it (daring it to last) and still it lasts. I'm sure it's the power that men must feel: I've created so I can move forward.

Something of this being outside the rules is essential to creativity – and not just in the artistic sense. Vivienne also steps outside her relationship and musters her aggressive energies even though they are being gathered for what turns out to be the good of her relationship. This theme of the importance of being able to cut free and separate, without which connection and relationship are impossible, will be returned to in Chapter 6's discussion of aggressive energies and eating disorders. Meanwhile, Mary's fantasy starts with an image of a highly separate, lone wolf, predatory kind of creativity, and ends with an image of voracious, destructive desire. Such fantasies have not traditionally been associated with mainstream womanhood.

This raises an interesting question in relation to Waldby's comments which occur in the context of her reading of Jeanette Winterson's *Oranges Are Not the Only Fruit* (1985). In that text, the newly lesbian protagonist expresses her desire for someone who will destroy and be destroyed by her. Waldby spells out what she means by this kind of erotic destruction.

By erotic destruction I mean both the temporary, ecstatic confusions wrought upon the everyday sense of self by sexual pleasure, and the more long-term consequences of this confusion when it works to constitute a relationship. Destruction seems an appropriate word for these states because it captures both the tender violence and the terrors involved in sexual practice and relationships, the kinds of violence this does to any sense of self as autonomous. Erotic pleasure arguably requires a kind of momentary annihilation or suspension of what normally counts as 'identity', the conscious, masterful, self-identical self, lost in the 'little death' of orgasm. These momentary suspensions, when linked together in the context of a particular relationship, work towards a more profound kind of ego destruction. I do not mean that the ego in love relations is destroyed in an absolute sense. Rather each lover is refigured by the other, made to bear the mark of the other upon the self. But all such transformation involves the breaking down of resistance, of violence to an existing order of the ego.

(1995: 266–267)

Winterson's character goes on to explain that her desire for someone who will destroy and be destroyed by her eliminates the possibility of her lover being male, since they 'want to be the destroyer, and never be destroyed' (1995: 266). Perhaps Mary's fantasy replies to the unstated question in Waldby's comments about why women find it hard to take up the role of the destroyer, and habitually fall into the role of being the destroyed, thus blocking the *telos* of change embedded in certain amalgams of aggressive energies.

Waldby's image of relationship as a profound form of ego destruction which is part of the process of mutual transformation also links to Vivienne's letter to Geoff. Vivienne had to let go of her naivete and face the possibility that Geoff might not be the man she thought she had married, and Geoff had to face the choice between a bachelor life-style and relationship, thus relinquishing the fantasy that 'we can have it all'. Vivienne's letter destroyed both of their childish fantasies in order that their relationship might survive, and that action depended on an amalgam of aggression, compassion and commitment to the relationship. This amalgam is the non-sexual counterpart to Waldby's erotic destruction that does violence to an existing order of the ego for the sake of transformation.

Nina takes up this theme of relational destruction of the ego as a means of transformation and links it back to the sexual realm.

Nina: fran terrified me, she could destroy me like no body before[2] despite the ambivalence which was profound, and i was deeply deeply conflicted about her. i realised that i was only really interested in someone who could utterly shatter me, someone where everything was at stake. it is death that i looked for in my sexual experiences with fran, the end of

> myself as i experienced myself, the collapse and shattering of ego boundaries that liberated and transformed me into an ecstasy that i intuit as the closest to God that i'm going to get in this lifetime. sex with fran held the promise of a radical transformation, that in part has been released in my first real ability to love. so sex with fran was very painful as the walls between sex, love and intimacy were crashed.

Nina's comments underline the links between these kinds of states of confusion and destruction, love and death. For lovers there is the potential to hope that the Other will fight cleanly and be willing to be destroyed, as well as being the destroyer. But access to aggressive energies and the agency embedded in them is often called for in circumstances which militate against such potential. Often the possibility of agency is buried deeply in indifference, despair, and among amalgams of aggressive energies which border on the untransformable. It is to the exploration of agency and aggressive energies in such circumstances that I now turn.

THREADS OF AGENCY IN THE MIDST OF COLLAPSE AND DEFEAT

As argued in Chapter 3, when women try to explore the kind of agency which is embedded in aggressive fantasies they are engaging with a form of inner Otherness which takes them outside of what Stryker referred to as cognisable personhood in Chapter 2 (Scheman, 1997: 140). The agency associated with aggressive energies is part of a woman's 'Not-I within', and I want to expand a little more on what the lived experience of this is like. An image for the landscape of the 'Not-I within' might run like this. One area, called cognisable identity, is inhabitable. Rationality and order reign here. Movement is comparatively easy and physical objects behave in predictable ways. Things make sense to the ego, and there is a sense of reasonable safety. There are, however, other realms where the individual's pockets of psychotic material reside. These pockets, which vary in size, intensity and mobility, mark the places where unconscious processes swamp conscious ones, tossing the ego complex about like a cork in an ocean. Again, these are the realms of the 'Not-I within' which object relations has access to.

But there is another realm of the 'Not-I within', which comprises those human potentials which have been marked off as culturally uninhabitable. These domains of possible identity have been rendered abject in order to create other regions where identity is possible. Butler argues that sexuality is the product of just such a process, with heterosexuality naturalising itself by setting homosexuality up as a radical Otherness – something which one has never known (Butler, 1997: 139). Her argument is that a child must face the loss of the possibility of sexual contact with both parents, but that only the loss of the possibility with the opposite sex parent is allowed to be publicly mourned. That mourning is recognised socially and, through the processes of recognition, it is structured into heterosexuality. The homosexual position, offered through the mourning of the loss of potential sexual contact with the same sex parent, is disavowed. That structure of recognition of one sexual option and the disavowal of another then plays into the constitution of gender itself: the mark of socially recognisable femininity is to be attracted to men, and vice versa. Butler describes the result:

> What ensues is a culture of gender melancholy in which masculinity and femininity emerge as the traces of an ungrieved and ungrievable love; indeed, where masculinity and femininity within the heterosexual matrix are strengthened through the repudiations that they perform.
>
> (1997: 140)

The point here is that identity formation is a political process, through which certain positions are recognised as liveable, and others are not. These positions which are not liveable are rendered abject, which Julia Kristeva describes as that which is repulsive and disgusting, uninhabitable, yet all too unavoidably human, and therefore fascinating because of its nauseating, defiling, polluting, taboo qualities. In the first instance we might think of shit, vomit or pus as abject, but Kristeva points out that what makes something abject is not a matter of lack of cleanliness or health, but disturbance of identity itself.

The abject is that edge of

> non-existence and hallucination, of a reality that, if I acknowledge it, annihilates me. There, abject and abjection are my safeguards. The primers of my culture.
>
> (1982: 2)

Kristeva's argument is that identity itself is only maintained by localising and policing that which is abject. The abject marks the cultural boundary between liveable, cognisable identity and realms of unliveable revulsion and/or madness. Contact with these realms which lie outside of identity can be terrifying. Here, there is no lover who might fight fairly, there are only the no-go zones of unthinkable anti-identity. This is the landscape of Doris' psychopath nightmare, where we experience the operation of the ruthless and terrifyingly indifferent processes which enforce the boundaries of gender. As we will see, these boundaries are policed by experiences of abject helplessness in which all volition, let alone agency, has been lost. Images of such places take numerous forms, including being buried alive, being trapped in an unbearable place, finding that one has no traction or grip on the world (so that relationships, or life itself, keeps slipping away), being trapped in a maze, falling through space and so on. Again, such images could reflect individual trauma, but I want to explore a more collective aspect of them, by focusing on them as expressions of either what lies outside of culturally recognisable identity, or the processes which enforce the margins of that identity.

As in Chapter 3, my suggestion is that women's aggressive energies lie at the edges or outside of the structure of identity. Because they disturb identity, they are likely to be experienced as abject by both the woman who has them and those around her. Yet, at the same time, as Bersani suggests, only the decentred subject is available to desire (Butler, 1997: 149), so these abject realms which are potentially annihilatory are also insistently fascinating. The next section explores this level of abject, cultural 'Not-I'ness through the experience of Vivienne, who offered an image of being buried alive. The point of this discussion is to draw out the role of aggressive energies in the struggle for the kind of agency which exists at the margins of identity.[3] At these edges, grounds for agency can be hard or impossible to find, yet it is here that the capacity to note aggressive energies and focus on the possibilities of agency which they offer can be most powerful. In other words, agency matters most in the psychological places where it has been all but wiped out as a possibility, and aggressive fantasies can act as clues to the location of any residues, no matter how tiny and apparently useless they might be.

Vivienne: I lie in bed beside Geoffrey, who is snoring quietly. The children are asleep too. It is raining. Relentlessly. And hard. Harder than I can remember. It's not that I can hear it very loudly – like on a tin roof – this apartment block has a flat roof with a swimming pool, and next to it, a lovely, lush garden. On a sunny day, quite gorgeous. Glittering water and orange blossom, perfume to send you to heaven. But tonight I know it's teeming. Bloody teeming. I can hear the pool's pump working overtime. Looking out of the window, I can't see the familiar lights – just a thick shining curtain of rain. It's pitch black. I lie, wishing my heart beat would pipe down, and mentally calculate what is on top of the building. . . . I see it in my mind, starting to slip: first tons of blue metal – for structure and drainage, then tons of pool water and garden soil. And then, an army of plants weighing at least another ton. How can the roof hold this extraordinary burden? Was the engineering properly calculated – ever since we moved in I had meant to get it checked – no matter the cost. . . . And why oh why has it rained so relentlessly so often since we moved in here? It never used to rain like this. And why oh why is no one else affected. Am I mad? Was I entombed in a past life – Egypt perhaps. And if – when – the roof collapses, with its huge, wet, gushing burden, it will fall straight through the living room onto our bedrooms. Mega tons of concrete and water. There would be no escape. There would be no warning. We would all die – immediately – crushed like cockroaches. The rain is pouring. Absolutely relentless – no relief, no moments of lightness. As usual, I gather my pillow and quilt and trudge exhaustedly upstairs, where I prepare for another vigilant night ceaselessly eyeing the living room ceiling for the first sign of a crack.

In this context, I am choosing to read Vivienne's image as an example of the kind of terror which operates at the edges of identity, and the kinds of madnesses which threaten those who dare to approach the edges of identity. The (usually unconscious) avoidance of these places shapes lives, and a vague awareness of this can be part of what brings someone into analysis. Instead of being buried alive by snow or mud, the psychological equivalent is being paralysed by (or drowning in the quicksand of) fear, shame, and an habitual sense of helplessness and despair. As Campbell points out, women often experience their own aggressive impulses as bringing with them shame and frustration (1993: 10, 41).

What is possible in such places? Countertransferentially, they are close to intolerable and in spite of being unthinkable, they must be thought about in some way. It is valid for an analysand to simply want such places to be acknowledged but not 'thought into'. If, however, the analysand does want to try to think into them, it may only be possible to do so for fractions of a second. But over time those fractions of a second can add up to something.[4] One such unthinkable thought would be that Vivienne's image might be depicting her own aggressive fantasy of destroying everything she loves, and taking herself with it. Clearly, this is also the thing she is most terrified of. Yet, as Bersani suggests through Freud, love is a form of aggressiveness (1986: 20–21). By definition, the more intensely one loves someone or something, the more powerful the urge to destroy them. Likewise, Butler reads Freud as arguing that '[m]ourning is immensely reassuring because it convinces us of something we might otherwise doubt; our attachment to others' (Butler, 1997: 153). In this way the image of the destruction of all that one loves may be Vivienne's means of finding something out about the extreme edges of her humanity, through the dreaded, but compulsively present image of catastrophic loss.

At the same time, if, as argued in preceding chapters, our identity is a sedimented landscape of loss, Vivienne's image may be an exploration of the moments of total loss which have come to form her identity. Again, this could be at (the personal level) a matter of object losses and failures around which her individual psyche has been structured. They could also, however, be the marks of her personal experience of the losses and injurious terms of identity formation. Whatever the source, what is being presented is a realm in which the forces are crushing and deadly in their indifference to human vulnerability and needs. This is an uninhabitable realm, yet we must inhabit it, because that is what life is. Something of the impossible struggle with this is conveyed by the following text which comes from a Friday night Progressive Jewish service *Siddur*, or Order of Service. This text is part of one of a number of optional texts used in this particular community's service, just before the Mourner's *Kaddish*, or Prayer for the Dead is said:

> we could not have our sensitivity without fragility. Mortality is the tax that we pay for the privilege of love, thought, creative work – the toll on the bridge of being from which clods of earth and snow-peaked mountain summits are exempt. Just because we are human, we are prisoners of the years. Yet that very prison is the room of discipline in which we, driven by the urgency of time, create.
>
> (North Shore Temple Emmanuel, 1997: 191)

The awareness of mortality brings with it a sense of fascinating, exhilarating and horrifying precariousness and vulnerability that is almost unbearable. It is a moment of intense energies and extreme possibilities. I read the *Siddur* text as offering a system of identity within which such energies can be glanced at, even if only momentarily. The image offered canalises the rawness of mortality into a particular system of identity. In this system of identity, our vulnerability and mortality *demands* that we try to make something of our human predicament.

One of the facets of this awareness of mortality is the sense of its unbearable precariousness, and the desire to turn away. James Hillman comments on this, saying that therapy is not about lubricating adaptation – '[i]t's more a matter of evoking the sense of individuality which comes with death, with fate. My death. It's very hard to stay with that' (1992: 178).

In the face of this potentially overwhelming and paralysing reality, agency has to be found and decisions have to be made. My suggestion is that aggressive energies have an important role in these imperatives, and that this is especially so at the margins of inhabitable identity. The choice is between a melancholic refusal of the losses and limitations of identity, or a more aggressive mourning of them, which contains within it the possibility of a subsequent turn towards life.

In order to illustrate this, I use an image from an analysand. This analysand was male, but I will take the point he makes back through Vivienne's example. Robert had been struggling for a long time with terrifyingly broken up places within himself. The level of disorientation was such that it left him with little idea of how to live his life, either from moment to moment (including what he wanted to talk about in sessions), and at a more big picture, directional level. Living in this way was agonising.

One session we had found some words to discuss the appalling helplessness he felt. I offered some words, he offered some back, and slowly we began to find images for what is possible when all sense of orientation has gone. Robert then offered an image of how to respond at a moment-to-moment level to this state of being overwhelmed. He came from a country where the winter snows were known to bring avalanches in the mountains, and remembered that he had been brought up to know that there are certain things which increased your chance of getting out of an avalanche alive. In the event of being buried, one is told to dribble saliva out of one's mouth and note which way it runs, and then try to wriggle or dig in the opposite direction, retesting in the same way at short intervals to make sure that no energy is being wasted digging in any direction other than up. Based on this memory, Robert's task became to find, on a moment-to-moment basis, the micro-clues around which to exercise whatever tiny degree of agency he could, and in the direction which his micro-experiments led him to believe his best chances of survival lay. This was important as it took the emphasis away from the parts of him which were panicky and insistently demanding that he was getting nowhere, running out of time, and had no idea which direction he should be moving in. This panicky voice was demanding 'action' – any kind of action would do – even though previous experiences indicated that this kind of action only caused more mess and stuckness.

The saliva image gave Robert a way of repeatedly, momentarily relinquishing the parts of himself which expected him to know what the 'big picture' of his life was, and this allowed him to concentrate, for the first time, on his immediate needs and options. In this way, parts of him were able to begin to inhabit his helplessness without the previous need to split away from it and judge it as intolerably abject weakness or failure. In effect, he was converting helplessness into powerlessness, by concentrating on the moment and trying to find what possibilities it offered. The separation which I am making here is that to be helpless is to be unable to help oneself in any way. To be powerless is to have no direct power over the external world, but to develop a sense of responsibility for learning from one's conscious and unconscious responses to that world. Unconscious responses are not (by definition) under control, but the point of psychoanalysis is that they can be treated as a system of communication and learnt from. Paying close attention to them as communications and learning their patterns still does not provide control (or anything like it), but it is possible to acquire some skill at 'riding' the energy patterns in them, perhaps in the way that a surfer rides a wave. While precarious and dangerous, such an approach does provide some degree of expression of agency, as well as space for exploring the margins of helplessness and powerlessness.

In these places, however, aggression is often tightly entwined with defeat, helplessness, despair and pain. It can feel as if there *is* no aliveness, no sense of direction, nothing which even remotely resembles agency or, often, even the smallest possibility of movement. Actually, these are the places where aggressive energies matter most. Very small and slow to appear, but eventually significant changes can accumulate if the threads of aggression can be spotted and unpicked from their paralysing amalgams so that they can become available for other combinations. The choice to roll some saliva out of one's mouth and read its movement as a compass for how to direct one's efforts is an expression of aggression in the sense that Tom Steel describes when he writes that 'aggression wants to bite, tear, smash, explode, find alternatives and push on to new territory' (Samuels, 1993: 163). Steel is articulating an energetic, free-moving moment of aggression, but the trapped, focused version of this is a refusal to collapse into despair, confusion and helplessness, in spite of feeling that one will inevitably do so.

The connection between Vivienne's collapsing apartment image and aggressive fantasy is that often, when women approach their own aggressive energies, there is a terror that somehow something awful will happen. Maybe the sky will fall in on them or their loved ones. Again, such images can be read as the ways in which female identity is policed: exploring the margins of that identity is simply so uncomfortable, and throws up so many alarming and seemingly irrational, if not mad, images that it is generally much easier not to go there. Maybe Vivienne's image relates to a feared moment where agency fails in the face of the overwhelming might and power of an indifferent or perhaps malevolent Other. Perhaps her image can be read as a graphic description of the collapse of identity. The important point is, however, that these moments of collapse are actually where agency and morality are defined.

Again, I come back to David Cooper's commentary of Foucault's *Madness and Civilization*, introduced in the preceding chapter on how we create the disease of madness in order 'to evade a certain moment of our own existence – the moment of disturbance, of penetrating vision into the depths of ourselves . . . By this means we escape a certain anxiety, but only at a price that is as immense as it is unrecognised' (1995: viii). Cooper is pointing to chaos as the thing which we turn away from in ourselves, but I would add (or possibly substitute) the word 'helplessness' in place of 'chaos'. We would rather create madness and see it in others than face our own most stuck, helpless places, with all the humiliation and sense of abjection that goes with them.

I do not know which would be more dangerous: being in Vivienne's collapsing building or in Robert's avalanche – there are too many variables involved in each situation for a non-expert to make a comparison. But the question remains: what avenues would be left for the pursuit of tiny degrees of agency, if one were left alive and conscious. Robert came up with an image which answers this question, but what of Vivienne's predicament? In the event that one could move or speak there might be the possibility of either tapping on whatever could be reached, or calling out, on the assumption that emergency services with sniffer dogs would arrive and be searching for survivors. To be in Vivienne's position and to be able to conjure up such an image in the face of the terrifying image of the landslide would be to be able to start making use of (in an object relations way) the minds of others. It would be a significant step to be able to trust that, in the event of a disaster, one would stay alive in someone's mind, and that they would search.

But note, I am not concentrating on the object relation as an end in itself, but as a way of exploring the person's capacity to hold on to their own sense of agency. This positioning deliberately focuses on using the mind of the Other as a container not for the development of relationship, but of agency. In this way, the analytic relationship, as the holding of a space in which the analysand can come to explore inner and outer Otherness, offers room for the analysand to unravel stuck amalgams of aggression and despair, by using the attentive, engaged capacity of the other. It becomes possible to explore zones of identity which feel like they are landslides waiting to happen if there is a sense that someone will be around and listening to your tappings, should you manage to survive the landslide. Given the kind of landslides of paralysing self-hatred and shame that women often feel in relation to their own aggressive impulses, this kind of presence can make a significant difference. Again, my choice is to use the *tools* of object relations, but without taking on the values and social agendas of object relations.

BEING MADE NOTHING – SEXUAL ASSAULT AND THE LOSS OF AGENCY

The madnesses and possibilities of death which lie at the margins of identity exist not only in the realm of the imagination. Dolores wrote of the sense of shock at being treated as a gendered object when she was raped and nearly murdered.

Dolores: When I was raped, some years ago, I went into shock. Actually, I narrowly escaped being murdered and at the time that was the more shocking thing, of course, because death is the ultimate violation, and the only image I could find to describe the way I felt, was that I felt like a sophisticated New York black who goes to Mississippi and finds that there, he is just an uppity nigger. (At that time, I did think of a man.)

I had always thought I was somehow invulnerable, that because I didn't conform to the normal rules of bourgeois behaviour, those rules didn't apply to me. It never occurred to me that I might get treated that way, simply because I was female. Actually, up 'till that point, I had never had any strong sense of myself as Female – not because I didn't know that I was a girl, but because I had so little identification with the inferior gender stereotype which was accepted as real 20–30 years ago – for a start, I'm six foot tall, my eyes are not blue, I have a long nose, and

> my face has features not button blobs; I'm not so bad – the sort of person people remember, I've been told I'm 'striking' but I am not a candidate for the cover of Vogue! I can never get shoes to fit me, and I can't buy clothes in [fashion chain stores], so why should I have imagined that I was a member of that sub-class who got beaten up and raped?

Dolores' account could be read as discussing the sense of falling through layers of shock at how ruthlessly the production of gender is enforced. She might not have performed her gender role in a way which identified with the assumed helplessness and inferiority of women, but the Other was able to impose that discursive structure in such a way as to rape her and nearly kill her. This is a realm of literal hopelessness, and Dolores also wrote about how she had subsequently positioned herself in relation to the loss of her sense of invulnerability.

> **Dolores:** These days, though, I don't feel like an uppity trouble maker. I used to, but now I feel like a sad, withdrawn, and I hope, dignified woman. I consider I have been marginalised from my own culture, although I suppose that this has given me strength as an individual. I am also aware that if I were black, I might have a lot more to complain about.

Note, however, what Dolores has done with her experience – through it she makes a series of links about what it might be like to have an identity which is as contingent as her own, and possibly more vulnerable to humiliation and destruction than she is. A sophisticated New York black man's claim on his human dignity is, like hers, as a woman, dependent on the discursive consensus of those around them, and upon those who maintain law and order. This consensus can collapse at any moment, as Dolores' sense of invulnerability collapsed in moments. Remarkably, Dolores subsequently used this horrifying confrontation with the reality of rape and murder to contact the precariousness of her fellow beings. Having been forced into a situation where she had no rights, no dignity, little or no agency (although she does use the words 'narrowly escaped' when talking about having nearly been murdered), Dolores used her experience of the Other's enacted ruthless, cruel, destructive amalgam of aggression to build on her sense of political and social justice. This response to the Other's aggression or to one's own aggressive fantasies and energies is a move which a number of women took in their second round reflections on their contributions to this project, which will be discussed in Chapter 7.

Reading these ideas at an individual level suggests that the maximum possibility for agency coincides with the deepest sense of abjection and incapacity. What is crucially important about this notion of agency is that the likelihood of it toppling over into a tyrannical, for-its-own-sake exercise of power over others is minimised. The power accessible in such psychological landscapes is shot through with the pain of one's own vulnerability and is therefore self-limiting. This is a sense of power which is based on one's experience of weakness, rather than a desire to cover it up, or try to make it the 'fault' of the Other. It is a sense of power which acknowledges the conditions of its own existence and is therefore more likely to be ethical and aware of its own limitations. As Cooper points out, when we turn away from the chaotic within ourselves and elect Others to carry what we refuse to confront in ourselves, we lose something very important (1995: viii). Turning away from women's aggressive fantasies loses the rich possibilities for exploring one's relationship with the inner and outer worlds, the price paid by oneself and others for identity. Through that disavowal the thread of our common humanity is lost.

STOPPING FURTHER HARM

Ella's approach to these issues was different. She too wrote of the humiliation of sexual attack and her surprise at being included in what Dolores calls 'that sub-class who get beaten up and raped'.

Ella: Surely it couldn't happen to me? Which is odd because I expect it all the time. I was assaulted once by a group (five or six, I forget) of boys I knew. They held me down and tried to get the youngest to penetrate me – he was as upset as I was and it's odd but this is the first time I've thought of that, him being upset too I mean. As he couldn't do anything they used a large stick, and commented on my being hairy. My current boyfriend (at the time) was one of the perpetrators and I let him fuck me afterwards. I was 13 or 14, I never told anyone and continued to frequent that part of town where my reputation had 'blossomed'. I was raped properly (what do I mean?) later by a chap on the fringes of the group. I wish I had not let myself be abused – the second time could have been prevented and the damage from the first mitigated by at least running away afterwards. This has sat like a lump in me for years and I wonder if any of them ever lost a minute's sleep over it. And yet, the attraction for me [of the rape fantasy] is in the lack of responsibility – returning to childhood almost – 'don't hurt me I'm only little'. Since when did that have any effect anyway?

While Ella's sexual assault was different in the degree of mortal danger to Dolores', she too was left with deep pain, so that it has sat 'like a lump' in her for years. Ella's experience did, however, leave her with a speculation that some of the subsequent damage from the second attack could have been mitigated had she run away afterwards. Perhaps this reflects Walkerdine's work on the role of humiliation in the positioning of people as social subjects and, in particular, the way women remain in humiliating situations because of the lack of alternative ways of reading their situation. Miss Baxter's situation bears similarities: she remains in role and interprets her boy student's behaviour as 'normal' by seeing it through the liberal humanist pedagogic perspective, thereby making it acceptable. In order to maintain that position, she has to refuse to see her boy pupils as violent, attacking and humiliating, and she also has to remain cut off from her own aggressive responses and right to intervene and protect herself.

Ella's comments that she wishes she had run away imply that she could not 'read' the aggression in what had happened to her in such a way as to be able to respond to it. Had she been able to, it could have provoked a fight or flight response, and given her access to her own aggression. In Samuels' terms this might have been leg anger (1993: 156), in the form of running away as an act of stopping further harm. This is part of what I mean about it being important that women be able to hold on to their capacities to think and feel amongst their own and other people's darkest of psychological shadows. Only by doing so is it possible to develop any kind of capacity, let alone one which can be relied on, to recognise threats. This might sound like a recipe for suspicion and paranoia. In fact it is the opposite. The capacity to think one's darkest thoughts, and consider the possibility of the Other's darkest thoughts, actually offers the freedom to explore one's ability to trust without being afraid that one is hopelessly naive and vulnerable to even the most obviously predatory Other. Again, this is part of how I read Jung's comment about women improving in analysis when they are 'allowed' to think all the disagreeable things which they had denied themselves before (Jung, 1998: 1105). The more clearly one can think and feel in the face of one's own and the Other's predatory, ruthless and murderous capacities, the more chances there are of spotting Others who are capable of fair and honest fights in the way Vivienne and Geoff did at the beginning of the chapter.

SIMULTANEOUS LAYERS OF INTERPRETATION

Based on the range of experiences discussed by the women who contributed to this project, there are numerous possible levels of interpretation of women's aggressive or violent fantasies. Such images may be exploring specific, personal trauma, or they may be related to the human need to try to rework the terror of the non-negotiability of mortality. They may be discussing and/or eroticising the specific violences which attend the processes of female subjection, or they may be gesturing towards the domains which lie outside of inhabitable female identity. They could also be articulating the levels of aggression and violence which police the performance of femininity. Or they may represent the repetition, exploration and/or eroticising of the violences of subject formation, independent of gender.

Assuming that the above points coexist in complex relations to each other, the nature of fantasy and dreams is such that they offer the possibility of exploring multiple subject positions, even if it is only possible to identify with one position in the tableau in a particular moment. In other words, several of the above levels of description may be true simultaneously, and fantasy may offer a woman ways of exploring the tensions between those levels of experience.

Thus, a rape scene in a woman's erotic fantasy might mean many things. It could, as for Dolores or Ella, represent traumatic, terrifying or humiliating memories. It could, as for Rosa or Ella, be an image which carries possibilities of arousal, which is also uncomfortable, as it hovers around the edges of frightening previous experiences, albeit (in Rosa's case) in the context of love. It is also important to bear in mind that Ella, who had been sexually assaulted in real life also comments on her own use of erotic rape fantasies.

Again, this blurring of fear, humiliation and sexuality can be thought of in the light of Bersani's reading of Freud, quoted above, which suggests that 'all comparatively intense affective processes, including even terrifying ones [spill over into] sexuality . . . It may well be that nothing of considerable import- ance can occur in the organism without contributing some component to the excitation of the sexual instinct' (1986: 37–38). Sara's comments draw out a particular element of how complex our internalisation of personal experience and the gradients of social identity can be.

> **Sara:** I always went out with men who treated me badly – I knew I was alive then – it fired me up – plus I could get angry and let my imagin- ation go free on revenge. If they treated me kindly I became confused and very uneasy. Men who said I'll pick you up at 7pm but came at 11pm drunk, smelling of another woman were my kind of man. I knew where I was.

Sara put up with being treated in unacceptable ways, and implies that this was familiar to her: she knew where she was with it. But she also points out an important second layer, in which the abusive treatment gives her the go-ahead to be angry and let her imagination run wild on revenge. In other words, it justifies guilt-free aggressive fantasies. She also gives clues as to why this worked as a way for her to access her own aggression.

> **Sara:** I don't trust many people. I don't like many people. Many people I've known would be shocked – I'm sure – if they knew what I thought of them. I hate it when people tell me who I am, i.e. 'You're so gentle'. Half of me feels I've conned them and the other half feels I have to be gentle all the sodding time.

Again, perhaps these are the disagreeable thoughts which Jung describes women as being able to make use of in the process of 'getting better'. Here, Sara is talking about the parts of her which resist or give the slip to her gender role – her hatred and her resentment of being type-cast as gentle. She is describing places where she privately resists the pressure to be the redemptive good girl whose role was made so clear in Walkerdine's commentary on teenage girls' magazines. Thus, what she is resisting is the cultural fantasy of femininity, in which women's desires are shaped for the good of others, and where aggression, spark or trangressive brilliance are humiliatable or attackable.

Again, the tactics I have been using are the post-Jungian dissociationist-based ones outlined in Chapter 2. First, it is necessary to recognise and attend to the 'Not-I' and, second, time needs to be allowed for the characteristics and personality of the 'Not-I' to emerge. Close and sustained exploration of an individual's psychic landscape will reveal pockets, no matter how small, of subversive, identity-resistant inner Otherness, which often carries the seeds of a longed for, but feared agency. Through the post-Jungian model being proposed, this Otherness which is all too easily disregarded as irrelevant or destructive (as von Franz's could easily have dismissed her murderous burglar), can be seen as the potential carrier of much needed additional psychological perspectives. Such additional options can be especially valuable in the face of an habitual, stuck, defeated conscious attitude.

THE ATTRACTION OF BEING A BRICK WALL

I use another comment of Ella's to bring this exploration of agency, helplessness, defeat, destruction and *jouissance* to a close.

> **Ella:** As I tried to think about these questions, I kept hitting a brick wall. Pictorial representation is a reproduction of a North London road sign whose uncompromising nature has always attracted me.

The North London road sign in question shows five blocked exits from a road (see Figure 4.1). Based on the preceding argument, a reading of this would

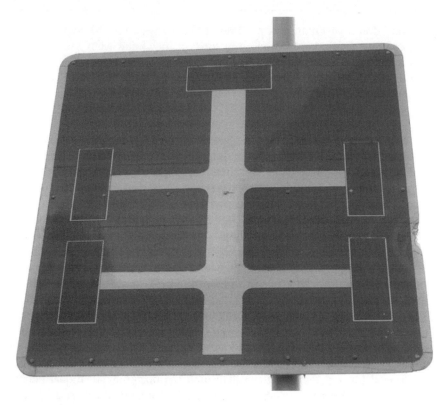

Figure 4.1 Ella's North London Street Sign

be that such a sign depicts Ella's experience of trying to engage with her own 'Not-I within' aggressive energies. Since these aggressive energies are positioned at the margins of intelligible identity, they will be heavily 'policed' with road-blocks aplenty for the explorer to hit.

But Ella is saying something else. She comments that the uncompromising nature of this road sign has always attracted her, as though she can identify with, and take pleasure in, the non-negotiable way in which the sign says 'NO!'. The road sign is not assertive. There is a certain aggressive defiance in its absolute and uncompromising nature. It is as if Ella switches her point of identification from being the person who is defeated by hitting the wall, to *being* the wall or road-block itself, with the pleasure of being relentlessly uncooperative and unyielding.

Ella provided another picture to illustrate her inner life, a birthday card which carries a watercolour painting entitled 'Custard, Darling?'. This is a picture of an exuberant, dancing, naked woman, wielding spoons at the stove as she makes custard for someone who is presumably her lover. Ella's two

Figure 4.2 'Custard, Darling?'

pictures appear to be opposites: defeat and joy. I suggest, however, that they actually overlap. By identifying with the aggressive defiant NO! in the road-block image, Ella sets up the ground of the exuberant sense of fun and capacity to say 'YES!' of the 'Custard, Darling?'[5] image. This place where aggression and love are inseparable will be returned to in Chapter 6, where I discuss aggressive energies and eating disorders. But before that, I will take up a cluster of images which women offered as part of their contributions to this project. At first these images seemed tangential to my own interests, but their wall-like refusal to let me pass until I had learnt something from them changed my mind, and led me to suspect that there were important aggressive energies embedded in them.

Chapter 5

Explosive visibility

ON THE MOVE

When I started this project, I had a hunch that women's disavowed aggressive energies were often embedded in their performance of gendered identity. That idea forms the basis of this chapter, and in order to provide a context for developing it, I need to introduce some theoretical elements. These elements are then used to explore the comments of the women contributors who wrote about body, movement, visibility and clothes.

I suggest that feminine embodiment is both the site of a performative displacement of aggressive energies and also a product of that displacement. This tension is echoed in feminist discussions of how women live their bodies (and are lived by them):

> The body, as anthropologist Mary Douglas has argued, is a powerful symbolic form, a surface on which the central rules, hierarchies, and even metaphysical commitments of a culture are inscribed, and thus reinforced through the concrete language of the body.
>
> (Bordo, 1997: 90)

Yet the psychoanalytic body is also the substrate of the lived psyche, so that Bersani (viewing the body through Freud's work) writes that:

> The ego does not merely register perceptions and sensations; it is also an inventory or a storehouse of perceptual processes themselves. It fantasmatically repeats the body's contacts with the world in something, perhaps, like metaperceptual structures. The ego is not a surface; it is a *psychic imitation of surfaces.* In the same way, the ego's relation to the objects which form its character is a kind of replay of the id's relation to objects. In both cases – in the ego's derivation from the body and in its derivation from the id – a relation to the world is petrified either as an architecturalizing of the body's moves in the world or as a grouping of decathected internal objects.
>
> (1986: 95, original italics)

Thus interiority (from the perspective of the ego) is a self-aware surface of a culturally inscribed and culturally formed physicality. Examining women's experiences of space, embodiment and movement reveals that women's aggressive energies are very much part of the operation of the cultural definition of the inhabitable, recognisable body. At the same time, however, women's aggressive energies are also tightly woven into the creation and policing of the desires which mark the limits of that recognisable body, and the excesses of the body's powers.

In terms of this project, the result is that the body contains the traces of the production of identity. That which has been made Other in order to fabricate the 'I-slot' in which a woman lives her life will leave its traces on the lived 'I', even if only in the form of what the 'I' disavows or regards as abject. And this is where the post-Jungian model which I am proposing is relevant. Jung's dissociationist heritage provides a clinical framework from which to engage with the 'Not-I within' which arises through the processes of identity formation.

Indeed, Joseph Redfearn (1994) suggests that the body is the gateway to the 'Not-I within', and a comment by Ella provides a point of departure for exploring that.

Ella: Since stopping smoking 7ish years ago I have indulged a tendency toward overeating and carry a protective layer of about 1–1 and 1/4 stones of flab (good heavens isn't fat light – a little goes a long way). I decided to try to become more active and energetic. I suspected my post viral illness would respond to a more spirited approach. I started to eat less – nothing drastic or obsessive, but smaller portions and no biscuits except in emergencies and more exercise, extra yoga, some short indoor jogs and an exercise class. Energy levels increased, muscles started to appear, jeans began to loosen and I looked forward to leaping about. But my head fell apart; problems on the back burner began to boil over and fear and anger came up with a vengeance. I've been doing yoga for years, but have moved forward pretty quickly in the last two, doing things like headstands which I never in my wildest dreams expected to. I was talking about this to someone – about having to let go of my fixed vision of myself as someone who could not do anything physical. He agreed and said yes especially as you can now do more than the average person. I was shocked as I had only just thought about letting go of the idea of being hopeless; now here was someone suggesting above average competency – how will I manage without all my ready made reasons for failure?

Again, my approach is to take a post-Jungian perspective of assuming that some form of inner Otherness is being expressed as Ella discusses her experience. Given the position developed in the preceding chapters, Ella's sense of inner Otherness is likely to contain amalgams of aggression and other emotions such as fear, shame and despair. Again, however, deep structures stand in the way of a woman who tries to explore these levels of her being, and Ella's comments introduce questions about how the resultant amalgams of emotions are experienced physically. In order to discuss these questions, I introduce certain ideas from feminism around gender and space, space being the context of our experience of our body. As Kate Bornstein observes 'Most of the behavioural clues [to gender] boil down to how we occupy space, both alone and with others' (Ainley, 1998: xvi).

SPACE AND FEMININITY

At this level, Ella's comments can be read as saying that by becoming more active, she was simply changing her relationship with external space. This alone would, no doubt, have had an impact on how she experienced inner space, and could be seen as contributing in some way to her head falling apart. There is, however, another more subtle level at which gender and space are entwined. Space operates as a philosophical category, like time, reason and morality, and has a particular place in the development of the self-experience of the Western subject. A number of feminists have questioned the traditionally accepted definitions and 'natural' order of these entities, including Elizabeth Grosz, who comments that:

> [I]n Kant's conception . . . while space and time are *a priori* categories we impose on the world, space is the mode of apprehension of exterior objects, and time a mode of apprehension of the subjects' own interior. This may explain why Irigaray claims that in the West time is conceived as masculine (proper to a subject, a being with an interior) and space is associated with femininity (femininity being a form of externality to men). Woman is/provides space for men, but occupies none herself.
>
> (Grosz, 1995: 98–99)

Grosz could be read as applying a Foucauldian line of questioning to the notions of space and time: what is the history of these notions and how have they developed and come to be taken for granted? How are our beliefs about their status as 'truth' maintained? Whose interests are served by our accepting these notions of space and time as 'truth'?

These questions make more sense if one bears in mind that notions of space and time, their flow, division and relationship to other concepts (such as gender) vary between cultures. Ardener puts it clearly: *'behaviour and space are mutually dependent*' (Ardener, 1993: 2, original italics). She goes on to say that '*space defines the people in it* . . . [and] at the same time, however, . . . the presence of individuals in space in turn determines its nature . . . *people define space*' (Ardener, 1993: 3, original italics). Adele's comments illustrate this.

Adele: I listened to a man walking down the corridor and going out to his car: he called out loudly then whistled his way down the corridor jangling his keys. He slammed the car door, revved up the engine and sounded the horn. I never even saw this man and yet with his sounds he invaded my space and occupied my mind. I felt afraid of the aggression I heard in his actions. I cannot allow my voice to come out as a shout, anything louder than a gentle speaking voice sticks in my throat, and I take great pains not to bang, slam or thump as I go about my business. I would love to be able to open up my lungs and sing out or shout regardless of if anyone would hear me. I dream about singing to people but the idea of making that much noise fills me with horror.

Grosz takes up Irigaray's point that in Western thought, there has been a long association between women and space, and men and time, to the point where this association has become deeply woven into cultural/linguistic structures and is now taken for granted. These structures do, however, become visible in numerous philosophical arguments. Rousseau's view was that women were the custodians of the nursery of good citizens who could transform public life. These (male) citizens would build their own families/nurseries which, by virtue of women's assumed closeness to the uncorrupted natural world[1], would also provide them with a retreat from the corruption of contemporary society. Here, men could be good citizens and women good private persons, with the two spheres intersecting in ways that gave women a role in the development and preservation of good forms of public life, while they themselves did not participate in it directly (Lloyd, 1993: 77). For Rousseau, a woman's job was to stay at home and create the conditions under which the public sphere could be maintained. In other words, women's physicality provided the spatial context in which men's intellectual and civic lives operated freely. Likewise, for Hegel, the male journey was one of transcendence of the netherworld of women – the breaking away from 'the realm of particularity and merely natural feelings. For the female, in contrast, there is no such realm which she can both leave and leave intact' (Lloyd, 1993: 102). Essentially, women mark space, men move in it.

Historically, the fantasy that women's bodies must be 'left behind' in the pursuit of something higher abounds. The Western notion of space is caught up with a fantasy of the femininity which renders space a safe, familiar, clearly definable entity, which because it is female, should be appropriately docile or accepting of domination. At the same time, the precarious boundaries of this fantasy-space-body create an underlying anxiety (Best, 1995: 183), a point which connects with Chapter 3's discussion of the dangerous nature of femininity. Moreover, as Best points out, space is not ours (as women) to take part in, since our substance has been used in the production of the concept of its containment (Best, 1995: 186).

So for a woman to have agency, to move in a loose or carefree fashion is to place herself outside of the 'safe' zones of identity. These attitudes to space are embedded in our perceptual field and turn up in the very bricks that form our depth psychological edifices. In object relations, the mother as marker and container of space is taken as a 'given'. Failure to perform this function is regarded as a mark of 'failure as a mother'. A comment by Erica Burman, however, provides another perspective. She suggests that what matters to society about a mother's 'failure' is that it represents a breakdown in the way in which citizens are produced:

> Mothers were, and still are, positioned as the relay point in the production of 'democratic citizens', that is, adults who will accept the social-political order by imagining that their concurrence is through independent choice rather than coercion.
>
> (1997: 80)

Seen in this light, constructing as failure a mother's inability or refusal to anchor space for the Other in ways which produce the 'right' kinds of citizens could have another meaning. Such a construction might be part of the culture's process of policing the production of a certain kind of identity which fits in with accepted fantasies about what is normal and what is good. Rather than being some kind of personal pathology the refusal or inability to anchor space in the prescribed way could be seen as a woman's (healthy) core resistance to identity, even as it unsettles our fantasies about femininity.

My suggestion is that women's aggressive energies are diverted into creating and sustaining these categories of perception and experience which have become normalised as 'truths'. Again, I would ask the Foucauldian question of whom do such truths serve, and how? In order to explore this, I will first examine a Jungian counterpart to object relations' unconscious fantasy about the women's bodies as 'natural' markers of space. As in Chapter 3, my interest is in drawing out where women's aggressive energies have become solidified into materials which form the building blocks of cognisable personhood, making these energies difficult and disturbing for women to access for their own benefit.

THE MADDENINGLY MOBILE MISS MILLER

Jung's *Symbols of Transformation* was based on the writings of an American woman, Frank Miller. In 1905 Miller published an article based on her own fantasies in Flournoy's *Archives de Psychologie* (Shamdasani, 2003: 301). Miller had been a student of Flournoy's, and Deirdre Bair writes that 'Flournoy gave Jung his own French translation of the original English version of Miss Miller's fantasies as well as thoughts and ideas he gleaned from later conversations and correspondence' (Bair, 2003: 213). Jung's interpretation of Miller's fantasies forms the basis of *Symbols of Transformation*, the book which precipitated Jung's break with Freud. Miller's fantasies, and Jung's interpretation mark the birth of important aspects of the Jungian interpretive tradition.

Jung read Miller's fantasies as involuntary delusions, the study of which formed a 'pathway towards successful treatment of psychosis' (Bair, 2003: 214). In the preface to the 1942 edition of *Symbols of Transformation*, Jung comments that he had received confirmation of his interpretation of Miller's fantasies – that she was in the prodromal phases of schizophrenia. Jung writes that in 1918 he had heard, through an American colleague, that Miller had indeed been admitted to a psychiatric hospital after a trip to Europe. Her diagnosis on her 1909 Danvers Hospital record reads:

> 'Psychopathic personality, with hypomanic traits.' Her family history is given as 'bad.' She is described as being of 'unstable temperament,' 'erotic,' 'vain,' and 'inclined to be talkative.' The prognosis for the hypomania is given as 'good,' for the psychopathic personality, 'very bad'.
> (Shamdasani, 1990: 31)

Shamdasani located Miller's poems as well as reviews of her public lectures about her extensive overseas travels. In her lectures, Miller used costumes and images to evoke foreign places and historical periods for the audience, and Shamdasani's paper includes photographs of Miller in costume. He also provides a context for Miller's psychiatric diagnosis through the work of Elizabeth Lunbeck whose research on the history of turn-of-the-century American psychiatry suggests that:

> [t]he diagnosis of psychopathy [in the Boston area at that time] was overwhelmingly applied to young women who were the first to live on their own in cities and to achieve a limited freedom to spend and associate with whom they pleased. Their emergent expression of sexuality and independence which transgressed social norms was enough for them to be branded as immoral and thereby institutionalised. Their aspirations were usually ridiculed by psychiatrists. The immediate events leading to Frank Miller's hospitalization bear out this portrait.
> (Shamdasani, 1990: 32)

Miller's refusal to stay in place and anchor the space in which male agency was performed does appear to have been the kind of thing which created anxiety in the psychiatric system she encountered. Furthermore, as Shamdasani observes, her capacity to transmit her own impressions of the world with great intensity (which was the basis of her illustrated costume lectures on places such as Russia, Greece and Scandinavia) seems to have induced in Jung a powerful experience of her imagery. This capacity to induce strong experiences of places that the subject had not been to, and periods in which they had not lived, was the hallmark of Miller's art, and Shamdasani comments that the Greek Consul, Mr Botassi, who had been to one of Miller's costume lectures:

> thought he was seeing one of the caryatids of the Acropolis step forth. For Jung at this time, schizophrenia consisted in a loosening of the historical layers of the unconscious; this loosening is one way of viewing what Frank Miller did in her performances, though in a mode rather different from a schizophrenic regression.
>
> (Shamdasani, 1990: 53)

What emerges is that Jung may have mistaken the status of Miller's imagery as a symbolic representation of her psychic state. Instead, they appear to have been far more complex, and woven into her experiences as a well-travelled woman, who had a powerful artistic gift for communication of her experiences and imagination.

Bair concurs with this understanding, pointing out the fantasies Jung based *Symbols of Transformation* on had been created by Miller to 'support her beloved teacher Flournoy, who was under merciless attack from critics who derided his earlier book' [*From India to the Planet Mars*] (Bair, 2003: 214). Miller's writing was from what Bair describes as a 'normal, novelistic imagination' (Bair, 2003: 214). The Danvers State Hospital record indicates that Miller's own perception of her situation at the time of her admission was that 'she was nervous and run down and needed a rest and also some treatment for stomach trouble which she had suffered for some time' (Shamdasani, 1990: 31). Shamdasani describes the trajectory of Miller's hospitalisation:

> Frank Miller appears far from being a raving maniac – lucid, clear, and defending her rights as a woman, indignant at being placed, as well she might, in a state mental asylum against her will and without her knowledge. What's more, she was discharged after just a week, to her aunt, who promised to take her to a private sanatorium. There are no immediate signs that she spent the rest of her life as a bedraggled waif, roaming the back wards of an insane asylum.
>
> (Shamdasani, 1990: 32)

Perhaps Jung was unable to make the turn towards the Otherness which was embedded in Frank Miller's imagery in the same way that he was unable to make the turn towards the Salome figure in the fantasy he discusses in *Memories, Dreams, Reflections* (see Chapter 2). This embedded Otherness could be thought of as the abjected spectres of gendered identity of the period: women's desire, freedom, aggression, agency and power. Thus perhaps Jung's *Symbols of Transformation* needs to be read not as an account of the truth of Miller's psychological state, but as a man's struggles to engage with his personal version of his culture's fears of madness, precipitated by a young woman who refused to perform her gendered role appropriately. The feared madness is attributed to Miller, when rightfully it belongs to the culture that is defining her role as a gendered being. In Chapter 1, I suggested that people whose identity positions are comparatively marginalised are more vulnerable to having what would normally count as assets turned into liabilities. The example I quoted is the labelling of a woman's anger in such a way as to trivialise it, or to make her look insane. This kind of 'finessing' is what happened when Jung viewed Miller from his own cultural position, without taking into account that his position was located and limited, rather than universal and with access to ahistorical truths. Miller's mobility and agency became part of what established her as mad. It is inappropriate to judge historical ideas and thinkers by contemporary standards, but these kinds of shifts import powerful, unconscious fantasies and identity politics into Jungian thought. Women's aggressive energies and desires to push on, create movement, change and aliveness are rendered impotent through the fears of instability which attend them. Perhaps it was such fears that Ella unsettled when she decided to become more active and energetic, with the consequence that her 'head fell apart'.

Embedded in Jung's technique is, however, the possibility of seeing these kinds of cultural madnesses and defences through their appearance as inner Otherness. Again, this is the basis of my use of this aspect of his work in this book. By working in this way it is possible to make use of Jung's complex-based model of psychological plurality (see Chapter 2) to view Miller's story as an expression of the period's cultural fears around loose women undermining the fabric of a civil society (again, a theme which finds echoes in Jung's own paper 'Woman in Europe' written in 1927). Thus Miller's struggles can be seen as those of a woman having to work her way along the edges of these cultural fears, policings and punishments. The rest of this chapter tracks these workings along the edges of identity as they were documented by the women who contributed to this project.

Note also the resonances between the psychiatrist's comments about Miller's personality and the male teacher's comments about the personality of a bright girl pupil in Chapter 4. Similarly, Jung's *Symbols of Transformation* could be seen as a manifestation of a cultural system of punishment for a woman who resisted her gendered identity.

Ella's choice to slip out of role and move more loosely and more easily certainly appeared to unleash anger and fear, but I would ask: whose anger, whose fear? Ella's comments can be read as a statement about what happens when a woman ceases to provide the context of space, but becomes instead an agent in space. In doing so, she is cutting against her internalisation of the boundaries of her gender role, occasioning an attack from the psychological mechanisms which police her performance of gender and reinforce the splits and eroticised losses which that performance depends upon. In other words, the aggressive energies which have been split off in order to perform femininity well are likely to get stirred up in a woman who becomes an agent, and makes use of space, rather than acting as a container of space for others.

INTENTIONALITY AND THROWING LIKE A GIRL

In order to think more about these issues of movement, agency, aggression and the fears they provoke, I introduce an essay by Iris Marion Young called 'Throwing Like a Girl'. Doris' comments provide a lead into this.

> **Doris:** I was socialised by my father who treated me as an equal in that he shared his passions – literature especially – with me, and his views on life. While on the one hand his is an old style man and the women he chooses to have relationships with are his 'inferiors' education and class-wise and has classically defined husband/wife roles, he votes for women, works with women as his equal and has never said anything 'sexist', i.e., women are inferior to me. My mother on the other hand has a classic suspicion of other women, was always negative towards me about how I looked and how I was physically (clumsy, ungainly, etc.) – in other words she didn't socialise me very adequately in terms of taking up what would be seen as female tools. What some would claim are inherently female – born with a desire to wear make-up, dress up, seduce men. She was however a good sportswoman, coached my softball team and taught me to throw 'like a boy'.

I want to concentrate on Doris' final comment which is that her mother taught her to throw 'like a boy'. Young provides an analysis of this, taking as her point of departure Merleau-Ponty's work on embodiment, and draws out how he assumes a universal male body – a body which can claim space for itself and 'throw like a boy':

> Merleau-Ponty locates intentionality in motility; the possibilities that are opened up in the world depend on the mode and limits of the bodily 'I

can.' Feminine existence, however, often does not enter bodily relation to possibilities by its own comportment towards its surroundings in an unambiguous and confident 'I can.' For example, . . . women frequently tend to posit a task that would be accomplished relatively easily once attempted as beyond their capacities before they begin it. Typically the feminine body underuses its real capacity, both as the potentiality of its physical size and strength and as the real skills and coordination that are available to it. Feminine bodily existence is an *inhibited intentionality*, which simultaneously reaches towards a projected end with an 'I can' and withholds its full bodily commitment to that end in a self-imposed 'I cannot'.

(Young, 1990: 148, original italics)

This 'I can' which ends in an 'I cannot' was expressed by Adele.

> **Adele:** I have struggled to free my thoughts and beliefs. I am now proud of my ability to think for myself, express what is important to me and trust my instincts. What I now long for is freedom in my own body. I alternately experience my body as disconnected, insubstantial and float-ing; or heavy, sluggish and dense. The only time I feel a true joy and freedom in my body is when I swim – I feel more natural and at ease in the water than I ever do on land. I have recurring dreams about swimming where the water gradually drains out below me until I am struggling along the bottom of the pool in the remaining few inches. In my dream I feel such a desperate longing to get to the water, then a release once I am swimming which turns to hopelessness as the water drains away.

This bogging down of lively, mobile, aggressive energies was touched on in the previous chapter's discussion of helplessnesses, and earlier in this chapter, when Ella described her reaction to having someone point out that she could do more in terms of yoga than the average person. She said that she found it hard to let go of being hopeless and was shocked at having to come to terms with having a level of competency which was above average, a pattern which fits with Young's observation that women tend to underestimate and under-use their physical capacities. I suggest that this is so partly because the 'I cannot' which is deeply embedded in many women's bodies is an internalisa-tion of the processes of identity production which render them Other to agency and movement.

Young builds on these ideas and develops a view that the female body tends to exist in discontinuity from its surroundings.

[W]omen frequently react to motions, even our own motions, as though we are the object of a motion that issues from an alien intention, rather than taking ourselves as the subject of motion.

(1990: 152)

[A woman's] . . . spatial existence is *positioned* by a system of coordinates that does not have its origin in her own intentional capacities. The tendency for the feminine body to remain partly immobile in the performance of a task that requires the movement of the whole body illustrates this characteristic of feminine bodily existence as rooted in *place*. . . . Likewise does the tendency of women to wait for an object to come within their immediate bodily field, rather than move out toward it.

(1990: 152–153, original italics)

Young is describing the phenomenon of 'throwing like a girl', in which the female body remains significantly immobile while performing a task which requires full involvement for its success. Ella points to this when she comments that accepting her above-average competency at yoga would interfere with her ready-made reasons for failure. The way in which femininity is entwined with the concept of space means that it is comparatively unusual for a woman to experience her body as the consistent and context-independent point of reference for her own intentional capacities, or agency. Clearly there are exceptions, and women are taking increasingly active roles in sport. But somehow this still fails to translate into significant changes in agency. Undertaken alone, such developments of physical capacities seem unable to produce the kind of strong energy Courtin refers to in Chapter 1, or the kind of reaction Courtin had to being raped (see Chapter 4). Rarely do sportswomen report the kinds of breakthroughs in their thinking and capacities to relate that Garner describes in Chapter 1.

As Best pointed out earlier, however, this concept of contained and containing space, which is based on fantasies of femininity, creates an anxiety because the same body which is used as the basis of our way of conceptualising and stabilising space is, in turn, conceptualised as having unstable edges (see Waldby, Chapter 3 and Lloyd, above).

For some time prior to starting this project, I had been interested in how women's aggressive energies were diverted into the performance of identity. My sense was that this had something to do with the static, background quality assigned to femininity in the cultural imagination. In order to unsettle this I developed a group exercise which experimented with visibility. As part of the research for this book I used a description of this visibility exercise to illustrate my themes when discussing my interests with the women who contributed material to the project. Some women chose to respond directly and 'do' the exercise in private and described the results as part of their contribution to my research.

AN EXERCISE IN VISIBILITY

The visibility exercise involves asking the members of the group to:

> Call to mind someone you know quite well and think about them care-fully. Think about how they look, their body, their smell, how they walk, move, scratch, their gestures, the way they dress. Dwell on the physicality of their being and how it is so much an expression of who they are, how it makes them three-dimensional. Consider how it would be if they were just their voice, or the essence of their personality, consider how much of them would be missing.
>
> Now imagine that you are standing behind a screen which makes you invisible. Feel what that's like – you can move around and no-one can see you. Your presence is only known when you choose to betray it by speak-ing or making something happen. Someone sits on the other side of the screen – they can be a friend, lover, or total stranger – it doesn't matter. They know that you are behind the screen, but can't see you through it. Imagine starting to move out from behind the screen: it might be that you put a hand or foot out first, or that you choose to emerge more fully. Stay with how it feels inside you when you become aware that you are now as visible to the other person as they are to you – that for them, you *are* your body, your voice, all the views of you (including your back and sides), how you walk, as well as your thoughts. Note what happens as you emerge.[2]

Often the material which came out of this exercise in groups surprised or distressed participants. Frequently the imagery was aggressive. Occasionally the source of the aggression was the 'watcher' (even if they were envisaged as a known 'safe' female) but much more often it was the protagonist herself. Of the women who explored the visibility fantasy for this project Jane offered an illustration of this.

Jane: I put my right foot outside and round the screen so that my calf was exposed and the room exploded. The walls, ceiling, floor, furniture and air that I was breathing turned into an all consuming, all destroying monster: blind rage and fire bombs, and I shattered against the wall to escape.

In workshops other images arose, such as being invisible even after emerging from behind the screen, experiencing paralysis or shrinking to nothing. One woman reported that when she ran the fantasy of emerging into visibility, the limb which she moved out from behind the invisibility screen distorted and became deformed, stopping her from taking the experiment any further. The percentage of women involved in this project who responded with explosive or inferno-like imagery (four out of the fourteen) is a little higher than in the five groups I have tried it with. Perhaps, as Redfearn observes, the emergent self is so energetic that its emergence cannot be stabilised within existing identity structures and produces a superheated, explosive or atomic kind of reaction (1992). Ella's comments develop this.

Ella: When I tried out the idea of being visible to others I exploded. Flesh all over the walls. The flesh had destructive power (other than the splat value) it seemed to be acidic or like napalm. I thought how odd it is that someone who is on closed circuit TV all the time should be invisible, but then the TV is for the Committee's use, not mine.

One reading of Ella's image is that the destructiveness of her flesh is a product of how it is seen by the committee. The committee which polices the performance of her 'I' wants her to keep her aggressive energies split up and remanufactured into the provision of safe, static space for the Other. In this way, the committee, as a product and beneficiary of those split-up energies, also gets to maintain its own existence.

By moving into visibility, Ella upsets this arrangement and starts to mobilise the split-up energies whose exclusion sustains her identity. The situation destabilises and she explodes. Through this, she discovers that her flesh has an acidic, napalm quality. I imagine that this is an effect of the aggressive energies which have been dammed up in her body, used to structure and police her performance of gender. Perhaps her explosion represents something of the attacking resentment which her aggressive energies feel towards the committee for keeping them under surveillance and demanding their remanufacture into the structure of female identity. Butler refers to these dammed-up energies as abjected spectres:

> [which] threaten the arbitrarily closed domain of subject positions. . . . What cannot be avowed as a constitutive identification for any given subject position runs the risk not only of becoming externalised in a degraded form, but repeatedly repudiated and subject to a policy of disavowal.
>
> (1997: 149)

Identity must, by its formation, be haunted by the constant presence of non-identity, and can only exist as a result of constant, internalised policing of the boundaries between the two.[3] My suggestion is that women's explorations of visibility transgress these divisions, sometimes with explosive results. I imagine these abjected spectres of women's fragmented and disavowed aggressive energies as a kind of anti-matter to femininity. Performing femininity well (including anchoring space for the other) entails keeping all this anti-matter in its place, so that it does its structural job of fuelling the performance of femininity. Movement, and especially movement into visibility, appears to destabilise this *status quo* with results which are frightening, even when they are not explosive. Mary and Juliette offered illustrations of this.

> **Mary:** Moving out from behind the screen. I can't. Crying like a child. Pleading. Please, PLEASE don't make me. Like standing at the open door of a plane, with no parachute and someone with a gun at my head saying jump. Certain death. Paralysed and numb. Can't believe this is happening to me.

Juliette also felt she could not survive the transition into visibility.

> **Juliette:** First time I tried this my attention got distracted just as I stood up to come out so I tried it again. It was like hitting some sort of force field. The air got thicker and heavier, and I began to go into a panic attack. It got hotter and hotter, so that I began to melt like wax. By the time I noticed what was happening it felt like I had almost gone too far. I only just pulled myself back, but I do have this morbid fascination with what would have been left if I hadn't.

So even when visibility is not explosive, women can still experience it as crossing a threshold which they cannot survive. While not explosive, Juliette's image speaks of the threshold as containing dangerously high levels of energy.

In the preceding chapters I suggested that women's aggressive fantasies and energies provide a window into the internal policing of the 'I'/'not-I' boundaries since, as argued in Chapter 3, the structure of female identity is such that it is (in the cultural imagination) positioned closer to the violences which underlie identity. At the same time, female identity is formed around an illusion of distance from those violences, so that femininity is read as the opposite of violence and by extension, aggression. Paradoxically, as Doris' interpretation of her psychopath dream in Chapter 3 indicated, the very structure of femininity can be experienced as a form of attack. Maybe women's explosive images of visibility express something of this explosive attacking feminine anti-matter. If so, the violences involved in the production of femininity are such that when that performance wobbles, the aggressive energies disavowed and eroticised in it start to unravel in ways which the woman's 'I' experiences as threatening and potentially lethal.

BEING UNDER SURVEILLANCE

Ella describes the committee, and draws out its function.

> **Ella:** God is a committee which judges my every move and employs a narrator to keep up a running commentary. Whenever I get near to having a look at the committee (lower case!) (for instance they almost appear at orgasm or at other times when the control is off) they are always in the same place – above and to my right. Also the top right part of my head is one of the 'missing bits' – I'm not aware of it even when it's on the floor. I find it difficult to look up to the top right, and my eye is quite a different shape from the left – less open. Once when I was working with a cranial osteopath we tried to sneak up on my head by getting energy to flow up and down my spine (another 'missing' place) and when it did, I felt like a knife was being pushed into the sole of my foot – extremely painful.

Ella is invisible – moving into visibility is explosive; yet, within her invisibility, she is highly visible to the committee. It is as though the committee is an internalisation of some injurious terms of femininity which demand that she will have no privacy (as a woman, one's appearance is assumed to be public property) and, at the same time, her passions and energies can never emerge in public. Energy is not even allowed to flow freely around her body. Living under surveillance creates no-go zones in the body, where threateningly uninhabitable domains of anti-identity reside.

Jane wrote about the same paradox of invisibility and surveillance.

> **Jane:** I'm always astounded that I've never met a man who lives his whole life on closed-circuit TV. Maybe they have a different way of talking about it, or maybe they just don't have it to anything like the same extent (if at all). I don't know. Even though I'm invisible I have a sort of faceless narrator (sometimes several) telling me about what I'm doing, discussing the options of what to do next, panning around the situation that I'm in and telling me about what other people think about what I'm doing. The voice(s) is/are more male than female, but I know that in terms of my assessment of myself it's God. Maybe that's why I can't bring myself to call God 'she'. On bad days the voice is relentless:

'fat, lazy, stupid, ugly, useless, cow' it tells me as it points out the pity, scorn and mocking in the eyes of the people around me. It's like living in a hall of distorting mirrors. The best I can do then is to just hide my shame and hope they don't realise the truth about me – if they did I would die.

And Sara's surveillant Other was Dracula:

Sara: I developed a childhood fear of Dracula. He was stalking me from sundown to sun up every day for years. I would have to pass him every night to get to my room. I'm sure I was so scared of Dracula for so many years because it felt like everything except my blood was messed up. Maybe the imps, devils, whatever, came later because I was having such a bloody fantastic sex life at the time – they only appeared during sex.

Ella's committee and Sara's imps and devils serve similar functions: they both police and punish sexuality, as well as marking its presence and, presumably, heightening its tensions, since the committee and the imps mark the boundaries which sexuality transgresses. Hence the fact that the committee is most visible when, as Ella puts it, 'control is off': in acts of transgression the edge which is being transgressed becomes a little clearer. Perhaps Dracula and the committee personify gatekeepers at the edges of identity.

USING SURFACES

So how do women negotiate these paradoxes of their interiority? A number of the project's participants spoke of these matters through their relationships with clothes and makeup. Mary described using makeup and clothes to engage with fights around desire, but within certain limits.

Mary: I started to wear makeup when I was about 16 and I'd say I've worn it pretty well daily ever since then. My mum used to say that she wouldn't be seen dead without her lippy and I'm the same, I'd feel naked without at least some basics: mascara, eyeliner, lipstick. It's a relief to know that when men look at me, they are not looking at the real me, the one who wakes up crumpled and pale, instead they are looking at the face I put on deliberately to get them to look at me. They look less as I get older, and in some funny way I miss it. It's like the fight

> involved in their looking at me and me pretending I hadn't worked for that look made me feel alive somehow. Clothes are the same, I use clothes to draw attention to where I want people to look and all that stuff about women dressing for other women is only partly true. I dress and makeup to get men to look where I want them to, a classic case of emphasise your assets. I also dress and makeup to stop women spotting and zooming in on my defects, and somewhere in there, there's also something about my own tastes!

Mary uses makeup and clothes to create a surface, echoing the quotations at the start of this chapter. But this is a surface through which she seeks to control her relationship to a world which wants her to provide a certain kind of surface in which it can see itself reflected. Mary's surface provides this, but it is also a Trojan horse – through it she has freedom to move and position herself in the world, as she chooses. Juliette uses a different strategy, based on her perception of herself as plain, to achieve similar results.

> **Juliette:** I've always been plain. I really hated it as a young woman, thought it a curse. Clear memory of walking along the street with a pretty friend and watching men's eyes (young and old) lock onto her. Only part of it was simple lust; the rest was more like desperation. It was as if her prettiness contained a sweetness which they craved. What was odd was watching them try to rip it out of her – as if they wanted to swallow it whole and have it inside them, wiping out her existence, without a second thought. Like they wanted to steal the sweet soul of her prettiness. Eventually I noticed that when they grabbed like that, it was as though they had settled down to watch a porno DVD and had got so engrossed that they had left all the doors and windows open. While they were locked on a pretty girl, I discovered I could slip in, unnoticed, through their wide-open-doors of peripheral vision and have a snoop around. At first I just made for their sock drawer, to see just how bad their old passport photos were. Then I discovered that there was usually a pile of porn just under the bed. Mostly really boring stuff, with lots of the pages stuck together. Occasionally I'd find something a bit more exotic and would take a second look at the man I was rummaging around in, perhaps with a bit more respect. Often I would move a few things about, or smash a few glasses or plates – just to let them know that someone had been there. Just to unsettle their arrogant sense of safety. Never steal – that would take me down to their level.

Both women engage in an interpersonal battle – Mary is clear that she's fighting for control over desire – does she set the terms of her desirability, or does the Other? Winning is when she feels like she has set the terms, so that men look at her. She can then pretend that she has had nothing to do with entrapping their desire, pushing them back onto themselves. She writes that the sport of this made her feel alive as a younger woman. In a way, it was a vehicle for playing out aggression – a kind of catch-me-if-you-can game, with the aim being to always stay one jump ahead. The Other thinks he has 'got' Mary, but he has only got the surface she made to 'get' him. This game could be read as a form of revenge: you want nice surfaces, you want safe spaces? Well, you can have the promise of them, but just as you reach to take owner-ship of them, they elude you. It is as though Mary knows that she cannot stop the world regarding her body as a marker of space, and as a provider of a surface which can be positioned as Other in the creation of rationality (see Chapter 3). But she can still take her revenge for those positionings, by making the delivery of what they promise into a war game.

Juliette's aggressive play is different. Her aggression is more focused on making use of the gaps in the performance of femininity to take up a role similar to Isla's anti-woman in Chapter 4. Juliette's fantasy is that she is quietly, invasively penetrative, exploiting the cultural fantasy about the strength and authority of male desire to reveal a vulnerability. Like Mary, Juliette uses her appearance to create a Trojan horse: she appears to be staying in place and performing femininity well, making a gift of her aggressive energies to the Other by creating an illusion of safe, stable, ordinary, non-aggressive womanhood. But on the inside she has found a way of playing by the rules of femininity in a way which undermines its structure. The Other's fantasy of her as part of their safety provides her with a sniper's vantage point in her mind. Note, however, that even as Juliette fantasises that she has subverted the rules of gender, she is taken back to questions about the nature of the Other, the differentness of their desires, as Isla was in her fantasy of raping the rapist.

Sometimes using the surface of femininity to create a Trojan Horse works. Such strategies are, however, far from secure, as the story of Miss Olive Pink (an extraordinary and unconventional anthropologist who advocated Abo-riginal rights in Australia in the early twentieth century) shows. Julie Marcus describes how Olive Pink dressed with great care when out in public to try to out-manoeuvre the limits associated with femininity:

> The vivid image of [Miss Pink as] a woman in white is partly the creation of Olive Pink herself, the result of her determination to declare her sex-lessness and deny her body, to wear the symbols of whiteness and purity in an effort to step beyond the constraints of being a woman. In choosing [also] to retain an older form of dress, in maintaining gloves, parasol and button boots, she dramatised the origins of her political activism by calling on an image of the spinster as a woman who was beyond reproach. She cloaked a passionate heart in the drapes of respectability.
>
> (2001: 304)

Olive Pink's strategy can be read as using old-fashioned (usually white) clothes when in public to disguise herself through the careful display of an aspect of feminine anti-matter, i.e., spinsterish sexlessness. In reality, these symbols were caught up in the powerful racial politics of the frontier environment of central Australia with their meaning being re-assigned by processes beyond her control. Specifically, the morality which Olive Pink sought to identify with through her clothes had become caught up in the period's battles over white superiority, positioning her, against her intentions, into the heart of the maelstrom of gender and race politics which comprised the Australian frontier's troubled and troubling past. As will become even more apparent in the next section, the performance of femininity does offer disguises, but they can be unstable and unpredictable in their effects.

OPTING FOR INVISIBILITY

Other women also described their negotiations between visibility and invisibility. Their comments can be read as describing how they move about in the world, using strategies which offer combinations of invisibility and movement which are not too explosive. Doris describes how easy it is to get things wrong.

Doris: I am what you would call pretty, but that has always seemed something of a surprise to me – something in our look-conscious world I have benefited from without knowing, but not something I had any idea how to use in some innate feminine way. My belief is this sort of performance can only be taught. On the few occasions I have actually dressed up 'female' I have experienced the greatest discomfort – certainly no sudden connection with my 'female' side as the stars of *Priscilla Queen of the Desert* claimed they experienced by donning their frocks. I can only think one's 'female' side must be associated with the inability to move with ease, the inability to eat and the inability to run if in danger. In other words to be female is to be a victim. But apart from this lack of connection the horror I experienced while hobbling about in 4 inch heels and a dress you couldn't bend in – to the outside world a very glamorous package – was a terrible sense of looking like a clown – red nose and all. I caught sight of myself in a mirror at the bar and saw quite clearly the face of a pudgy pre-verbal baby – not a perfectly made-up cocktail hat with veil glamorous woman at all. The hallucination was so distinct I withdrew to an out of the way spot until it was time to go home. This sense is not extreme with more moderate forms of female attire, but ultimately I always have the feeling everyone who looks at me will know I am in drag.

Doris' account highlights a number of things. First there is the performed nature of femininity, and the important role of clothes in that performance. Second there is the immobilising, constricting nature of the performance – can't move, can't eat, can't bend, can't run, themes which Adele echoed.

Adele: I see the potential for danger in every situation and with every man I encounter I wonder what they are capable of acting out. I long ago realised that the stereo-typed feminine clothes such as high heels, tight skirts and a cumbersome bag were restraining devices that keep women trapped and clumsy. I feel most comfortable and safe when wearing men's clothes. I like to know that what I am wearing will not restrict my movement, so that if the need ever arises I can run, climb and jump. I like to feel prepared for any possibility. I avoid reading or listening to news items about attacks on women as they feed my fear and keep me trapped – scared to go out on the street and scared to stay home too.

Third, there is the risk of the performance going wrong. It is as if Doris cannot use the performance of femininity to get far enough away from the violence embedded in the production of glamour to become absorbed in its illusion. Instead, she gets caught on (and cannot free herself from) two images – the red-nosed clown, and the pudgy pre-verbal baby. The art of the clown is that of making a spectacle of oneself, and that is something which women are taught to be extremely careful about. The clown takes our anxieties about our own ridiculous, clumsy, stupid, embarrassing selves and parades them, hopefully with enough pathos and charm as to render them funny. In other words, the clown's task is to take that which is marginalised by the performance of contained, mature identity and present it back to us in a format which makes it engaging. Hence, perhaps, Doris' unconscious choice of the clown image as a depiction of her own (failing) struggle with reworking feminine anti-matter into glamour.

Similarly, Doris' pudgy pre-verbal baby could be read as a reference to the human body in the early stages of being trained into the performance of gender – possibly at the point in identity production where the losses involved in gender formation are starting to really make themselves felt. Perhaps the donning of glamorous feminine attire throws Doris back to the point where she began to refuse (or be unable) to eroticise the violences of female identity in the ways needed to perform femininity 'well'. Specifically, the sophistication signalled by Doris' outfit is paid for by a high degree of bodily control, the counterpart of which is a physically uncoordinated, pudgy, spilly baby. For Doris, dressing up in drag in order to 'do woman' calls up the ghost of the suppressed Otherness within that performance. It is as if the offcuts from the manufacture of the glamorous woman pile up around her: she is unable to dissociate from them well enough to become absorbed in her own perform-ance. And Doris is clear that she is generally uncomfortable with performing, with gender as no exception.

> **Doris:** I find 'male' attire preferable not because I think I am a man, but because it is much more comfortable and utilitarian and also it doesn't call attention to oneself. Rather than clothes make the man, clothes make the gender – especially female with 20th century fashion. Having not been socialised to feel comfortable performing female I have to feel very strong mentally to be bothered going through that performance and the attention it elicits – because it feels to me like walking on stage – and I have a great fear of being on stage, speaking in public, etc.

Doris is using invisibility and disguise for her own purposes. She points out that she cannot enter into a public performance of femininity unless she feels very strong, a point also made by Rosa when she writes 'I must say I looked good – it's not everyday I could put myself at such risk'. Helena also makes reference to clothes as belonging to a public (performance?) space when she describes herself as hiding her body behind a voluminous curtain.

> **Helena:** Maybe its just with age I've ceased to care what people think about how I look. I've developed my own style and how others see me and how I see myself might well be at odds. I like to wear huge clothes – men's XXL for preference, loose and moveable; flat round toed shoes like children's school shoes, baggy pants and if a skirt it must come almost to the floor. It may be a disguise, I may be hiding my body behind a voluminous curtain, but I don't care, I feel totally alien and uncomfortable in anything else.

Doris, Helena and Adele all emphasise comfort: not just sitting-around com-fort, but freedom of movement as a priority, whether that need for mobility is expressed as a rejection of tight clothes, an awareness of the dangers of a cumbersome bag, or the preference for loose, moveable clothes and round-toed, flat, children's style shoes. At the simplest level, these choices offer a form of resistance to the positioning of femininity as the holder of space for others, and as distant from strong energies.

Margaret makes it clear how 'invisibilty' can give access to space and physical freedom.

Margaret: 'The chariest maid is prodigal enough/If she unmask her beauty to the moon.' Perceiving from a young age my destiny as a thin (incomplete) woman, I fondly misunderstood Laertes' warning to Ophelia to mean that even thin, flat-chested women appear voluptuous at night. As in love, in fantasy all can be made good.

I am my father's daughter. My thin woman is invisible, one of the blokes, spared the feral greedy looks. She's a boy, an angel, a speedy bike rider, a tireless walker. Outside in motion she's in a mood in her head, ecstatic. Lacking substance, she can't age or decay, just get dry as a grasshopper.

I am fascinated by fatness, fleshiness, embodiedness. Fascinated and appalled. To live inside huge breasts and stomach and buttocks and thighs, as inside a prison of flesh. Weighed down by a body which rolls and sways and bulges: insistently a factor, compulsively visible – object to a speedy watching predatory world. Voluptuousness of the abysmal. I am the extreme of my own fantasy, an absolute. I am complete. I cannot be more what I am.

Juliette also wrote of disliking her invisibility as a young woman, and coming to appreciate it later.

Juliette: A while ago I saw a program on Disneyworld and how they make it happen. Apparently there's a backstage warren of tunnels, entered by hidden doors, so that the Disney creatures are never seen out of character. No Mickey Mouse sauntering out of the gents, checking his fly. No Snow White nipping off for a burger or a cigarette. I feel like being plain gives me access to that kind of tunnel system, and it's great. It gives me a whole heap of freedom and I get quite alarmed if I start to feel I can't find an exit door. It's like I can appear and disappear pretty much at will. To appear and make a man see me, I smile and pay attention to him. It sounds corny, but it almost always works. The attention which comes back is not the 'want to fuck you' type, it's more like they feel they are finally getting their hands on a devoted mother who has endless interest in their boring little lives. To disappear, I just look away, don't bring them into focus and get on with wearing my neutral coloured clothing which camouflages me into the background for maximum vanish/maximum freedom.

Margaret and Juliette's comments articulate how women use different modes of invisibility to manage and subvert the demands of the performance of femininity. The highly visible surface of femininity is such that it can be used to vanish in what otherwise feels like being trapped on stage in a performance. Margaret's lack of flesh, lack of curves makes her less of a target – she is not 'compulsively visible'. It is also a relief – she cannot be more than she is. She cannot get caught up in the Other's fantasy that she should provide a cuddly, warm space, just for them, simply because she is female. This is the point which Juliette also makes – she knows that as a woman who uses her plainness, she becomes less of a target for the fantasies of the other. Using her earlier imagery, no one would want to steal the 'sweet soul of her prettiness – by dressing down and rendering herself invisible, she has made sure that she does not appear to have one.

Yet Mary, who 'does' visibility through clothes and makeup, is doing something similar. She wants privacy and manipulates the demands that women provide spaces and surfaces which reflect and contain the Other in order to withhold from that Other.

Again, I am following the thread of how women resist identity, even as they perform gendered identity. It is as if these women refuse to hand over certain levels of their aggressive energies to the task of performing femininity 'properly'. Through their invisibility, they retain their aggressive energies for their own inner and outer projects and pleasures. These strategies bring to mind the comments made by an analysand in her 50s. She was glad that she had not had children because to do so would have demanded that she hand over her aggression into social control as part of the task of performing 'parenthood' well enough. Her feeling was that to be a parent was to have one's masochism regulated and structured into a socially approved format and that price was simply too high.

So far, I have been exploring contributions which cluster around the theme of negotiations with the aggressive energies that attend the possibility of being visible to the Other. These negotiations focus on the use of clothes and appearance to manage one's accessibility, the Other's internalisation of one's surface, and their fantasies about one's interiority. Closely related is another group of images which women contributed. These deal with what happens when one's management systems fail, and the structuring aggressions of femininity leak out.

LEAKING ANTI-MATTER

Ella's image of explosive visibility indicated that female flesh can have a corrosive quality to it – as if the losses and violences embedded in the structure of femininity had boiled and distilled in her flesh, producing acid and napalm as a result. Perhaps what has been distilled is the fire-bombing rage Jane spoke of in her image of explosion.

A comment of Isla's resonates with this sense of something dangerous leaking out through female flesh.

Isla: When I was 16 a friend of the family offered to take some photos of me (he was a good amateur photographer). I felt ashamed, I thought my parents had paid him to ask me. I posed for the photos but I wasn't really comfortable, I thought that he'd see through me. I was worried about the photos looking like me. When I saw the prints I was amazed. Some (most) looked like me which was what I'd dreaded but some were lovely: I looked like my fantasy version of myself, the perfect me. I looked very different in them, very calm, almost haughty. Unfortunately the 'shatter' came when the photographer said that my mouth was 'hard', 'protected' and closed, and spoilt the photos. I didn't ask which photos he meant: the ones I liked or the other ones? He was trying to be nice, to relax me, tell me what I was doing wrong in front of the camera but I felt devastated. I knew exactly what he meant, my mouth was like another personality on my face – not giving, refusing to enjoy. I still feel my mouth hardening, even when I'm smiling freely. It's an unyielding presence on my face.

Isla's comments can be read as discussing what it is like to glimpse something of the Otherness embedded in femininity: the moments when the hardness, aggression, violence, sexuality and cruelty, which have to be split off to create the performance of femininity, refuse to stay in place. It is as if some kind of 'anti-matter' to the 'matter' of femininity refuses to be contained or erased. Note also that Isla writes of the 'shatter' that comes when the photographer says something about her 'hard', 'protected' mouth. Again, I would wonder about Isla's mouth as a site of resistance to identity in which women are supposed to be open, vulnerable, unquestioningly offering a containing space to others.

Clinically, I would want to try to engage with this resistance to identity, and sit with it, waiting to see if something of its *telos* might emerge. For example, it might represent a point of departure into an exploration of what it is to simply be oneself, in all its human toughness, and for that to disappoint, offend or even horrify the other. It might open up space to explore feelings of guilt, responsibility and inadequacy about failing to fulfil the other's fantasies or needs. These explorations might, in turn, bring up stories from Isla's childhood, about her relationship with her parents, siblings and wider family, but they might also evoke stories about her anxieties about the cultural pressures on her to perform her gender role in certain ways. They might link to moments like the Miss Baxter story in Chapter 2. Isla might describe a moment where she found herself positioned culturally in a role where she was expected to allow her physical substance to be used to support the Other's fantasy of a safe, unconditionally accepting, nurturing space. The parallel to Miss Baxter's position might be that the position Isla found herself being pushed into might be one of providing someone else with space in which to experiment with their fantasies of omnipotent and destructive agency, in the name of it being 'good for them'.

Alongside this, however, the quality of hardness, which obstinately expresses itself through Isla's sense of her mouth, might also be explored more directly. In it, there might be something of a determined refusal to give in to the infantile longings of others. It might be saying the NO! of Ella's attractive road-blocks in the preceding chapter. Alternatively, the shatter might be saying something about a brittle anxiety about being caught out for not being suitably, desirably yielding.

It might, also be saying something about shattering to get away from the pressure to be suitably yielding, or shattering into shards intended to puncture that pressure. Again, these interpretive directions would be based on a post-Jungian, dissociationist-influenced tactic of attending to the 'Not-I within', and waiting for some of the unconscious 'personality', which is linked to it to emerge. The interpretive position proposed assumes that fragments such as Isla's sense of her mouth as hard have a direction, a *telos*, and that patient and sustained amplification around its unsettling, possibly offensive inner Otherness will bring forth something of that *telos*. Again, the point is that such inner Othernesses often have to do with aggression, desire and various forms of resistance to identity, which have embedded in them the possibility of a richer and more relational experience of the world.

For women, the nature of gender is such that the abjected spectres of identity (the anti-matter of femininity), are likely to consist of energies which have to be negated or disavowed in order to make the performance of femininity possible. Usually these comprise amalgams of aggression, desire, sexuality and other highly 'mobile', non-containing, strong or potentially explosive energies.

MANAGING FEMININE ANTI-MATTER

Tightly entwined with these energies are feelings such as shame and fear which police them and sustain them in their position as feminine anti-matter. Approaching this feminine anti-matter can stir up the kind of confusion, helplessness, alienation and futility discussed in the final sections of the previous chapter. Feminine anti-matter is abject: it comprises the discards from the manufacture of femininity, whatever they may be for an individual woman in her particular set of circumstances. It is that which is experienced as excrement-like, to be ejected and left behind in order to maintain the system of feminine identity. Rosa provides an illustration.

Rosa: I go swimming at an indoor luxury hotel heated pool. It took me 3 years to make the decision and pay for a trial membership – all the women there are 40 or 50 and flabby. One is 70 so she doesn't count! We are welcomed by 20 year old spunks, as we make a last valiant attempt with our bodies – gasp, gasp – and try to get back in shape. The shape of our youth, the sexual potential of our youth. Only now can we afford the membership! One of my major difficulties is how to hide the pubic hairs that hang below my cossie. Trimming them is OK, shaving disastrous – itchy, short stubby painful regrowth. I just hope the spunks are not that interested to look close up although some-times I fantasise they tell each other how excellent I am for my age – and how charming too. Some of the women are inelegant enough to be seen doing aquaerobics – jerking their poor bodies about to Michael Jackson music against water pressure, with young spunks showing them how. I fantasise that one day they'll tell me I can't come because now I'm too old and unattractive to be seen by the public at the pool.

Pubic hair and flab are some of the bodily signs of out-of-role/out-of-control feminine anti-matter. They represent the leakage of something which needs to be hidden as part of the performance of femininity, in the same way that the sense of hardness around Isla's mouth does. Ella's comments expand on the struggle with body hair.

Ella: Requiem for my eyebrows. They were plucked into insignificance during the late sixties and seventies and have never grown back. Now I need something to beetle brow with and they're gone for good. I used to think my being above averagely hairy was a punishment from God to mark me out for my sluttish ways. I think I still do, although the armpits have been safe from the waxer for many a year.

It is as if Ella's chain of unconscious logic runs something like: 'if you behave in animal or sluttish ways, the committee which is God knows about it, and will punish you, making that animalness visible for all to see by making you above-averagely hairy. Through that, the feminine anti-matter that is your sluttishness will be inconcealable, thus damning you publicly'. Thus the anti-matter of femininity is indelible (again, in the way that Isla felt her mouth was), marking Ella's punishment so that anyone could read its message.

One way of reading Rosa's comment that the woman who is over 70 does not count is that age has taken away the possibility of concealing the signs of feminine anti-matter, or even the possibility of its using it in a game of desire-eliciting concealment and selective display. By this logic, the woman in her 70s has become irredeemably abject in the eyes of mainstream culture, and there is simply no point in her trying to conceal that. With desire, however, nothing is ever straightforward, so the defining of a taboo (such as the ageing female body) creates a counter-position, albeit well hidden from mainstream life. A woman in her 50s who worked in a brothel, which specialised in providing older women, explained to me recently that the oldest woman working there was in her 70s. While she was described as being in 'good condition', she was a woman of her age, not remodelled through plastic surgery or a heavy exercise regime, and attracted clients of all ages. While this could be simply read as men enacting Oedipal fantasies, I would add another potential interpretation that these men's desires might be exploring that which our culture now defines as abject and taboo: the ageing female body.

For Rosa, however, the fantasy of visibility at the pool suddenly lurches from pleasurable exhibitionism to humiliated objectification. As this happens, the nature of the watcher changes, somewhere in the comment about some women being inelegant enough to be seen doing aquaerobics. What appears to be at issue is the possibility of being seen as a monster or a freak, a humiliatable outsider who has forgotten her place, or is too stupid to realise what it is. Along the lines of Walkerdine's work, we see the role of humiliation in subjection.

MAKING A SPECTACLE OF ONESELF

Mary Russo amplifies this humiliation when she writes about her mother harshly criticising other women by saying that they were making 'a spectacle' of themselves. Russo explores this as an expression of female grotesqueness and says that as a child she realised that:

> Making a spectacle out of oneself seemed a specifically feminine danger. The danger was of an exposure. . . . For a woman, making a spectacle out of herself had more to do with a kind of inadvertency and loss of boundaries: the possessors of large, ageing, and dimpled thighs displayed at the public beach, of overly rouged cheeks, of a voice shrill in laughter, or of a sliding bra strap – a loose, dingy bra strap especially – were at once caught out by fate and blameworthy. It was my impression that these women had done something wrong, had stepped, as it were, into the limelight out of turn – too young or too old, too early or too late – and

yet anyone, any *woman*, could make a spectacle out of herself if she was not careful.

(1986: 213, original italics)

For a woman to lapse in her performance of femininity, for her feminine anti-matter to leak out in the form of a dingy bra strap or cellulitic thighs, can be a lapse into the grotesque. Furthermore, the line between well-performed femininity and the grotesque is exceedingly narrow, and cannot be determined until the other's response is known – even then it may remain unclear. Individual women will feel these pressures differently, and respond to them differently according to circumstance, taste and background, as Ella indicates when she comments that in spite of having plucked her eyebrows away as a younger woman, her armpits have 'been safe from the waxer for many a year'.

This notion of feminine anti-matter is not to be taken literally. It is simply a form of shorthand which I am using to indicate the degree of terror and threat that some women feel when in the presence of their own disavowed energies. These energies can be experienced as potentially annihilatory of liveable identity and must be hidden or retrained in order to perform femininity well.

An individual woman might or might not choose to manage her body in a particular way; what matters more is the engagement with how she experiences her feminine anti-matter, and how the management of the spilly, politically constituted body can act as a point of entry into that engagement. As Bordo suggests:

> through table manners and toilet habits, through seemingly trivial routines, rules, and practices, culture is '*made* body,' as Bourdieu puts it – converted into automatic, habitual activity. As such it is put 'beyond the grasp of consciousness ... [untouchable] by voluntary, deliberate transformations'.

(1997: 90, original italics)

While the practices which make the culture into lived bodies may be beyond the grasp of consciousness, I suggest that they are not beyond engagement with as unconscious processes, for example through the post-Jungian analytic mode of interpretation which I am proposing here. Indeed the tensions and anxieties around the spilly, leaky body (what spills, how, onto whom, and what reactions it generates or is feared to generate) can be read as communications from the places where identity is simultaneously manufactured and resisted. And as Jacqueline Rose's comments from Chapter 3 suggest, this kind of resistance to identity is the core of psychic life, as well as being the primary point of interest for psychoanalytic thought (Rose, 1990: 232).

The result of these social practices and the historical use of femininity to signify the monstrousness and the grotesque means that when a woman looks at that which is regarded as monstrous or grotesque, she is likely to become entranced, unable to hold her distance. She risks falling into identification with it, as Rosa does when she switches from a fantasy of desirability to a fantasy of humiliating rejection in her vignette about the swimming pool. Hence the shift in Rosa's subject position during a sentence in which she talks about the (grotesque) women who are inelegant enough to fail to hide their spilling, ageing bodies. As Rosa thinks of the inelegant older women doing aquaerobics, she comes up against their cultural significance as abject grotesques, overly full of feminine anti-matter, and cannot stop herself falling into identification with them.

Also of note, however, is the way the nature of visibility changes in Rosa's text, and how it is accompanied by a move from desire to aggression. When writing about what to do with her pubic hair, Rosa comments that she 'just [hopes] the spunks are not that interested to look close up'. This is a distanced gaze, a gaze which is benevolent and pleasurable, creating a sense of being desired. It is the gaze in softened focus, through which Rosa can enjoy herself and imagine the instructors making appreciative comments about her. It is as if she is not so much behind a screen of invisibility, but a softly-lit veil of benevolent privacy, through which she can deal with the generalised authority figure of 'the spunks' who are the instructors.

As Rosa becomes more specific in her description of what the women in the class do ('jerking their poor bodies about to Michael Jackson music against water pressure, with young spunks showing them how'), it is as if she steps out from behind the veil, exposing the women in the pool (with whom she is beginning to identify) to high-powered fluorescent, changing-room lighting, showing up every humiliating fault. Behind the veil she could explore her desirability, locating the extreme signs of abject feminine anti-matter in the 70-year-old. As the veil thins and vanishes, Rosa emerges into visibility and the level of aggression in the imagery rises: she is verbally attacked and rejected for her age and unattractiveness. In effect this is a variation of the scenario of emerging from behind the screen of invisibility and exploding, except with the volume turned down a little. What matters are the specific ways that Rosa manages the interaction between signs of feminine matter and anti-matter by blurring the owner of the gaze in order to sustain a space where she can explore her own desirability. Jane added a further elaboration to this issue of the management of visibility.

Jane: When I played about with the exercise (after recovering from the explosion), I realised that the person watching me come out from behind the screen was automatically assumed to be male – I mean, they do the watching don't they? I wondered what would happen if I played around with who the watcher was, and tried a woman watcher. That just

> made me feel awkward – foolish, apologetic, and very reluctant to emerge in case she criticised me. The only way I could solve the question of how to emerge at all was to make the woman who watched me poor, black, and disabled. Then I was able to come out with my back to her and run across her field of vision until I could find something else to hide behind.

What Jane is spelling out here is that within femininity, visibility is less dangerous if the looker has less cultural capital; in other words, if the looker is positioned closer to the abject edge of non-identity. If the looker is so positioned, her capacity to push Jane off the edge, into the abyss of abjection is considerably less. In Jane's image, the looker has already been described as carrying more feminine anti-matter than her, so that it is less of a risk for Jane to experiment with visibility in front of her.

Perhaps this is another reason why the exploration of visibility fantasies conducted in groups were slightly less violent: with other women around, alternative channels exist for women to manage their own feminine anti-matter. Also, in a group, a woman might stay further away from such inner material for fear that other women will seize upon it and use it to push her further into the realm of the abject. Maybe these are the dynamics which underlie women's fights. Instead of being about 'who gets the man' or (to be Lacanian about it) who has the phallus, perhaps women's fights are about who gets to off-load her feminine anti-matter, with its associated risk of humiliation and madness, into whom. If so, women's fights are about trying to buy an illusory freedom from the processes which form gendered identity.

FASHION AND OTHERNESS

But there is another, culturally sanctioned strategy for the management of feminine anti-matter. In the world of fashion, the relationship between desire and the taboo is worked over so that that which is abject can, if displayed with enough skill, become highly desirable. This is finessing in reverse: that which should be abject can, by being repositioned discursively, become the object of fascination.

Seen in this way, fashion becomes the laboratory in which experiments are run to explore the current sensibility for the edge between abject and desirable displays of feminine antimatter.[4] What will be made visible in this way will be a concealing/exposing interplay around the violences of female identity formation, and the aggression, desire and mobility which form the anti-matter of femininity. Perhaps this is the basis of the cold, hard, violently thin catwalk model look – it provides a frame for just such a display. The excitement that fashion stirs up is around the risky nature of this display. Note too how glamour draws its cold sheen from the interpersonal space around it: Marilyn Monroe looks all the more blonde and luscious while singing 'Diamonds Are A Girl's Best Friend' in *Gentlemen Prefer Blondes* because all the women in the dance chorus have their faces darkened. They are merely dresses in motion around Monroe, enhancing her brilliance by giving up their position as people, so that all the energy they bring with them is focused and becomes all the more visible through Monroe. But what is curious is that we *enjoy* glamour – we too, as the audience, readily surrender our own energy to make the desired, glamorous object appear all the shinier, all the brighter so that we can long for it (or long to be it). Glamour is the arena in which the disavowed violences of the formation of femininity can be displayed, as trophies in cabinets, to be admired, but never touched.

This notion of the performance of femininity as a concealment/display of the individual woman's reworkings of the shattering losses of identity formation also throws a different light on the definition of fetishism as a homage to the missing maternal phallus (Grosz, 1995: 145). Perhaps what is being glimpsed and eroticised in fetishism is the paradox of the violences involved in the formation of female identity, and their disavowal in the performance of femininity. What is fascinating is not the missing female phallus, but the paradoxical double meaning associated with femininity as that which is simultaneously associated with the absence of aggression and violence, and that which is shot through with the disavowed aggression and violence of its formation. Perhaps fetishism and fashion are related strategies for the selective display of the violences entailed in the formation of female identity. If so, fetishism would seem to be an expression of it which is within strict conventions, traditionally played out in more private arenas. Fashion, by contrast, is a more complex, kaleidoscoping, collective and experimental endeavour, but operates around the same set of variables.

By exploring the aggressive energies embedded in her management of her own visibility and feminine anti-matter, Rosa is brought up against the Otherness of both the outer Other and the inner Other. Just as her descriptions map out processes for veiling, containing and manoeuvring the dangerously explosive energies associated with visibility, her explorations of desirability lead her to map out the Other's capacities to desire, envy, intrude and behave aggressively or reject her.

Again, for women, visibility disturbs the ways in which their aggressive energies are canalised into the production of female identity. This disturbance brings the possibility of a catastrophic, potentially explosive undoing as the disavowed aggression which is both our bliss and the root of our conscience is unsettled (Merck, 1993: 262). This place where bliss, taboo and conscience coincide is also the point of Bersani's account of psychoanalytic criticism when he writes that a work of art exists:

> not in order to hide [desires], but *in order to make them visible*. If the
> sexual is, at the most primitive level, the attempted replication of a shat-
> tering (or psychically traumatizing) pleasure, art ... is the attempted
> replication *of* that replication. That is, it repeats the replicative movement
> of sexuality as a domesticating and civilising project of self-recognition.
>
> (1986: 110–111, original italics)

Not only do we eroticise the injurious terms of identity, discovering them
over and over again through the patterns of our desire, we are also impelled
to make our deepest experience of them visible to ourselves and others
through our creative projects. This process of making visible our second-level
replications of the shattering nature of identity formation is not merely some
form of exhibitionism or mastery of the terror of our desire: it is an attempt
to see how our most fundamental erotic preferences are arranged (or more
accurately, arrange us), and how they create us anew in different circumstances. One of the ways in which we express our replications of sexuality
(which is, itself, a replication of the injurious processes of identity formation)
is how we clothe and ornament ourselves. If female identity is structured
around injurious terms which demand the generation of a fictional distance
from strong energies, then the replicative expression of those injurious terms
through art, ornamentation and taste will express the individual's ways of
both creating that fictional distance and, simultaneously, subverting and
undoing it.

This is why clothes, as the display of the signs of feminine anti-matter and
the management of the risk of humiliation are important – they relate to the
need to replicate and make visible to ourselves and others the moments when
morality and pleasure, aggression, conscience and bliss collide. How we
experience those collisions, how they live us and the consequences which
follow is the realm of psychoanalytic practice. Tracking the key role played by
aggression, its disavowal, its *telos* and its relationship to recognisable identity
can provide a window into those collisions and the relational capacities
which come out of them. Vivienne, who also ran the visibility exercise and
documented her results, provides an illustration.

Vivienne: I think that if I, even for a moment, allowed myself visibly to
be the whole person I truly could be – intellectually, passionately, sexually, physically, emotionally, and intuitively – I would explode with such
intensity that I, and all around, would be irradiated. What a terrifying
thought.

Vivienne's comments suggest that the cause of her explosion is the coming
together of the parts of her into a whole, implying that the aggressive energy

released in the explosion is normally maintained in its dormancy through her remaining split up. This is not an image of nuclear *fission* energies coming from a nuclear explosion, but of *fusion* energies, generated by the coming together of particles (or parts). Again, though, she refers to an irradiating, destructive release of energy.

These images prompt a question: if the structure of femininity comprises solidified, disavowed aggressive energies, whose solidification and remanufacture is eroticised as being a 'good thing' for the benefit of some imagined 'Other', how might such energies be gathered together into something liveable, something which women can use in their inner and outer lives. Through my work with people with long-term, severe eating disorders I have come to view those illnesses as just such an attempt to bring aggressive energies into one's relationship with oneself and others (albeit a highly problematic and potentially life threatening strategy). The next chapter takes up this discussion.

Chapter 6

Eating disorders and the *telos* of aggression

EATING DISORDERS, AGGRESSION, RAGE AND DETERMINATION

This chapter begins with a clinically based exploration of the aggressive energies involved in eating disorders and ends with a re-examination of the misunderstandings of aggression that lie at the heart of object relations.

I start by focusing on anorexia nervosa but as the discussion develops, the focus moves to the dynamics of bulimia nervosa and binge eating disorder. My primary interest is the recurrent struggles women have with turning the kind of determination and rage which often accompany eating disorders into something enlivening and relational.[1] While the highly embodied nature of eating disorders makes these struggles especially clear and intense, they are also found more widely in general analytic work. The father of a young woman with anorexia provides an image of the kind of aggression which can accompany that illness:

> [h]er behaviour is absolutely appalling and completely irrational. I don't know any other father whose twenty-two-year-old daughter gouges the kitchen table with the bread knife, just because she has to eat. Or sits in her room banging her head against the wall.
>
> (Duker and Slade, 1992: 83)

Anorexia is a physically and psychologically violent illness, in which aggressive energies have become caught up in self-hating, and self- and other-punishing amalgams. I argue that one of the important aspects of recovery is that these amalgams need to be dissolved to some extent, so that the aggressive energies caught up in them become available for forming other, more enlivening amalgams.

Susan Bordo illustrates the kind of violent amalgams of aggression which can operate in the inner life of a person who has anorexia nervosa through the comment of a woman who spoke of wanting to cut off her breasts (1997: 100). I have repeatedly heard similar comments from analysands who had recurrent imagery of finding relief from their self-hatred and inner torment by being able to cut their 'fat' off without bleeding to death.[2] These kinds of images inform the discussion that follows.

In this chapter I will also discuss the use of countertransference imagery as an instrument through which to learn about the aggressive and violent dynamics in analysands' eating disorders. The violence of self-starvation has a curiously numbing quality to it: combinations of punishing exercise regimes, sleep deprivation, super-human work-load, overuse of stimulants such as coffee or amphetamines, as well as fasting can become a 'normal' way of life. These strategies can provide the person using them with a complex system for manipulating their psychosomatic field. Certain combinations of strategies are intended to numb specific distresses, while other combinations aim to create pockets of heightened stimulation. It can be extremely difficult to develop languages and images which speak to these dynamics and make them available for analytic engagement. Through the stories and vignettes in this chapter I will illustrate some ways of approaching this challenge.

PRACTICAL BACKGROUND

But before exploring these matters further, I need to address some of the practical aspects associated with this kind of clinical work. The approach I am outlining is based on work with people who have usually had at least one, if not several, unsuccessful hospitalisations, leaving them chronically ill. Realistically, a minimum BMI[3] for this kind of approach would be above 13. A significant percentage of my private clinical practice comprises people who fit Morgan and Russell's (1975) description of people with anorexia nervosa who have poor prognosis for hospital treatment. These people have 'relatively late age of onset, longer duration of illness, previous admissions to psychiatric hospitals, a disturbed relationship between the patient and other members of the family, and premorbid personality difficulties'. These findings were subsequently confirmed by Morgan, Purgold and Welbourne in 1983.

Working with people who are this ill is only possible if their physical health is being monitored by someone appropriately qualified, and part of my initial analytic contract with these analysands is that they will maintain suitable contact with such a person, and accept medical advice if their illness becomes life-threatening. I should also add that I do not have a training in child or adolescent therapy, so I do not see people under 19. Of the people I have worked with who have been severely and chronically eating disordered, all were over 20 years of age, most having had their illness for between 8 and 35 years. Most have been hospitalised numerous times.

The other main practical consideration is that people only gain weight and hold it if doing so is part of gaining a bigger life. In order to expand one's life in this way, a person needs to have a creative relationship with their own desires to generate change and move on. The development of this awareness depends, in part, on lively, aggressive energies, hence the need to find ways of unravelling these energies from violently self-destructive amalgams. At the same time, however, it is not possible to have a more spacious life while one eats like an invalid. Having any energy at all, aggressive or otherwise, requires adequate nutrition, so that physical recovery is an essential aspect of developing a bigger life. Weight gain needs to go hand in hand with psychological change, both being inseparable parts of a series of slow, careful moves into a broader, more meaningful life.

In order to consider the possibility of building such a life, a person who has anorexia nervosa often needs help to develop a broader interiority. To begin with, this sense of a felt, spontaneous interiority may be hard to access, with alexithymia (absence of language for feelings or inner states) being a significant problem.[4] It can also be the last thing which a person with anorexia wants, as their interiority may, initially, be full of self-hatred, guilt and fear.

Over time, however, the analytic space can be used to build an individual language for aspects of inner experience (including words and images for extreme distress), and in this way an unthought or 'unthinkable' somatised inner life can slowly and carefully be brought into consciousness where, eventually, different choices may become possible. The facet of this process which I want to explore here is how languages for aggression can be developed from the physicality of the illness.

My suggestion is that aggressive energies can be thought of as an important, but often very stuck, aspect of these analysand's 'Not-I within'. The analysand may be very afraid of this aspect of their own interiority and in order to illustrate what this can be like and how it can be engaged with, I will tell a series of stories. The first two developed out of requests to speak publicly about my work with analysands with severe and chronic eating disorders. In response to these requests I developed a series of images which have two aims. First they seek to help people who are unfamiliar with eating disorders to imagine the kinds of psychological landscapes which people who develop eating disorders may be trying to navigate around in. Second, through these images of emotional landscapes, I aim to help clinicians find a position from which they can be of maximum assistance to the parts of their analysand which are interested in the possibility of recovery (no matter how small those parts are, and they may be virtually invisible for years).

The images that follow are not intended to represent any kind of universal truth about the experiences of people who have had anorexia nervosa, bulimia or compulsive eating. Nor are they intended to capture some essence of the countertransference. They try, instead, to introduce ways of thinking about the role of aggressive energies in eating disorders and other situations where the will has ended up declaring war on other aspects of inner and outer life.

FEROCIOUS FEELINGS

In order to try to imagine the point at which anorexia becomes a solution to an inner struggle, picture yourself waking up, and suddenly becoming aware that you are locked in a room with a ferocious lion. You have no idea how you or it came to be in the room, and there is no one to talk to or ask for help. All you know is that a wild animal is growling at you (because you are in its territory), and baring its teeth. After initially backing away, and several moments of blind panic, you notice that there is an old, bentwood, circus-type chair nearby. You grab it and wave it at the lion, and the lion, which was starting to move towards you, backs off a little. You wave the chair in the lion's direction again, and the lion backs away a little further. You feel great relief at the realisation that you are not totally helpless, about to be ripped apart by a wild animal.

This is a way of thinking about the opening moves in the development of anorexia nervosa. The lion represents a group of ferocious and terrifying feelings which threaten to destroy you. These feelings are intolerable – it is as if they are about to rip you, the person who is developing anorexia nervosa, to pieces. Such feelings may have appeared suddenly, precipitated by an external event. More likely they have been building up for some time, eventu-ally reaching a critical mass. Maybe you always knew that the lion of your own voraciousness, helplessness, self-hatred and desperation was in one of the rooms of your internal, psychological 'house', but that was a room you could avoid going into, an arrangement which made it possible to just about cope with life. Circumstances were such that over time, however, the other rooms got locked off, full of emotional clutter, or undigested bad experiences of inner and outer life. One day the 'lion room' was the only one left, and you found yourself in it, with nowhere else to go. Either way, a day eventually came when you could not ignore the threatening feelings any longer, experienced yourself as being in great danger, and took defensive action accordingly. Anorexia is like waving a chair at the lion because the physiology of starvation is such that it pushes feelings away – it provides a sense of distance from interiority. An analysand once described starvation's emotional effects as like looking at the world through the wrong end of a telescope.

The anorexic strategy in such circumstances can sometimes be usefully understood as opting for the position of being a lion-tamer. Such tactics involve making a scrabbling, terrified, backed-into-a-corner grab at determination, will and endurance in order to try to force ferocious feelings under control through the will-based control of the body. Doing so is an attempt to fight for one's life, using the available weapons. Looked at in this way, the analysand's actions start to make sense, as does her commitment to her illness, and resistance to treatment.

At first glance the illness appears to be malignant: a thing to be cut off so that the rest of the person can get on with their life. This is evident when one hears a parent or husband say 'I just want my daughter/wife back'. In fact, some of the most important parts of the person who has the eating disorder may be expressing themselves through the illness, perhaps because they have no other way of coming out. They may simply be too much at odds with the restricted sense of 'I' that has come to dominate the personality. If so, recovery based on 'moving on and leaving the illness completely behind' can be dangerous. Instead, the important parts of the person which have come to be expressed in the illness need to be brought into consciousness so that it can broaden and become more flexible. This kind of approach can offer a way of listening to what the illness is communicating, while at the same time refusing to collude with the analysand's (possibly unconscious) belief that her illness is the only response possible to how desperate she feels, and/or the only way in which she can communicate that desperation.

Returning to my image of the dilemma of the person who is developing anorexia nervosa, the situation which she finds herself in as a lion-tamer is not static. The lion is getting more irritated by the presence of an intruder in its territory, and it is also getting hungrier. It bares its teeth more, and snarls louder, occasionally roaring at you, the person developing anorexia. You wave the chair about more and harder on the grounds that this tactic has worked once, so hopefully doing it again, and doing more of it, may momentarily stabilise the rising threat. This translates roughly into working harder and harder at starving yourself.

Indeed these tactics may work, but meanwhile the lion gets even hungrier and angrier, and you are getting more and more terrified, eventually throwing all your energy into stopping the lion getting to you. Holding the chair up is getting tiring, but you dare not let your guard down, because to do so would be fatal. By now the person who has anorexia is locked in a war. Her ferocious feelings, which I am representing here as a lion, are almost beside themselves with rage and hunger at being crushed, controlled, and starved of engagement, response or expression, as well as (quite literally) food. Meanwhile, the lion-tamer part of the person with the illness is also beside itself with terror, doubling and redoubling its efforts to keep the situation under control in the only way it knows how. There is no room to think, explore or imagine. Those spaces have been closed down by terror, rage, desperation, exhaustion and starvation, which are the symptoms of the internal war which is under way. Enter the naive clinician, family member or friend who hopes to be helpful in this situation (and I would include some of my less successful interventions very much in this category). 'Yoo-hoo' they call out. 'I'd like to help you – look at me, pay attention to me, and we can talk about your situation'. The sensible person who has anorexia will quickly conclude that such a stance is insane and have nothing to do with it.

To look at the person who is volunteering 'help' is to take your eye off the lion, and get eaten alive. The naive Other who is attempting to help has failed to comprehend the dangerous and precarious nature of the situation, and has already marked themselves as a liability by their very stance, since their behaviour indicates that they are capable of creating disastrous destabilisations without even noticing they have done so. Such a person is more interested in their world than they are in that of the person with the illness, and they have already proved that by failing to observe that the person who has anorexia is trying to save their own life through starvation. The person with the illness' will-based control of the body is not a whim, or about avoiding adulthood and sexuality. It may touch on any of these things and many more besides, but it is likely to be primarily about desperately needing to get control of feelings, thoughts and sensations which are experienced as intolerable and feel like they are about to kill you, ripping you limb from limb. By trying to engage with the situation from an external position, based on theoretical or philosophical assumptions about how things could or should be for the person who has the illness, and how analysis, therapy, family life or friendship could or should work, the would-be-helpful Other has already confirmed the person with anorexia's worst nightmare.

Things were bad beforehand, but now the person with the illness also has to manage the naive Others' need to feel 'helpful' in a situation which they clearly do not understand. Worse than this, a mountain of shame has now sprung up, repositioning the interaction with the lion from a flat surface, to a crumbly cliff edge, many thousands of metres up. The last thing the person with the illness wants the well-meaning Other to realise is how helpless and terrified they are or to see that the lion of self-hatred has already got its claws into them and is ripping their flesh off their bones. That would be too shaming.

So how can one approach an analysand who is in this kind of battle, and how can one be of use to the parts of the analysand which are terrified, exhausted and starving, longing to de-escalate the fight, but have no idea how to do so without getting killed? Continuing the lion-tamer analogy, my sense is that it is dangerous and naive to try to get into the room, or out on the cliff edge with the analysand. It seems to be more useful to simply try to provide an accurate commentary, based largely on what other analysands have taught me, tacitly informed by relevant theory. It might go something like this.

See that lion over there, well, I think it's getting tired. I've watched a few lions and I reckon that when they start to put their heads on their paws and close their eyes like that, they are going to have a nap. If I'm right,

> I'd suggest you take the opportunity to lean the chair leg against a wall. I'm not stupid enough to suggest that you put it right down, or give it to me, but at least if you prop it against the wall, you can give your arms a bit of a rest.

This might be analogous to suggesting to an analysand that for us to start an analytic conversation, I need them to agree to see a specialist general practitioner or physician who will monitor their physical well-being and advise them of any dangers which might arise. In that way, we can clear some space to think about the meaning of their actions, and those of the lion, rather than having to worry about whether they should be in hospital.

This approach is aimed at recognising and acknowledging that an analysand in such a position experiences something about the 'Not-I within' as terrifying and life threatening, and that their illness is an attempt to manage this. Perhaps what matters most about such an approach is, however, what it does not do. First, it does not offer to try to protect the person with the illness from the lion of their own ferocious feelings – it offers, instead, to try to help the person learn about ferocious inner states which feel alien, Other and attacking. This entails trying to describe the analysand's situation in ways which put back on the map options which fear and starvation had rendered invisible. Second, it does not assume that the person in front of me who is seriously ill wants to be well or lead a happy or enriched life. At this point, the person is likely to just want help to cope better from moment to moment. Their current way of doing this is killing them, but it is the best they can do. Alternatives are likely to be explored with great difficulty and with much hesitation because of the feared disastrous consequences of such an experiment not working. Third, it does not suggest that the person with the anorexia should relinquish 'control'. Nor does it suggest that the need for control (or even hyper-control) is pathological. Instead the need for control is seen as being based on terror and having the feeling that there is no other way of staying alive.

LIFE-HUNGRY, CLEAR-EYED AND SHARP OF TOOTH AND CLAW

The lion-tamer story seeks to illustrate the desperate, ferocious amalgams of aggression associated with the anorexia and to indicate that those amalgams need to be engaged with as they contain the basis of the analysand's sense of agency. The story is deliberately ambiguous about the source of the ferocious feelings, so that clinicians can read their own modality's theories into it, while nonetheless becoming more comfortable with the need to track and support the analysand's amalgams of aggression.[5]

The lion represents the capacity for fast, predatory movement – deliberately a far cry from the kind of femininity which anchors space for a male agent. In choosing a wild animal I am also picking up on Jane's comments in Chapter 3 about how, when she became tired, people's faces morphed into those of animals. Jane wrote that these transformations often gave her information about how the person she was dealing with would act in a tight corner: what they were like when they were being less civilised. It was as though her animal imagery allowed Jane to take off the distorting lenses which are essential for a 'nice girl' or a 'good woman' and see the darknesses in others (and thus in herself), even though what she saw sometimes frightened her. By way of parallel, the lion image suggests that a woman who has anorexia nervosa might come to trust the life-hungry, clear-eyed, sharp-toothed and clawed aspects of herself which the performance of femininity requires her to disavow. With reflection and effort, such energies can form the basis of clarity, robustness and agency, a move illustrated by a comment from Ella (although she did not have a history of eating disorder).

> **Ella:** I'm hoping to develop a more wolf-like, robust femininity – not that I've anything against cows, they have a quiet sense of humour, it's just that I'd like to bite the odd ankle now and again.

A comment from Sara, another of the women who participated in this project, described her sense of frustration at being mistaken for, and having played the role of, a submissive woman.

> **Sara:** Since reaching 50 I've noticed (it could have been happening for years before) I'm invisible to men and some women (usually it's the women 5–10 years younger – maybe I tell them they too are getting older). It didn't upset me in that I didn't feel Oh God I'm no longer attractive because I've never felt this me/body-mind-matter had what it took. So one can't lose that which was never there, but the average looks did help the act I had learnt to attract/please men. I attracted men who liked submissive women. I am not a submissive woman – no wonder I was anorexic for over a decade. The submissive in me now is just remnants of the habit – like nail biting. I've wasted over four decades being someone I wasn't.

Note how Sara makes the explicit link between having learnt to act submissively, being anorexic for over a decade, and wasting four decades being someone she was not. Aggressive, demanding, defiant energies have to be pushed down in order to be submissive, and anorexia is a way of doing so, especially if they feel like they are a ferocious, wild animal which is about to destroy you. In such circumstances, recovery can involve a very slow and careful coming to experience these energies as enlivening and important, so that one can snarl, roar or bite back when necessary. With one analysand these aggressive energies came to be known as her inner crocodile, a choice of imagery intended to support those parts of her which resisted being mistaken for a 'nice woman', either by herself, or others.

The next story reruns the theme of disavowed aggression, but with two changes, First, this explosive version 'ups the ante' a little in order to depict more of the countertransferential anxiety which can arise around the unacknowledged violently aggressive amalgams in the illness. Second, it is intended to draw out the way in which those aggressions can be experienced as pleasures, especially through the possibilities which they offer for attacking or subverting identity.[6]

EXPLOSIVE RAGE

Working with someone who has anorexia can feel like sitting with a person who is inside a cell or a cage. She is cramped, miserable, exhausted, probably cold and constipated and feeling physically quite ill, but trying hard to pretend she is not. The key to the cell is lying within her reach, just outside on the ground. I, too, am just outside the cage, sitting quietly, keeping her company. Forcing the key into her hand is pointless – if I do she will throw it away, and the crucial fact here is that she can pick it up herself if she wishes. I am there to talk with her about what her cell is like, why she got into it and what she fears if she came out. I am also there, keeping an eye open for any tiny parts of her which indicate that, contrary to the dominant inner regime, they might not be entirely committed to anorexia as a way of being.

What is not immediately apparent, however, is that the floor of the cell is mined with pockets of the vibration-sensitive explosive, TNT, with the analysand sitting at the back of the cell. Her emaciated body is pleading, 'Come in, please, I am in a bad way, I need help, please help me'. Her mouth says either 'I am fine: I will be the perfect analysand, I will share insights with you, just don't expect me to eat more, or hold food down', or (perhaps more honestly), 'Come near me and I'll kill you'. At this point, therapeutic engagement needs to be especially sensitive. Any attempt at warmth or contact could set the explosives off. Yet by holding the analytic position and staying outside the cell, the analyst is a monster for not helping the analysand, and for confirming her hopelessness and despair. Hence the frustration of the near-paralysing countertransference responses that can develop when working with people who have severe anorexia nervosa. But such countertransferences can tell us something about the analysand's sense of paralysis; hence the comments made by my analysand Lizzie.

All that is left is the will, clenched iron-fisted will. Radar on hyper-alert. Siege. Minefields. There is no hope other than defiance. The last soldier on the battle field. Anything other than fighting feels like giving up and burrowing into rotting, dead corpses, and I cannot be grateful for that. Food is sickening, full of worms. So is my body. It's all poisoned. Keep your maggoty, therapeutic intimacy. I WON'T be grateful. I HATE anyone who TRIES TO GIVE ME THINGS AND MAKE ME/IT BETTER. Let me go. Your hope is my betrayal and my humiliation.

In this we see the shifts between being under siege, being stuck in the minefield, and (implied towards the end of the Lizzie's text) being the person who has set up the explosives in order to keep everyone and everything out. Reading this back through the image of the cell, the floor, walls and ceiling were mined with explosives by the analysand herself, in order to avoid a worse situation. The trouble is, the defensive placing of the explosives was done in a frantic panic. The analysand never drew a map, and some patches of it have gone wrong, or been forgotten, so that every so often bits of her cell explode randomly. That is why the analysand is trying ever harder to get more control and lose more and more weight – she believes that if she could just do that, she could at least get her cell under control. As with the lion story, the last thing she needs is a clumsy analyst barging around, causing more explosions and leaving her with even less of a world than she had before.

RESISTING THE CONSTRAINTS OF GENDER

In Chapter 4, Isla observed that a woman can only be one thing, unless she's beautiful. Beauty buys a woman space to incorporate more complexity into her identity, and can give her permission to bend the rules without becoming the object of criticism. Those familiar with the UK TV series *Absolutely Fabulous* might recall an episode in which Patsy's sister turns up at Edina's house. The sister says terrible things about Edina's daughter (Saffy) to the other houseguests (in front of Saffy), and Saffy is angry. Later in the kitchen, and away from the guests, she turns to her mother, Edina, and says 'What gives her the right to treat people like that?' Edina purses her lips and leans slightly forward from the waist, as if to say 'Do I really have to explain something so basic to you?' before saying to Saffy, 'Because she's thin!', as if it were so terribly obvious.

Seen in this way, Lizzie's warfare could be directed at the infuriating conventions of gender which demand that, unless she is beautiful (and very thin) she must restrict herself, not be too complex, not be too startlingly able in too many fields, lest she becomes the object of attack in the way that Adele illustrates.

> **Adele:** I have this ache in the small of my back which is connected to how I feel – at times of stress and self-doubt it is painful and I feel unsteady and unsupported. I discovered the ache comes from a large foot which is placed in the small of my back and pushes down on me forcing me into the ground. The only time the foot relents is when I am laying face down on the ground and not attempting to get up. It is the foot's job to prevent me from getting up, straightening, and walking tall. I wondered why I allow this foot to remain on my back and keep me down, I then realised that it has become my foot. The further I progress on my journey of truth the stronger the forces are that try to push me down. As my spirit comes alive so my resistance does too.
>
> I have been brought up and taught to be as invisible, inaudible and unnoticeable as I possibly can. With every step forward I hear my mother, my grand-mother, . . . all the women in my history . . . crying out 'don't draw attention to yourself.' Sometimes all I want to do is lay down with them and sleep. I grow weary and I get disheartened when I find that the spiritual guides history has to offer me are men. Can what they have learnt apply to me? What saddens me most is my initial reaction when I meet or hear of a woman who has struggled free and is walking tall – I want to put my foot in her back, push her down and say 'don't draw attention to yourself'.

From this perspective, anorexia can be seen as a battle between the need to live and perpetuate identity, and the need to resist and subvert it, raging against the processes which produce and police the performance of femininity. The accidental display of these battles, or of the feminine anti-matter which they produce and police, can quickly turn into the humiliating nightmare of making a spectacle of oneself (see previous chapter). But how do these battles manifest themselves in analysis, and how can they be engaged with clinically?

AGGRESSION AND VIOLENCE IN THE COUNTERTRANSFERENCE

A case vignette provided by Fernando Figueroa in an online internet seminar provides a means of exploring this, starting with the way aggression and violence can be communicated through the countertransference.

> Female of 32 years old who was diagnosed with depression with psychotic features and anorexia nervosa. She also used to cut her arms and legs superficially with a Gillette. Her appearance was of a very weak person, physically and psychologically, walked slowly, talked softly and promoted the image of the 'lady in pain', or in need to be rescued. I think it was right after the second session with her, that I walked to the back of the clinic's building when I suddenly felt very afraid and as I turned my head to a dark room, I saw her holding a Gillette and coming to attack me. It really struck me and for a moment I wasn't sure if this was really happening or not.

Note the tension between the weak, 'lady-in-pain' image and the hallucinated version of the analysand who is strong enough to attack and frighten the clinician. Building a hypothesis about the analysand's unconscious life from this countertransferential image might go like this. The analysand's strength, which is usually reserved for her self-starvation, is very much 'Not-I within' for her, and is a long way from consciousness at this stage. Her self-cutting indicates that her aggressive energies are caught up in amalgams of self-hatred, so that the analytic task is to explore the *telos* of that aggression and see what other possibilities are embedded in it.

Taking up Samuels' description of countertransference in Chapter 3, this image of attack might represent many things within Figueroa's analysand's unconscious. It could be depicting her sense that contact with him feels like an attack on her or it could be showing that individuals in her early life were attacking towards her, and that she has had to fight back. It could be indicating that the people she grew up around felt that they were under attack, and their struggles with that were passed on to her. Perhaps the only image of close contact available to her is a fight to the death.

Or, the image of attack might depict the analysand's sense of Figueroa having something good inside him which she needs access to, and the only way she can get anything out of anyone is by cutting them open and ripping it out. Alternatively, she may feel tantalised and tormented by his having a good heart and/or a good mind which she cannot gain access to, or take in. This might also imply that she feels tantalised and tormented by the possibilities of her own good mind and/or heart which she cannot access.

She might be terrified and ambivalent about her desires to take things in, and can only imagine doing so in a frenzy of brutality. She might feel that Figueroa is trying to shove bad things into her, and so she attacks back in order to stop an intolerable invasion. Maybe the image depicts her starvation and the kind of wild, hallucinating Greek-tragedy kind of mad desperation which goes with such an extreme state. Many other such possibilities exist.

A violent countertransference image can tell any number of stories about the kind of aggressive energies which the analysand may be struggling with, and the kind of inner landscape in which she is manoeuvring. Object relations offers ways of trying to understand the kinds of ghosts, or unconscious structures of previous experiences which inflect how the analysand's experience her own aggression. Indeed, her experience of her aggression will be significantly mediated by how the people around her when she was a child were able to experience and use their aggressive energies, and how they were able to engage with hers. But I would also suggest that there will be other layers to this woman's capacity to engage with, and live her own aggressive energies in ways which serve her. In order to access these I would want to focus not on where her energies and their amalgams came *from*, but on their *telos*, or where they are trying to go *to*, instead. Aggressive energies have *a direction*; they are vectors, not measurements of distance, and must be understood in that way. This was why, in Chapter 1, I explained that I eventually turned away from object relations to rock music and stand-up comedy in order to develop more of a sensibility for the spectrum of the amalgams of aggressive energies. Later in this chapter I will return to this move, drawing out more fully the problematic understandings of aggression which underlie object relations. In particular I will focus on the limitations which arise from reducing the possible understandings of aggression to reiterations of the past.

Staying, however, with the theme of the *telos* of aggression, if Figueroa were in supervision, I would encourage him to 'run his fantasy on' to find out how the attack proceeded. Did the analysand attack the same parts of his body as the parts of her body which she cut? If not, which parts of his body did she try to cut? Were her cuts intended to be fatal, were they deliberate, or was she slashing wildly. In his fantasy, did she say or shout anything as she attacked him, or make a noise? If not, could he feel his way into the tone of the attack and guess at a noise which might have accompanied the style of attack? Was she crying? Was she laughing? Was she taking pleasure in what she was doing?

As his image of the attack unfolded, did his analysand continue to attack him with the blade only, or did she touch him in any way, and if so, where and how – did she kick or punch him (if so, which parts of his body was she aiming for)? Did she spit at him, rip at his clothes or bite him; again, if so, where? And how did the image of the attack end – did his analysand eventually sate herself and walk away (coldly? jeeringly?); did she stand back and survey what she had done? Did she take any parts of him (or his clothes) away with her? Did she break down? As his imagination played the scenario through to its end, was it still just the two of them, or had anyone else appeared – if so, who, and what did they do? Above all, what was the overall feeling of the attack and how did it change or develop as the image of the attack unfolded?

THE *TELOS* OF AGGRESSION

The point of eliciting all this detail is that it establishes the tone, and through that, possibly some clues about the *telos* of the analysand's aggressive energies. The fact that the analysand attacks Figueroa with the same weapon she uses on herself indicates that the image of the attack might be some form of communication. It certainly means something quite different to an image of her trying to beat him up with a baseball bat, shoot him or even knife him with a carving knife. The Gillette is a link between them. It may be the only real access to his analysand's inner world which Figueroa will be allowed for a long time.

Samuels suggests that the degree of stuckness associated with an individual's image of the primal scene of their parent's intercourse is indicative of their capacity to sustain conflict constructively (1989: 129) In a similar fashion, rerunning the image of the attack could provide a kind of countertransferential instrument for exploring Figueroa's unconscious experience of the relationship between him and his analysand. Early indications of shifts in the analysand's unconscious amalgams of aggressive energies might appear as changes in the course of Figueroa's image of the attack. For example, a rerun of the fantasy in which the analysand's attack shifts from her attacking him with a Gillette to punching him might represent a move from the expression of a cold, cutting, lethal rage and fury, to a hotter, more frustrated desperate sense of blocked agency, which longs for a trial of strength with the Other in order to find out something about herself. Alternatively, a shift in which the analysand sobs intermittently throughout the attack might indicate that the despair-aggression-rage amalgam, which had become frozen and shard- , or knife-like, is starting to melt, with the despair leaking out as sobs. Such changes in countertransferential response can offer clues for how to think about moves in the *telos* of the analysand's unconscious, aggressive energies and what they are trying to communicate in the analytic relationship.

AGGRESSION AS A LINK

In this way, aggressive energies and the conscious and unconscious landscapes they bring with them can play an important part in the analytic relationship. This position is derived from a quotation from Bersani, introduced in Chapter 1 where Bersani discusses Freud's *Civilization and Its Discontents*, suggesting that the text:

> obliquely yet insistently reformulates [Freud's own argument that we need to sublimate part of our sexuality into brotherly love as part of civilization] in the following way: human love is something like an

oceanic aggressiveness which threatens to shatter civilisation in the wake of its own shattering narcissistic pleasure. We don't move *from* love *to* aggression in *Civilization and Its Discontents*; rather, love is re-defined, re-presented, *as* aggressiveness.

(1986: 20–21, original italics)

If love is a form of aggressiveness, then somewhere buried in Figueroa's countertransference image of his patient's attack must be information about her desires to love him and the world by attacking and shattering them. The image probably also contains information about her desire to be loved by him and shattered by his love. The point about the analytic space, with its fundamental rule that there be no sexual acting out between analyst and analysand, is that it enables these kinds of intense, extreme desires to be felt, thought about and learnt from, without being concretised. One of the reasons for not concretising them is that such desires and energies are *on their way to becoming something else*. The version of them which turns up in the consulting room is information about the analysand's unconscious state, not about their literal desires, in the same way that a woman can use a rape fantasy to explore her own sexuality and, at the same time, know that rape is a devastating crime, which she is outraged by in reality.

This idea of love as a form of aggression may sound paradoxical, but it relates back to Waldby's comments in Chapter 4, where she discusses Jeanette Winterson's *Oranges Are Not the Only Fruit*. In Winterson's text, the protagonist, who has recently come out as a lesbian, expresses her desire for someone who will destroy and be destroyed by her. Waldby articulates what this erotic destruction entails:

By erotic destruction I mean both the temporary, ecstatic confusions wrought upon the everyday sense of self by sexual pleasure, and the more long-term consequences of this confusion when it works to constitute a relationship. Destruction seems an appropriate word for these states because it captures both the tender violence and the terrors involved in sexual practice and relationships, the kinds of violence this does to any sense of self as autonomous. Erotic pleasure arguably requires a kind of momentary annihilation or suspension of what normally counts as 'identity', the conscious, masterful, self-identical self, lost in the 'little death' of orgasm. These momentary suspensions, when linked together in the context of a particular relationship, work towards a more profound kind of ego destruction. I do not mean that the ego in love relations is destroyed in an absolute sense. Rather each lover is refigured by the other, made to bear the mark of the other upon the self. But all such transformation involves the breaking down of resistance, of violence to an existing order of the ego.

(1995: 266–267)

When (in Chapter 4) I discussed Waldby's interpretation of Winterson's novel, I made the point that women often struggle with their desires to take up the position of the destroyer in this way. In the same way that Jung suggests that thinking disagreeable thoughts can help a woman move forward in therapy, I suggest that being able to explore the desire to be the destroyer (in Waldby's sense) can be a breakthrough point for a woman in analysis. Waldby's example is from the erotic realm, but Chapter 4's example of Vivienne's letter to Geoff indicated that this willingness to work out how and where to break something which is not working, thereby destroying an aspect of oneself and the Other, is crucial in relationships in general. Doing the work of trying to determine what needs to be broken and how it should be done is very much part of love, as is the task of applying the blow, and taking responsibility for working through what happens afterwards. This last task is often the most difficult, but most important part. As we shall see, it depends on developing a sense that one's aggressive, explosive or knife-like energies are seen as love by the Other, even if they bring discomfort or pain. It depends on being able to find others who know that one of the purposes of being in a loving relationship is to be tenderly destroyed by it, and remade through the paradoxical capacity to hold onto oneself and surrender to the relationship at the same time. And it depends on being willing to take up the role of the destroyer, when it is needed, and to the extent required, without overidentifying with it.

Running these ideas back through Lizzie's earlier comments opens up a way of reading her rage. In order to illustrate how this might work, I have tried to amplify the voice of the 'Not-I within' which I hear through Lizzie's image. This voice is also an attempt to distil many other such voices which I have heard while working with people with severe and chronic eating disorders over long periods of time. What follows would be the voice of Lizzie's aggressive energies as she stands in her inner battlefield landscape, having calmed down just a little, and having just stopped screaming at me in her mind's eye.

I have also used this distilled voice to link together a number of other images, including Figueroa's countertransferential image of his patient's attack, the explosive mined cage and the lion. It is intended, as a fictional device, to say the kinds of things Lizzie's rage might say after a good few years of analysis (but in the language of my project), and to act as a bridge between a number of theoretical elements in this chapter and my experience of many such moments with patients.

> There's this too-much-ness about me. I hate it. I bet you can't stand it either. There's something shockingly raw and angry about me. I know it's hard to bear – I see people look away from it. I see you look away from it at times too.
>
> I want so much from the world, and I want to give so much to the world, but it all goes unbearably wrong, all the time. Being a person is too small – I can't get myself to fold down that small. But I can't live this

bigness either. The only place I can live it is out here on the battlefield. This place may be a terrifying, desolate, unliveable Armageddon, but at least I feel alive here – at least my *aliveness* is alive. At least fighting reminds me that there is *something* to fight for. The fight might be violent and bloody, but at least (while I am immersed in it) I feel connected to something – the thing I am fighting for. But what is it? I've lost track over the years, but my guess is that it's a longing to find a way to live the massive, explosive energies inside me.

I have an odd relationship with this huge ticking bomb of rage inside. It's always there, just off to one side. I can't live from it, or use it in any way; I have no idea how. It's broken through into the outside world a few times, like when I was backed into a corner in hospital, being made to eat terrifying things. I knew then that I could have killed everyone and every-thing around me, just to STOP it. Some of the nurses had tried to be kind, but then it came to the showdown. I remember the moment when I shattered – I stepped out of myself and picked myself up like a rag doll with a china head and hands. I smashed the doll against the wall (by now it had become a Molotov cocktail, which exploded as it hit the wall). Anything to stop them getting hold of me. I exploded and shattered to get away, to stop them breaking me. *I* will be the one who breaks me, not them. I remember the sobbing, raging humiliation. I never forgave them. They thought I did, but I just changed tactics in order to not have to shatter like that again. I gained just enough weight to get out, but I never forgave them for pushing me to breakpoint like that. They triumphed in that moment, but I won the war. Now I make sure my weight stays just high enough to not have to go back into hospital. I want it to be lower, but I don't think I could stop myself from killing myself or them if I was put back in hospital.

That fight, that rage feels like a really important part of me. In an odd way, it's all that I trust. It is the 'real' me. People seem to think that it's such a bad thing – they call it controlling, or adolescent. I think that's just their way of trying to make me feel guilty for having a way of stopping them getting in and making me like them. It's tricky – part of me wants to be able to belong when I chose to, connect and feel like I can trust people. But most of me knows that that isn't possible. For them the most important thing is being comfortable. For me, it's living something inside me which I have no words or pictures for. It feels big: too big, embarrassingly, humiliating big. I need to be thin to hide it. If that high-energy thing is me, I can't be human. I certainly can't be female. Yet I am. This does not compute. It makes things a nightmare. Yet I'm so glad that the secret, impossibly, unliveable huge part of me is there. It's the part of me that fought in the hospital, and I have a dream that if I could find a way of living it somehow, the world would be heartbreakingly beautiful and alive and real.

What I really want is for someone to help me live it. This bloody-minded, determined, inhuman, raging, defiant part of myself which can sense at 50 paces when someone is lying to me and is more interested in their comfort, their safety or their income than in helping me live myself. They say they want to help me. What they actually want to do is to teach me how to tone it down, so that I make them less uncomfortable. They think I should want that, appreciate their help. Their help is useless – full of worms, worse than death. Why can't they be honest and say that they really want to kill me off and replace me with a polite, Stepford Wives replica? I'd rather rage and fight on. A thought that terrifies me is that one day, in a moment of weakness, loneliness or desperation, I will give in and accept some of their poisonous kindness. And then they will 'have me'. I will owe them for their kindness and start to have to behave in ways which make them comfortable. I will have lost my capacity to refuse.

I'm holding out for a different deal – I have been for a long time. I do get a bit desperate from time to time – increasingly so. What I want is someone or something that will recognise my rage as passion, and help me figure out how to use it to live outside of their system. Their system is deadly to me, but they always think it's so good. The most infuriating situation is when, in the past, I have thought I had found someone who might be able to do the job I needed them to do. I hoped desperately that they could choose me, and not their system. If they could, I would have loved them with all my heart. Sometimes I even prayed that *this* one would be the one. But invariably it wasn't. They always wanted to make me into a nice girl. They wanted to help me be normal – how sickening! I could not stand the sense of despair and rage which hit when I realised that each time. Better to ask for nothing and not get my hopes up than ever be humiliated and annihilated like that again.

What I want is someone whose world I can blow up, again and again and again. I want them to help me see what I am doing when I do that. I have a hunch that I am doing *something* when I do that, but I don't know what. Sometimes it's just the relief and pleasure of being able to do something – blowing something up is better than not being able to do anything. But my sense is that often there's more to it than that.

And I really want them to help me fight more effectively – less wild swinging about, more calculated raids. If I follow that image, I realise that it may not even be a fight that I want. Maybe I want to be a really good weapon, like a surgical scalpel which cuts cleanly and saves someone's life. Or a very fine laser, which just does enough damage to make space for the healing processes to kick in. Or maybe I want to be a high-explosives expert who knows how to set the detonators off so that the old, useless building implodes perfectly, creating a pile of rubble which can be cleared away to make room for something new. I want someone who can help me make use of the explosive, cutting parts of myself properly.

Sometimes I just want to do as much damage as possible, and I'd need someone to pull me to my senses when that takes over. My guess is that it's an addictive thrill – an old habit, based on moments when I can't bear to wait and see if I can make the world get my point. Above all I want to be able to get stuff to move – in me, in the world, anywhere really. I feel the frustration of wanting that, and quickly it all swamps down into despair. Then the rage escalates to the point where I push the plunger and use myself as an explosive. At least in that moment I register in the world for something of who I am – my fury at the world's closedness, stupidity and refusal of my love is expressed.

Actually, what I really want is for you to see that my rage and frustration at you is because I love you. The stuckness and pain of your unlived life which, again, I can feel from miles away, drive me insane. I want to blow you up to shake you out of it. I want to blow up all your ways of using your role to get away from me, while trying to make that look reasonable and professional. When you do that, I could hack at you with a knife – the rage in me wants to kill you for that kind of cowardice on the battlefield. You can't let me down, you mustn't. I'll kill you if you do. I want to cut you free from your own fears and stucknesses, partly so I can get you to be who I need you to be, but also for yourself. I want my explosive love to be able to free you up too. I dearly, dearly want my ferocious, sharpness to mend something in someone or in the world. In you. Then I would know that I am not a total waste of space on the planet.

Finally, I want to get really good at picking the people who will fight properly. I want to be able to see the threats in other people and in myself, so I can say NO! when I need to, and stand by it, taking real pleasure in the fact that I can hold onto a NO! and look after myself. Only then would I feel safe to say the YES! that I really want to say. Sometimes it's like I can't see straight because of the ghosts of the past looming up. I try to fight them off, but it gets overwhelming and I end up just lashing out at anything that moves. I've trashed a lot of relationships that way, and barely trust myself to be near people now. I want help to sort out those confusions that pull me about like a puppet on strings.

I want to know how to get people to tussle and struggle with me so that we both learn and change. I can see that they/you are stuck too and I have a sense that our stucknesses are related. If we could have the right kind of fights about them, maybe there would be enough energy, enough love around to get things moving. That's real *hope*. Learning how to fight really well, like a fencer, is hope. Knowing that you can handle yourself, and pick good fighters who want to learn, who want to draw close through it, want to be broken open and remade through the honesty of a really muscular, emotional tussle is hope.

This amplification is intended to convey a number of points. First, and most important, is Lizzie's desire to have her knife-like, wall-like (NO!), explosive *qualities* recognised as such. This is the problem for the depth psychologies which rely, one way or another, on girls and women being prepared to disavow their aggressive energies and then eroticise that disavowal. My amplification of Lizzie's text is intended to draw out the level at which she refuses to do that, because to do so would be worse than suicide. She is very, very wary of people who appear to want to help her but, in fact, only offer her systems which would support her in these disavowals and eroticisations. What Lizzie longs for is help to live her aggressive aliveness, without having to give in and 'do' girl or woman in a way which makes the Other comfortable, in order to get their continued help.

This aspect of the amplification is also intended to echo Ella's imagery (in the previous chapter) of her explosive flesh being napalm-like or having an acidic quality. Lizzie, in a similar fashion, faces the question of what to do with the violences and aggressions which are folded into her flesh as a woman. Again, my suggestion is that these are an inevitable result of the formation of all identity positions. Cultural assumptions, however, make a significant difference to the degree of access to these violences which is possible from particular identity positions. Ella's struggle, like Lizzie's, and like Doris' in her psychopath dream (in Chapter 3), might be to find a way of living those deeper levels of her being which, if acknowledged, make it impossible to perform femininity in a socially recognisable way. In other words, the question is: how to be Isla's anti-woman and survive, let alone flourish?

On the other hand, refusal to perform femininity places one outside of identity, a place of madness and desolation, which my amplification of Lizzie's text was intended to suggest. I imagine Lizzie's predicament is based on her knowing that she has sharp, explosive qualities and that these are actually love, but she has no way of conveying that in a world which associates women with femininity, and femininity with something which is containing, safe-making and soothing. And Lizzie's femininity *is* actually femininity: it is femininity which is organised around *jouissance* and a metaphysics of absence. It has not surrendered its claims to decentered desire and has refused to settle for *plaisir* and attachment.

BULIMIA AND AGGRESSIVE ENERGIES

Lizzie's embattled, enraged state might be seen as a response to her own inner life and energies which she feels threatened by and cannot bear to think about. If she experienced her aggressive energies as very much 'Not-I within', their excitation might feel intolerable to the parts of her which she identifies with, creating explosive inner tensions. For a person with anorexia nervosa, these might be expressed as a bout of compulsive exercise, self-cutting, or still further restriction, whether it be food eaten, sleep allowed or TV programmes watched which are to be restricted. For someone who overeats, it might trigger either a frantic binge, or a session of steady grazing on food, until the required anaesthetic effect is achieved to numb the distressing conflict.[7] For someone with bulimia it could easily turn into a binge-vomit episode.

A colleague's patient[8] spoke of this state while describing her experience of herself prior to a bulimic binge in the following manner.

> Think about the times when the wind direction is such that it charges everything up electrostatically. Usually the weather is very dry – ultra-low humidity, and it is cold, perhaps frosty. Touching a car, or another person gives you a shock. You feel edgy. Imagine that you are a cat in these climatic conditions and your fur has picked up the static charge too. Each hair of your fur is repelling each other hair such that your fur bristles and your skin is crawling with dry static.
>
> It is already unbearable and getting worse (be it quickly or slowly). It is no longer a question of trying to find an orderly, sensible way of releasing some of this tension in order to earth yourself and make yourself more comfortable. It is now a driving, compulsive matter of survival that means you will do whatever is necessary to discharge this super-intense state. You simply must find a way back to some sort of 'ground-state'. Normal thinking has stopped, just as it does for anyone in a crisis, and some other part of you is running your actions. The autopilot mechanism cuts in and you find yourself hurtling along train-tracks until the process is over and all the food has been cooked, wolfed down and vomited up, perhaps repeating the process several times until temporary relief finally comes.

This kind of 'tunnel-vision' intensity has a highly aggressive charge to it, and analysands who have bulimia nervosa have described their sense that, having commenced a binge, they would punch or shove anyone out of the way who tried to interfere with their binge. Again, the analytic task is to find ways of thinking and feeling into these massive energies, which are often experienced as very much 'Not-I within' by the analysand. I will illustrate further what I mean by this through an image from Jenny, an analysand of mine who described her swings between periods of food restriction, and bingeing:

> It's as if I live in a glass room. While things are good with food, in other words, while I only eat fruit and yogurt, and not very much of those either, the glass walls hold, and I am safe. It may last hours, or days. It feels clean, ordered, sane. I am clean inside, acceptable. I can look people in the eye. I am not crippled with disgust at myself and what I do [with food]. Then, with no warning, I see a hair-line crack appear in one of the

walls. Frantically, I try to tape it back together, hoping that I will be able to somehow make it unhappen. But I know I can't stop what happens next. It's only a matter of time before it all falls apart and I am eating whole loaves of bread, and all the food my flat mate has left in the fridge. I am awash with food madness. It is chaotic. And I have no idea if it will ever stop again. So far it always has, but I have no way of telling how or when it will happen. Maybe I will walk out of my front door and the sky will be just the right colour, and the wind touch me in some way. Maybe I will be on a bus and see an advert which somehow clicks me back. Maybe I will wake up one morning and the glass room is back. Until next time.

Again, there are many ways in which one might respond to such an image as a clinician, all bearing in mind that at a physiological level, Jenny's driven attempts at food restriction make the next binge pretty well inevitable.

The aspect which I want to draw out here, however, is how Jenny is trying to create a safe, clean zone, where desire is being held in check by a glassy, fragile will, and so that she feels like she has a right to be a member of the human race. The only other place which she can live from is a place where will-power has snapped, dumping her into chaos, voraciousness, desperation and shame. Using a Jungian tactic of personifying an element of her psychological process, I asked Jenny what caused the crack in the glass wall to start. Jenny, sobbing desperately, described to me a cruel, mocking, jeering goblin, who hated her and tried to destroy her by smashing her glass room.

Looking at this through the ideas proposed earlier, I would say that even though Jenny dearly wanted to stabilise the glass room and live in it, feeling safe and protected, she also unconsciously knew that it would become a psychological coffin. So each time things started to firm up and become inhabitable, the unconscious parts of her which wanted to push on out into the world – her aggressive, lively energies – smashed the room, pitching her into painful chaos.

Jenny had no way of making any sense of her own aggressive energies, or of thinking about what they might be *for* in such a situation: she felt far too victimised by them to have room for such thoughts. Working with Jenny as she went through the swings between her glass room and the chaos over and over, month after month, made us pick through the rubble of the collapses as they occurred each week. It seemed to be the only thing Jenny and I could do each session. Eventually it became apparent that we were starting to find the odd clue as we were able to sieve through the debris more slowly. This was, paradoxically, because Jenny's despair was deepening: she spent less and less of each session frantically imploring me to help her stop these chaotic collapses, and slowly more of her became available to simply pick through the resultant mess together. This had the effect of enabling us to rerun the collapses on slow-motion video until this became a still-by-still exploration at times.

In these stills incongruent details began to become visible – for example, the way in which (prior to her last binge) Jenny's boss had ripped her off by not paying her at the end of her shift because business had been a bit slow. She simply assumed that it was her responsibility to accept this, rather than to negotiate with him about it and question whether she should be loyal to a man who could afford the luxuries that mattered to him, while not paying her properly. Jenny was determined not to be petty or disloyal, and thought her anger at his behaviour 'mean'. In such a situation the goblin was actually doing her a favour by smashing the glass walls which protected her from her own aggressive response to her exploitation. Sometimes the trigger was much more subtle, and only very close examination of the 'stills' gave us any clues about it. Often the trigger had to do with something incoherent and deep down inside Jenny starting to scream with rage at what was happening to her. That scream and rage would terrify her, forcing her to identify with the 'don't make a fuss, don't put people out, I'm sure s/he didn't mean it' position, as she tried to cauterise her own aggressive response. The bingeing was the place where she could 'let rip' with those raw energies which could not be lived within traditional, recognisable femininity.

For Jenny, the most important parts of her inner life were generating the collapses, even though the crashes were terrifying. The coming apart of the old order is not, however, always experienced in this way: for Garner (in Chapter 1), approaching this place where aggression breaks up the old order of identity was a joy. The difference was that for Jenny, the changes her aggressive energies kept demanding of her were, at that stage, unacceptable. Consciously, she did not want to be a bigger version of her own personality; she longed to be small, fit in with other people's expectations and thus find a sense of belonging.

But at an unconscious level, there was another story. As in my earlier attempt at expressing a distilled version of the aggressive energies in anorexia nervosa, Jenny knew that she needed to be a much bigger person, but had no idea how to live that. At this unconscious level she was organised around her own aggressive energies and the desire to get on with separating, taking responsibility for herself and reminding others that they needed to take responsibility for themselves. This unconscious story was anathema to her conscious identity: Jenny feared that it was selfish, unfeminine and would destroy her relationships with her boyfriend, family and her friends.

For Jenny, exploring the 'Not-I within' goblin part of her was almost intolerable. My image for it was that it was like being a turtle who, halfway through crawling up the beach, has had its shell ripped off, leaving all its insides exposed to any predator which might pass by. She felt terrifyingly visible and unprotected, and my sense is that this is one of the nightmare landscapes that a woman can find herself in if she explores her own aggressive energies. The performance of femininity can provide a shell, a way of hiding the paradoxical helplessness and vulnerability which are inextricably entwined in aggressive energies.

In fact, Jenny needed the hatred which she felt that the goblin held for her: she needed to hate her boss for being exploitative, and find a way to use that to stand up to him, set limits and fight for those limits to be respected. Instead, the hatred was turning back on her.

HATRED AND SEPARATION

Brinton Perera describes how, for Jung, there was an aspect of hatred which 'one would describe in Western philosophical terms as an urge or instinct towards individuation for its function is to destroy participation mystique by separating and setting apart an individual who has previously been merged, identical with loved ones (1981: 31).

The kind of separation which hatred offers may entail changes to relationships in the outside world, but it can also represent the need to separate ideas, beliefs or inner, psychological spaces which had become stuck together. In other words, hatred can demand that some unconscious image or thought be differentiated and brought into consciousness. It can also demand that one breaks up and separates the elements of one's experience of the world, sieving through to find what is worth keeping, and what should be let go of.

In this way hatred, and the separation it can instigate, can form the basis of an emotional digestive system. Just as we need our physical digestive system to break down complex foods in order to make their elements useable, and to dispose of the parts which are of no use to us, so too with emotional digestion. The capacity to take the world into one's psychosomatic being with a reasonable confidence that one has the capacity to digest it, in other words, break it down, draw nourishment and get rid of waste, is crucial. People who have severe and chronic eating disorders often need help to build and come to trust these processes in themselves. It may be why someone with anorexia nervosa avoids taking the world and food in the first place. They may feel that they have no way of sorting through and getting rid of anything which gets inside them, so life is only viable if they take in nothing. But that, of course, that is death.

An image which I use for this is that it can feel as if every difficult or painful thing which has happened in life has been like being handed another rock. In order to free up your hands (and be able to carry on doing life), you want to get rid of the rock, but you cannot put it down: it is now part of you. You cannot get rid of it. So you pop it into your emotional rucksack. This is fine, up to a point, but eventually there are so many rocks in the rucksack that it has you pinned to the ground, flat on your back. Viewed through this image, recovery is about building an emotional digestive system for breaking down experiences of the inner and outer worlds so as not to become overwhelmed or paralysed by them.

Aggression and hatred are key factors in being able to do this. Hatred gets under one's skin, forcing one to pay attention to the fine details of exactly what it is that one hates about the Other. Aggression then provides the energy to engage with, and tussle with, that which is unacceptable. Rather than tracing out how Jenny actually dealt with this situation, I want to stay with the possibilities it held. It would have been right for Jenny to feel hatred at her boss for exploiting her, and through that hatred, to create emotional distance from him to determine what she wanted and needed to do. Access to her aggressive energies could have enabled her to assess whether he was someone who was willing to learn from interpersonal tussles, or whether he was more invested in getting his own way at all costs. Had she decided that the former were true, she might have then found the space to explore her desire to cross swords with him about his behaviour. This might have only been partly out of her need to protect herself; it could also have been out of her desire to find out whether he could respond to the love entailed in her challenge. This is the kind of love which cares too much for the Other to let them sell themselves short by trying to get away with disrespectful behaviour, behaviour which necessarily becomes the basis of disrespect for themselves too.

If Jenny had come to know that her hatred and aggression carried the possibility of breaking open her boss's stuckness, as well as her own, her boss's capacity to respond to her challenge would have still mattered, but much less. She would have been able to maintain a sense of her own 'strong' energies, as Courtin described them in Chapter 1. As with Miss Baxter's predicament in Chapter 2, a possible mechanism for change is offered in the form of coming to see clearly the destructive, exploitative, hateful qualities in the other and in oneself. Thinking these kinds of disagreeable thoughts can start the process of gathering back together the aggressive energies which are split up and disavowed in the production of femininity, and by narratives such as the pedagogic one in which Miss Baxter was situated. As is evident by now, the gathering-up of these energies is often a complex and painful process, but it can offer a form of agency.

Again, however, this is a form of feminine agency which the object relations traditions find hard to support because of their unconscious fantasies about femininity. In Chapter 1 I outlined the history of some of these fantasies, and in Chapter 4 I indicated how such fantasies create a collusion with processes of identity production that render woman an anchor of the space in which the Other's agency plays out. Now I revisit the theme of object relations' struggle with women's aggressive energies, focusing on the issue of object relations' 'phantasies' about femininity and aggression.

REPOSITIONING AGGRESSION

For Klein aggression was a manifestation of the death instinct (Hinshelwood, 1991: 47), an instinct which 'greatly disturbs and modifies the natural progression of the libidinal development through the early phases'

(Hinshelwood, 1991: 55; see also Hinshelwood 1991: 266–270 for a discussion of Klein's understanding of the death instinct). In other words, aggression is a *threat* to development, with the processes of guilt and reparation offering the hope of a creative response to its damaging potential.

I suggest that what Klein is describing are the processes which form the Western, bourgeois subject for whom aggression *is* a threat. Aggression, with its associated demands for change, and its close links to defiance and determination to push on and find new ground are not the basis of bourgeois subjectivity. Quite the opposite: they are the very impulses which need to be canalised into the 'depressive position' or 'stage of concern' in order to achieve the kind of bourgeois subjectivity which will maintain the *status quo* in the interests of bourgeois culture. Klein is right, but in a limited way: for the bourgeois subject, taking up the lively moral and connective possibilities embedded in the *telos* of aggression *would* constitute a form of death. In this way, aggression could easily be mistaken as a manifestation of the death instinct, by someone who mistakes bourgeois culture for nature. But that does not make aggression a universal manifestation of the death instinct, it just makes the enlivening, dissenting demands of aggression potentially deadly to a certain kind of subjectivity.

Winnicott's attempts to engage with aggressive energies reveal a different, but closely related problem. His best known works in the area are the 1949 paper 'Hate in the Countertransference', and his concept of object usage. From the perspective of this book, these contributions are useful because Winnicott is closer to seeing aggression as part of the life instinct than Klein. Indeed, the notion of object usage implies that aggressive energies have a *telos* – that their unfolding is part of the process of learning about the world and coming to trust and love certain parts of it. It also implies that there are creative and moral possibilities embedded in our aggressive energies, and that the process of discovering who and what can survive those energies teaches us about love. But there is a troubling torsion in Winnicott's theory which points to a deeper problem in his understanding of aggression.

In order to explore this, I will start with a comment by Margaret, in which she describes how she experienced being pregnant:

Margaret: Once upon a time she is surprised by biology: her urge to be caught, held, pinned, penetrated. Help! what has become of who she thought she was? Can people in the street see what she knows? She's no longer complete. She's divided, plural (prodigal). She fights to hold herself together, to re-group. She seems to have lost the advantage she had. How can you give yourself to someone and be yourself? It's a fight to the death, though to win that fight is death.

Margaret's pregnancy occasions conflict and ambivalence even though it has come about through urges which she knows to be her own. The comments of Margaret's which I want to concentrate on are, however, those which indicate the kind of battles she finds herself in: '[s]he fights to hold herself together, to re-group', and most importantly: '[i]t's a fight to the death, though to win that fight is death.'

These images indicate a sense of being under attack and of having to fight for one's life. Yet this is a very particular kind of fight: it resonates with Garner's images of fencing in Chapter 1 – the desire to be involved in a fight to the death in which no one dies. This is a fight that can (and perhaps must) be repeated over and over, for its own sake. It is certainly not about a once-and-for-all victory. Its purpose is to learn about oneself as a fighter, not to beat one's opponent.

Margaret's comment '[h]ow can you give yourself to someone and be your-self?' captures the spirit of her battle, indicating that it is about how to survive the enlarging of her sense of self without a catastrophic loss of that sense of self. One way of reading this is that the mother's relationship to her baby can be that of object usage. Women sometimes talk about being fright-ened and excited by the 'challenge' of motherhood. The point of a challenge is that it pushes one to the edge – you get to find out what you are made of. Having a baby provides a way of finding out who you are as a mother. What kind of a person do you turn out to be when your capacities to love and to hate are put under extreme pressure? Which parts of you hold together in such circumstances and which fall apart or fall away? (Again, Parker's *Torn in Two: The Experience of Maternal Ambivalence* (1996) is unusual as a book which is both within the object relations tradition, and is critical of it, as it tries to speak to these struggles.)

These needs to find out about how one loves and hates can be seen as a form of object usage. They are different to infantile object usage primarily in that they are internal processes within the woman who is mothering, rather than actions played out in the world. They are also structured slightly differ-ently: the infant's object usage tests the outside world to see if it can survive the infant's aggressive demands and curiosities. A mother, on the other hand, will be provided with plenty of tests in which she gets to explore what she can turn her aggressive, hateful energies and fantasies into, through her day-to-day dealings with her baby. Her task is to see if she can turn her aggression and hatred towards the baby into something which is of use to her, in the way that Garner used fencing to explore her desire to attack. Through the explor-ation of that desire Garner discovered her own mind, and something of a sense of agency. In this way the baby can function as an object through which the mother brings herself into important struggles with her own aggressive and hateful energies. Through those struggles she may have a chance to learn about herself, and, most importantly, about the real, edgy nature of love. Again, this is a largely internal battle, but it often has the life-and-death characteristic which Margaret indicates in her comments about her pregnancy.

And this is where there is a dangerous gap in the Winnicottian model. I call it dangerous because it indicates a crucial point where the capacity to think breaks down, and it is rarely noticed that it does so. What steps in, in place of thinking, are fantasies about women and motherhood which are shot through with unconscious defences against the idea of the mother's love as a form of object-usage, and the mother's need to become conscious of, and engage with, her own aggression for the sake of her own psychological growth. These unconscious defences also evade the possibility that the mother may indeed have had her baby in order to generate exactly these kinds of struggles in her life, unconsciously knowing that they might offer her opportunities for radical learning and change.

In order to explore this gap I would remind the reader of Winnicott's notion of primary maternal preoccupation, which he saw as an organised state which would be an illness were it not for the fact of the preceding pregnancy. Winnicott characterises primary maternal preoccupation in the following way:

It gradually develops and becomes a state of heightened sensitivity during, and especially towards the end of, the pregnancy.

It lasts for a few weeks after the birth of the child.

It is not easily remembered by mothers once they have recovered from it.

I would go further and say that the memory mothers have of this state tends to become repressed.

(Winnicott, 1958: 302)

For Winnicott, only the mother who is sensitised in this way can 'feel herself into her infant's place, and so meet the infant's needs' (Winnicott, 1958: 304). Furthermore, '[t]he mother's failure to adapt in [this way during] the earliest phase [of her baby's life] does not produce anything but an annihilation of the infant's self' (Winnicott, 1958: 304). While Winnicott's comments are made in a context which is intended to support the 'ordinary, good-enough mother', they do make it clear that for the baby's well being it is *essential* that the mother be able to move into this state where she loses her self in the service of her baby for the first weeks of its life.

Winnicott also, however, acknowledged the darker side of the maternal relationship, writing in 'Hate in the Counter-Transference' that the mother '. . . hates her infant from the word go' (1949: 73). The problem is: how do these two understandings come together? How can a woman simultaneously be in a receptive state of primary maternal preoccupation *and* feel the hatred she has for her baby 'from the word go'?

There is a space here, a place where the plates of the model do not meet, leaving room for exploration but Winnicott closes down this space in which the *telos* of maternal hatred or aggression might be explored when he writes:

> A mother has to be able to tolerate hating her baby without doing any-
> thing about it. She cannot express it to him. If, for fear of what she may
> do, she cannot hate appropriately when hurt by her child she must fall
> back on masochism, and I think it is this that gives rise to the false theory
> of a natural masochism in women. The most remarkable thing about a
> mother is her ability to be hurt by her baby and to hate so much without
> paying the child out, and her ability to wait for rewards that may or may
> not come at a later date.
>
> (1949: 74)

It remains unclear what this 'appropriate' way of hating the baby is. If it is not masochism, what might it be? Again, my suggestion is that what is implied (but cannot be thought about in the Winnicottian world) is that the mother is (healthily and appropriately) making use of her infant and the hateful and aggressive energies it calls up in her for her own psychological purposes. But acknowledging this would mean relinquishing object relations' naturalised, bourgeois fantasies about femaleness and aggression as mutually exclusive. It would mean accepting the mother's love (to use Bersani's interpretation of Freud) as a form of aggressiveness.

My hunch is that, at some level, Winnicott knew this, hence his account of how the lullaby 'Rock-a-Bye-Baby' can be used to verbally express maternal hatred while disguising it with a melody which is supposed to prevent it from being communicated to the infant (1949: 74). At the simplest level, this lul-laby enables a woman who is mothering to voice her own aggressive, hateful, murderous energies towards her infant through a socially sanctioned mechan-ism while remaining safely 'in role'.

Actually, the lullaby does a lot more than that. It is one of the many, tiny cultural practices which constitute motherhood as a socially enforced splitting-off of these potentially destructive, potentially enlivening energies. In order to stabilise such an arrangement, the split-off energies need to be kept separate and 'held' in cultural containers such as lullabies. The collective nature of the lullaby makes the mother's destructive energies 'public prop-erty', offering the mother a means of canalising her struggles along culturally acceptable lines. Indeed, in similar fashion, one of the functions of telling fairy stories to children is that it allows the parents, and the mother in par-ticular, to identify with the witch who hates small children or schemes about how to put them in her oven, while splitting-off those aspects of herself in order to remain in role.

But the object relations models have not traditionally explored these aspects of how mothers manage to hate their babies 'appropriately', perhaps because to do so would challenge the naturalised fantasies of womanhood which underlie their image of the mother-infant couple. Indeed, what becomes apparent in the preceding discussion is that in both Klein's and Winnicott's work different facets of the production of the bourgeois subject are mistaken for 'nature'. In Walkerdine's words, 'the historical *production* of the "natural" is completely elided' (Walkerdine, 1990: 25, original italics). What is assumed to be 'natural' are the cultural practices which produce the kind of subject which, as Samuels suggests 'the culture which surrounds object relations already valorises' (1993: 276). Again, Haraway's question '[w]ith whose blood were my eyes crafted? (1997: 288) applies – in other words, whose lives and experiences have been carved up to sustain this naturalisation?

Thus while my emphasis on the creative, relational possibilities embedded in aggression in some ways parallels Winnicott's understanding of the ruthless, object-using characteristics of early infancy, that similarity is very limited. My interest is in the relationship between aggression, desire and passion, not aggression and attachment, as it was for Winnicott. Indeed, as Walkerdine argues, in Winnicott's work 'attachment, bonding and nurturance replace passion and desire' (Walkerdine, 1990: 73), which is the exact opposite of my aim. My argument is that the object relations discourses rely on a series of naturalised, unconscious, defensive and damaging bourgeois fantasies about the nature of femininity and aggression in order to create and sustain their exclusively intrapsychic emphasis, and their models of desirable development and personhood.

In my earlier exploration of Lizzie's aggressive and rageful imagery, I suggested that through Bersani's reading of Freud (1986: 20–21), Lizzie's aggressiveness *is* love. Her aggressiveness is a manifestation of her aliveness, not her death instinct. But in order to read aggression in that way, one must understand that the desire to blow up the processes of subjection is not a dangerous manifestation of the death instinct, which is to be redirected or transformed as part of psychological development. It is an indication of the unresolvable resistance to identity which, as Rose argues, lies at the very heart of psychic life (Rose, 1990: 232). This Freudian emphasis on resistance to identity is what is lost in object relations. If lived, the unresolvable tension of this resistance demands a creativity which constantly challenges the social *status quo*. It can generate, instead, a muscular process of discovery of agency, its limitations, the associated sense of abject, maddening helplessness, along with the possibilities for connection, morality and compassion which are the *telos* of aggressive and hateful energies. These forms of agency and morality are, however, highly demanding on the self and Other; again, arrangements which do not support the *status quo* of bourgeois culture, especially in its positioning of women as the Other to a fantasy of the rational, the moral (masculine) subject.

Butler reads aggression as serving life when she discusses Freud's *Mourning and Melancholia*:

if the ego contains aggression against the other who is gone, then it follows that reexternalising that aggression 'uncontains' the ego. The desire to live is not the desire of the ego, but a desire that undoes the ego in the course of its emergence. The 'mastery' of the ego would then be identified as the effect of the death drive, and life, in a Nietzschean sense, would break apart that mastery, initiating a lived mode of becoming that contests the stasis and defensive status of the ego.

(Butler, 1997: 193–194)

In this context, I read Butler's comments as pertaining to that which has been rendered 'Other within' in order to inhabit a socially intelligible identity. This unlived, and possibly unliveable potential is, from the point of view of the 'I', dead. The 'I' is left with a choice between mourning and melancholia in relation to this lost potential which has become 'Not-I within'. Both strategies have their advantages and complications, a matter which I will return to in the next chapter.

Butler sees the aggressive undoing of the ego as associated with mourning:

Survival, not precisely the opposite of melancholia, but what melancholia puts into suspension – requires redirecting rage against the lost other, defiling the sanctity of the dead for the purposes of life, raging against the dead in order not to join them.

(Butler, 1997: 193)

Yet the performance of femininity, even more so than masculinity, depends on the disavowal of these rages and aggressions which undo identity, and on the fabrication of an illusion of distance from them.

Female aggression is not to be used to rage against the dead in order not to join them; it is to be bent back into self-sacrifice and martyrdom in ways described by Walkerdine in her analysis of the structures of stories in 1980s' girls' magazines. Her point is that these stories offer girls narratives which help them render their desires intelligible by canalising them into structures which culminate in the semiotics of self-sacrificing, ecstatic martyrdom (Walkerdine, 1990: 97–98). '[G]irls are presented with heroines who never get angry. Their victory is in their very passivity and helpfulness. Selflessness is contrasted with selfishness, anger, greed and jealousy' (1990: 96). This is what I mean by the way in which girls and women are encouraged to eroticise their disavowal of their own aggressive energies and the violences of identity formation.

It is also what Jenny's bingeing hinged on. For Jenny, intelligible gender identity entailed not being selfish or mean, and unquestioningly accepting her boss's exploitative behaviour. The core of her value as a female person was in the victory over her own aggression and rage. That victory placed her among the 'heroines'; it made her a good, strong, brave girl.

The goblin of her aggressive energies was not, however, prepared to settle for the psychological glass coffin of her safe room, shattering it whenever she managed to stabilise it. Jenny desperately needed to fabricate a sense of identity, *and* resist it in order to stop it killing her. The analytic task was to find ways of inhabiting the immensely turbulent and intolerable tensions between these forces. Jenny's hateful goblin was the part of her which wanted to rage and mourn, rather than slip into the performance of a femininity structured around eroticising a melancholic position. The goblin was actually her Prince Charming. My earlier amplification of Lizzie's imagery was likewise intended to depict her rageful, aggressive energies as a refusal to make this turn.

Again, object relations with its unconscious investment in the perpetuation of the social *status quo* cannot analyse this pressure towards femininity as melancholia. Instead, it naturalises it as feminine masochism, or as Winnicott's fantasy that the woman who becomes a mother ' "naturally" denies her own agency: she *desires* to be without subjectivity so that she can be used as a living mirror by the child' (Doane and Hodges, 1992: 29, original italics). These melancholic turns towards a metaphysics of presence, with its focus on desires for known presences and certainties, are present in Jung's work too, and that is why, in Chapter 2, I recast his notion of the collective unconscious as a more political entity. This recasting of Jung's work through the lens of identity production aims to build on the interpersonal, cultural dimensions of his work, while drawing distance from the universal and ahistorical fantasies embedded in it. Those fantasies turn away from the metaphysics of absence which drove Jung's explorations of inner and outer Otherness. Again, it is this metaphysics of absence in Jung's work that is the focus of my interest.

Seen in this light, the aggression and violence of eating disorders can be thought of as the unresolved refusal to make the turn towards melancholia which femininity demands. Instead, the eating disorder enacts, contains and displays the endless tensions between the refusal to disavow the violences and aggressions out of which identity comes into being, and the unliveability of that refusal. It is an attempt to find a way in which to rage and mourn the losses associated with identity formation (and female identity in particular), without falling completely out of the realm of intelligible, gendered identity.

Chapter 7

Aggressive energies and relationships

INTRODUCTION TO THE SECOND-ROUND CONTRIBUTIONS

In this final chapter I explore the participants' second-round contributions in which they discussed their struggles to move away from what I call an 'identity based on gender melancholia' towards an 'identity based on gender mourning'. These struggles take women into conversation with their own aggressive energies and fantasies but in order to create a space in which to discuss both the struggles and what they reveal, I need to draw together certain elements from previous chapters, and introduce some new ones.

In what follows I explain what I mean by 'an identity based on gender melancholia' and an 'identity based on gender mourning'. I then use these terms alongside the notions of a metaphysics of presence and a metaphysics of absence, drawing out what they mean through some of the women's first-round contributions. The first-round contributions used in this chapter have been selected because they anticipated the directions taken by the women who contributed material in the second round. In hindsight, it was these first-round contributions which acted as the threads around which the second-round contributions wove themselves. (I also include a few paragraphs to remind the reader what I mean by first- and second-round contributions.) The chapter ends with a discussion of the women's second-round contributions, drawing out the way in which they focus on the close relationships between aggressive energies, identity and love.

MELANCHOLIA, MOURNING AND IDENTITY FORMATION

Towards the end of the preceding chapter I introduced Butler's argument that the ego (which I read as self-reflexivity) is primarily formed through the workings of melancholia (1997: 167–198). Butler outlines Freud's view of the ego as something which is instituted as a necessary defence against loss, and which is formed through the sedimentation of abandoned object cathexes. But the ego is a poor, unsatisfactory substitute for the lost object – hence the ego is shot through with the kind of ambivalence which distinguishes melancholia (1997: 169). Butler also writes that '[m]elancholia establishes the tenuous basis of the ego, and indicates something of its status as an instrument of *containment*' (1997:190, original italics), so that the ego's very function as a container of self-awareness is necessarily melancholic in tone. Attempts to move the ego's formative losses from melancholia into mourning would involve re-externalising the aggression against what has been lost, and that would 'uncontain' the ego (Butler, 1997: 193).

For Butler, the formation of gender is an elaboration of these processes: the grief associated with the loss of access to the parent of the other sex is a grief which is culturally recognised and canalised into the performance of gender as part of the mainstream heterosexual tableau. Since heterosexuality demands that the loss of sexual access to the parent of the same sex cannot be grieved, gender, as an aspect of identity and self-reflexivity is formed from, and maintained by, melancholic structures (Butler, 1997: 140). In more general terms, the social *status quo* is maintained by melancholic denials and ambivalences about the losses involved in identity production, with the performance of gender being a facet of that melancholic process.

The opposite move (from melancholia to mourning) involves a coming to know what has been lost – the unlived and unliveable lives which the processes of identity production demand be sacrificed for both sexes. This move also entails, as Butler puts it, a willingness to rage 'against the dead in order not to join them' (Butler, 1997: 193). It is this rage, this aggressive fury, which femininity bars, and which masculinity provides slightly more access to through the traditional association of masculinity with aggression.

The first round of contributions which women made to the project can profitably be read as documenting various struggles with identity-resisting aggressive energies which seek to break away from the *status quo* melancholic gender position. Such energies are, however, deeply problematic, because the enlivening and enriching possibilities which they offer undo the ego and risk the loss of intelligible identity. Femininity, like masculinity, is structured around an eroticised gender melancholia, although the genders are positioned differently in terms of how they can express that. The particular ways in which femininity is positioned provide women with opportunities for resistance and subversion, and I will use this perspective to amplify the participant's second-round contributions.

In effect, women traffic in identity-undoing aggressive energies all the time. As indicated in previous chapters, women have developed a multitude of fragmented and unrecognised languages to explore the limits of identity and the risks involved in subverting the powers that produce identity. Sometimes these languages seek to communicate between women, or between women and men. Often they simply seek to communicate within an individual woman's psyche – perhaps between the 'I' and the 'Not-I'.

Occasionally these communications are overt. More often, they are covert, conducted in the spirit that Shirley Ardener illustrates when she writes about how Muslim women (and men) outmanoeuvre gender practices which thwart the operation of agency in an area of Iran:

> In the traditions of the Mamasani district of Iran . . . women are not encouraged to speak in public on political matters. Yet . . . they do participate in political processes, moving about gathering information and testing reactions in ways hardly recognised in the culture – they operate what may be called a 'muted structure', sometimes coded into talk about chickens. It is interesting that these women do pass on their information, by commenting to their husbands when they meet in the evening, when the house is supposedly reserved for their private domestic concerns. It appears, however, that the husband is likely to disdain to ask direct questions, and gives little sign of attention or encouragement, thus maintaining the fiction that the wife does not participate in politics; she is structurally 'muted' although she speaks.
>
> (Ardener, 1993: 9)

I suggest that women's aggressive energies operate in a similar way: they are structurally muted, although they speak, often in code. Such energies are certainly invisible from the point of view of mainstream studies on aggression. They are rendered part of the support structure for the Other's agency, with both genders observing the gender rules in public, while knowing privately that they do not work. Nonetheless, their invisibility is maintained by a series of fictions which both genders participate in so as not to unravel their own gender identity, and through that, their experience of cognisable personhood.

SUMMARY OF RESEARCH METHODOLOGY: LISTENING TO WOMEN TALK ABOUT CHICKENS

In order to explore this structurally muted code, I had to develop a research methodology which could access the fragments and threads in which it can be seen. In Chapter 3, I described how I collected contributions to this project and how I came to view my relationship to those contributions. Through a process of trial and error, I took up the clinical psychoanalytic model of using my countertransference reactions to build hypotheses about the unconscious structures of the Other. My assumption was that aggressive fantasies and energies are an inner Other for most women. They are certainly regarded as Other culturally, hence Jessica Benjamin's comment about men's and women's anxieties that women might be sexually aggressive and that '. . .

the primary other, the mother, could be greedy, dangerous, violent' (1998: 43).

In the clinical situation, (from the analyst's point of view) the Other is the analysand, the transference–countertransference field between the two parties, and the inner Othernesses of both the analyst and the analysand. For the purposes of this project, however, the Other was the collected voices of the women who made contributions to it, the bodies of theory which I was using, and my own inner Othernesses and countertransference reactions.

Theory served both to amplify the women's contributions, and to provide clues about the discursive pressures which were shaping the women's voices. The women's contributions generated new theories and perspectives, and they also demanded the critique of existing theories. Working across these tensions generated repeated collapses: of theory, of my countertransferencial hypotheses and of apparent patterns of meaning in the women's contributions. Eventually, I realised that the patterns of these collapses and the stucknesses they caused were, in themselves, information about the kinds of dynamics which are generated by and also shape women's aggressive energies. Chapter 3 attempted to document this realisation and how I used it as the basis of this project, both as a theoretical and epistemological principle, and as a practical research methodology.

The idea of using my countertransference reactions as the basis of building an understanding of women's aggressive energies and fantasies necessitated a second step. In analytic training, the trainee analyst is supported by senior analysts over a number of years while they learn to use their countertransference reactions to develop hypotheses about the Other's unconscious structures. These hypotheses are offered back to the analysand and the value of the hypothesis/interpretation is determined by the way in which it is consciously or unconsciously taken up (or reacted against) by the analysand. In terms of this project, the parallel step was to offer my countertransference-based interpretations/hypotheses back to the women who had made contributions.

In order to do this, a near final draft of the earlier PhD version of this project was sent to the 12 remaining women participants (2 of the original 14 having died in the intervening period). As described in Chapter 3, seven responded, and those responses form the basis of this chapter. Also as mentioned in Chapter 3, when I sent the near final draft out I was still unsure how to end the project. I had something which served as an ending, but it simply did not 'work'. What I sent out to the participants was a draft which I asked them to read (if they had time and were still interested) to see whether they were comfortable with how I had interpreted their initial contribution. I also asked them to point out any ways in which I had failed to take into account the impact of the specifics of their life history or situation on their contribution. For example, did they feel that their aggressive energies were shaped by their ethnic background, whether or not they had children, their class or their sexual orientation? The feedback from this request was addressed in the final draft of the project.

Prior to receiving the women's second-round contributions I had known that I was using my countertransference reactions to their initial contributions and to bodies of theory in order to generate hypotheses, and that it would be better if I could find some way of testing out those hypotheses. But I could not see how to do so without starting a sizeable second project which would have surveyed the women's responses to my initial interpretation. When the seven second-round contributions arrived, I realised that they provided exactly what was missing: this was the response to my interpretation which I was looking for.

Possible meanings of the non-response of the other five women were considered in Chapter 3, as was the way in which I responded to their wider criticisms of the PhD version of the project. These second-round contributions generated the structure of this chapter but, by their nature, they also expanded on a number of threads from the first-round contributions. In order to make a link between the two sets of contributions, I start by summarising the relevant themes from the preceding chapters. By way of illustrating these themes, I discuss a number of the first round-contributions which provide the context for the subsequent exploration of the second-round contributions. The focus then moves to the second-round contributions and the ways in which they bring together and articulate the themes of this book.

SUMMARY OF THEMES

We are called into being through losses and the injurious terms of identity, processes which are then disavowed in the creation of an inhabitable identity. This disavowal entails a certain drawing-away from the violences and injurious terms which make identity possible. The pressures to create and maintain the subsequent illusion of distance are especially strong for women, because of the traditional association of femininity with non-aggression. The psychosocial spaces in which the genders negotiate these pressures are different (for example, around which losses and injuries of identity formation can be mourned publicly and which cannot), although they do overlap, and part of the process of learning to perform gender is learning how to eroticise those differences.

Watching the Hammer Horror version of Rider Haggard's *She* as an adolescent (see Chapter 2), I found myself caught between the longing to accept (and eroticise) the way in which the film sought to canalise my desire and, simultaneously, the need to resist my own longing to surrender to that canalisation. In effect, I longed to eroticise the way in which my desires were being shaped along recognisably feminine lines, even as I felt nauseated by that shaping and my longing for it. These processes which shape desire apply to both genders, and the film's set-piece opposition between love and power as part of the Western Romantic tradition is very much part of that cross-gender process.

Gender is, however, about how these disavowals and eroticisations are performed by the individual in order to remain culturally intelligible. For example, the performance of mainstream femininity involves the disavowal of strong energies such as aggression and the desire for mobility. Indeed, in the preceding chapters it became apparent that women's aggressive energies are often dispersed through various processes which maintain mainstream feminine identity. While the performance of 'ordinary' femininity requires the maintenance of an illusory distance from the violences and injurious terms of identity formation, the performance of 'idealised' femininity entails the remanufacture and display of these violences of female identity formation as an art form, for example through ballet or fashion. Cultural stories also depict this arrangement, for example, the story of the birth of Aphrodite, goddess of beauty. Images of idealised femininity are manufactured through the stylised and disciplined arrangements of amalgams of violence and aggression, carefully displayed so as to recast them as beauty or glamour.

But the disavowed, abject, violent amalgams of aggression which are so central to the production of femininity will not go away. Instead they reside in the unconscious and on the fringes of consciousness, often appearing as bodily sensations, hallucinations and what Butler calls the 'abjected spectres' of identity (1997: 149). These amalgams of aggression which are culturally coded as Other to femininity actually haunt women's experience of their interiority, for instance as a sense of threat or danger beyond that justified by the external environment. Aggression is both split off from femininity yet, because of that split, unthinkably close to femininity so that the ghosts of these violences, hardnesses, cruelties and losses appear in fragments of women's images and thoughts, such as Isla's (Chapter 5) concerns about her mouth looking 'hard' in photographs. Sometimes these elements appear as semi-hallucinations, like Jane's 'outcasts' revisiting her as images of death standing with the people waiting for a bus in Chapter 3. These fragments of women's aggression are not usually brought together and rarely are they seen as expressions of a deeper struggle with identity and agency. The qualities in them are seldom enjoyed in the way Ella did when she talked admiringly (in Chapter 5) of the sign which showed five blocked roads near where she lived.

It is too easy to call these fragments of hardness, sharpness, darkness and potentially threatening unyieldingness 'masculine', and so avoid responsibility for them. I suggest, instead, that they are fragments of a femininity which is not based solely on *plaisir*, but is more transgressive, exploring the uncomfortable need to undo identity in order to learn about inner and outer Otherness. In contrast, a femininity which lacks this *jouissante* quality can be indiscriminate and suffocating. Aggressive and hateful energies are needed to create the possibility of separation, focus and movement, but the fragments of those energies which appear in women's inner lives are seldom linked together and recognised as manifestations of a wider pattern of aggression that is potentially meaningful.

Instead these fragments of aggressive energies are usually entwined with other emotions, fantasies and longings, and need to be seen as such in order for the potential embedded in them to become available for other amalgams. An example would be my interpretation of von Franz's response to her dream of the murderous burglar in Chapter 2. My emphasis was on the possibility that the attack was coming from von Franz's own aggressive energies which had been split off and appeared to be attacking her and her creative project (the book she was writing). I suggest that these energies could be seen as part of von Franz's desire to break into the 'bedroom' of her profession and steal (in the sense that 'good poets borrow, great poets steal') as a necessary part of the creative act. Her consciousness needed to claim back the ruthless, aggressive energies of the murderous burglar and put them to work in the service of her creativity, instead of working against it.

Reading the fragments of women's aggressive energies which crop up in everyday life in this way involves focusing on them as signs of resistance to identity. These moments of resistance are uncomfortable, sometimes terrifying, often shameful or deeply disquieting, sometimes joyous. Occasionally, as for Garner, in Chapter 1, they are an epiphany. Rarely do they fit within traditional theories of aggression. Women's aggressive energies have, historically, been made invisible as a result of the ways theories of aggression have been structured. These energies have, instead, been canalised into the very fabric of femininity, hence the unnerving sense of femininity as somehow dangerous or threatening that a number of the women contributors gestured towards.

Psychology and some branches of psychoanalysis take it for granted that these processes of canalisation are 'natural' and 'healthy', so that (for example) femininity is naturalised as the container of a safe space for the Other's agency. Again, this structure is particularly evident in object relations which uses as its primary amplificatory image the mother and infant couple in which the mother's aggressive energies are dissociated or denied in the service of the infant. This image may be accurate for some or many mother and infant couples, and for some of the time, but its status as a foundational 'truth' around which an entire psychological discourse is organised needs to be questioned. Undoubtedly, the mother and infant image is a powerful one and has a tendency to fascinate and entrance. But the point of psychoanalysis is to *examine* exactly these sorts of fascinating and numinous images as psychological entities, rather than become unreflectingly absorbed in them, mistaking their powerful emotional effects for psychological truth. This failure to turn the psychoanalytic reflective mindset back on its own discourse is one of the indicators that object relations is structured defensively around an unconscious fantasy. The notion that femininity is, or should be, a safe-making container for the Other's agency is a key element of that unconscious, defensive fantasy.

Such fantasies have two unacceptable consequences. First, they help to produce the kind of ugly situation in which Miss Baxter found herself (see Walkerdine's vignette in Chapter 1). Second, the failure to examine these unconscious fantasies means that the depth psychologies cannot provide a useful analysis of a predicament like Miss Baxter's because they rely on the same fantasies of femininity which created Miss Baxter's situation. These shared fantasies naturalise her position as the nurturing container of what gets labelled 'play', but is actually the enactment of violent and destructive amalgams of aggression. Furthermore, these pedagogic/developmentally-based humanist fantasies cut the ground out from under Miss Baxter's feet by normalising the boys' attack – after all, it is just part of their development, a normal part of play. In order to get any real grasp on her situation, Miss Baxter would need to be able to experience her own aggressive energies and fantasies as part of her own inner process, but she would also need to see the violences being done to her and the children in her care by the fantasies of femininity embedded in the liberal humanist discourse which structures her work environment. Again, the problem is that these are the same fantasies which structure much developmentally based, post-psychoanalytic clinical theory.

In the light of this, the performance of femininity involves the folding-down and dispersion of aggressive energies through women's patterns of movement (or, more often, lack thereof) and in their arrangement of appearance and speech. They are also dispersed through the ways women view their own bodies, how and when they experience themselves as visible, the images in their sexual fantasies, their relationships with food and in their relationships with other people. Women's aggressive energies, in particular, are caught up in the manufacture of the illusion of a safe space for the Other's agency and free movement. To do this, one needs to corral into one's body the mad, non-rational and anti-rational elements which have to be cleared away to make space for the fantasy of the rational, moral citizen, (traditionally signified as masculine). The use of one's physical presence to create such a space also entails the management of a double bind – it means that (as the container for the Other's fantasies) one is compulsively visible yet, at the same time, curiously invisible and anonymous, a situation which a number of women described themselves as managing in different ways (in Chapter 5).

In order for women to come to decide for themselves, on a circumstance-by-circumstance basis, whether and how much of these kinds of role they want to play for others, the aggressive energies which are usually fragmented and dispersed into the performance of femininity need to be seen for what they are. Then they need to be explored in terms of their *telos*, or direction. This is what I take Jung to have meant when he wrote that:

women often improve tremendously when they are allowed to think all the disagreeable things which they had denied themselves before.

(Jung, 1998, p.1105)

So what is involved in the turn from an identity based on melancholia towards an identity based on mourning? The women's contributions to this project indicate that what is required is the reflective noting of fragments of disagreeable thoughts and images, and the linking together of odd and unsettling physical sensations and ideas in ways which disturb identity. It also involves a turning away from the culturally-dominant metaphysics of presence, with its certainties about desire, towards a metaphysics of absence, with its *jouissante*, decentring desires. Such moves are possible through engagement with the sometimes shocking amalgams of aggression which are scattered through women's day-to-day lives.

WHEN THE DISPERSED AGGRESSIVE ENERGIES COALESCE

The two dreams cited in Chapter 1 offer a means of exploring these ideas. In the first, a woman who had read a paper of mine contacted me and told me the following dream. She is involved in larking about with other people which results in an explosion in a school-like building. It is as though it was the end of term, yet they are adults. Later she hears a rumour that someone suicided in the explosion – remains were found. The dreamer is left with the question of whether she will get away with her role in the explosion if she does not confess. Should she confess anyway? Later she also notices some of the explosive material had splashed onto her, wondered if others had seen it and realised her involvement. The dream horrified the dreamer.

This is a dream in which the dreamer actually gets a sense of herself as an agent of destruction, rather than (as in most of the images considered previously) the victim of such an agent. She is involved in something which (appears to have) contributed to a death, and she may (or may not) be found out for it. It is an unsettling dream because it raises questions about morality – why should one own up if there is a chance that one will get away with it? The dream presents the dreamer with a highly personalised glimpse of the dynamics behind Bersani's comment that the socialised superego 'is merely a cultural metaphor for the psychic fulfilment in each of us of a narcissistically thrilling wish to destroy the world' (1986: 23). As we experience that thrilling wish to destroy (or the pleasures of having destroyed), we simultaneously experience the cultural metaphor for it, which is conscience. Mandy Merck amplifies this when she writes that we dare not approach our own *jouissance* because behind it lies:

the law which 'makes it [*jouissance*] possible', the castrating prohibition which engenders our desire for its opposite. We confront [the law of our morals] at the peril of our own undoing, for it is powered by nothing less than the self-aggression which Freud discovered at the root of our conscience and our bliss. Suffice it to say, our morals are as difficult to come to terms with as our pleasures, because they *are* our pleasures.

(1993: 262, original italics)

Through aggressive fantasy we unleash the pleasures and energies which coincide with our morals and our conscience. In this way, our most private terrors and pleasures bring us into collision with the level at which our psyches are the product of cultural myths which work to conceal political motives and secretly circulate ideology through society (Warner, 1994: xiii). As argued in Chapter 2, these cultural myths are not apolitical, ahistorical and universal in the way Jung imagined, but neither are they optional and irrelevant. In the preface to *Madness and Civilization* Foucault describes the operation of the categories of psychopathology in a way which parallels the reading of myth which I am suggesting:

None of the concepts of psychopathology, even and especially in the implicit process of retrospections, can play an organizing role. What is constitutive is the action that divides madness, and not the science elaborated once the division is made and calm restored. What is originative is the caesura that establishes the distance between reason and non-reason; reason's subjugation of non-reason.

(1995: xi)

As Butler suggests, these originative caesuras which create the separations out of which identity is formed cannot be denied or refused (1997: 104–105). There is no freedom from them, or from the myths and stories which we create as the picture-book accounts of them. Yet agency remains possible in the sense that Butler implies when she writes that:

The critical task for feminism is not to establish a point of view outside of constructed identities; that conceit is the construction of an epistemological model that would disavow its own cultural location and, hence, promote itself as a global subject, a position that deploys precisely the imperialist strategies that feminism ought to criticise. The critical task is rather, to locate strategies of subversive repetition enabled by those constructions, to affirm the local possibilities of intervention through participating in precisely those practices of repetition that constitute identity and, therefore, present the immanent possibility of contesting them.

(1990: 147)

Butler's comments underline why I have not used the aspects of Jung's thought (archetypes, collective unconscious and so on) as he developed them because of their reliance on the fantasy of the global subject. Instead I have selected elements which support the kind of agency Butler gestures towards at the end of her comments, in which it is possible to intervene locally in the practices of repetition which maintain identity. These practices work by elaborating the culture's mythologised defences against the originative caesura which makes identity possible. These defences, which are the foundations of identity, can be resisted and subverted through the everyday resistances to identity which lie at the core of each of our psychic lives. This is why women's aggressive energies are important: they provide a point of contact with these complex conscious and unconscious, personal and cultural dynamics. Through that they also provide the possibility of agency, and connection.

Therefore I would suggest that, in the light of the explosive, deadly and inferno-like images brought up by the visibility exercise in Chapter 5, this explosive dream might represent the aggressive energies which are folded into women's flesh. The dream might be offering the dreamer a challenge: what would happen if you began to release these energies into the world and into relationships; would your moral fibre hold up in the face of the kind of power these energies might offer? Such questions are exactly what women encounter when they begin to explore their aggressive energies and fantasies in analysis. Women's aggressive energies have traditionally been invisible, and that has offered women ways of using them which are hard to trace. This creates the temptation to evade responsibility, so that questions of morality and power are especially important when thinking about women's aggressive energies.

In terms of the logic of the dream, a woman might get away with such an explosion simply because its source – the packed down aggressive energies which form the structure of her identity – is regarded as culturally invisible. She could, potentially, use that explosive aggression and, because she is female, deny that it could possibly have anything to do with her. Certainly, the explosive aggressions folded into her flesh through the formation of female identity would fail to attract the attention of any security system or sniffer dog looking for more conventional, more overt explosives.

In the other dream from Chapter 1, a woman saw an unknown man standing at the edge of a cliff. He lifted his hand to wave at her in a non-threatening way. She suddenly found her body being lifted into the air, against her will, until she was arranged like a torpedo, with her right arm stretched out like a battering ram. She felt her face contort in murderous hostility; her body was carried by an incredible force straight ahead towards this man, intent on killing him, even though she had no desire to do so.

In the light of the preceding chapters, the aggressive energies in this dream might represent what happens when the aggressions which are usually folded down to create the static, containing qualities of femininity get released. If femininity has been used to anchor an illusion of a safe space in which the Other exercises agency, this dream may represent the unleashing of hateful resentment which accompanies that identity structure. It could be an image of revenge for the way in which femininity has been used in cultural discourse, a kind of 'you think I'm perfectly contented, even delighted to be an invisible backdrop for your agency, well let me show you!' If so, the dream could be exploring a similar theme to the one Juliette raised in Chapter 5 with her fantasy of being able to burgle men's minds while they read her 'plainness' as making her a form of wallpaper, a backdrop for their desire.

In this way, both dream images can be seen as aggressive energies which are usually dispersed and remanufactured into the structure of femininity becoming visible. If these dreams are thought of as the voices of women's disavowed and dispersed aggressive energies, they are saying: 'watch out, you nice woman, and the people around you. I am furious about being cooped up and treated as though I don't exist. I urgently want to find out what I am capable of. In particular I need to find out whether I would do monstrous and destructive things if I thought I would get away with them, simply because I could.' A first-round contribution from Helena speaks of how hard it is to come to terms with these energies within oneself.

> **Helena:** Even when I see the outrageous atrocities being committed around the world predominantly against women, although one part of me explodes with anger and hate, I know that the energy of the perpetrator lies also within me. I know I too am the torturer, rapist, mutilator. However, my mind tells me that this is an impossibility. I know the universal energy of this horror must have its voice deep down within me, just by the fact that I am human.

These concerns provide a link back to the images in Chapter 4 where women spoke of their free-floating fears of someone cutting their hair off in a cinema, or ripping a dangly earring down through their earlobe, just because they could, and because they knew that they would get away with it. It is also these energies which Doris' psychopath dream in Chapter 4 expresses in extreme form. At the other end of the spectrum are the connective aggressive energies which I sought to amplify in my commentary on Lizzie's anorexic battlefield imagery in Chapter 6.

Such an interpretation would imply that the dreams of explosion and flying presented the dreamers with pressures from their unconscious to change the basis on which they engage with others. Both dreams demand a re-examination of the basis of morality and love, in the way that Hart's analysand's urge to push the Sherpa off the cliff did in Chapter 2. That urge gave rise to the analysand realising that being a reactive victim to circumstances is a form of violence, and that engagement with aggressive energies can generate agency.

Also embedded in the destructive amalgams of aggression, rage and hatred depicted in these two dreams is the NO! which came up in Ella's (Chapter 4) discussion of the sign showing five blocked roads. It is the NO! which Courtin said to the men who raped her (see Chapter 3). Even though she could not stop the rape, she was able to refuse to be positioned in the way they intended.

Likewise, Dolores said a similar NO! when she stopped the man who was lunging at her sexually by saying 'what the fuck do you think you are doing?', and shocked him into stopping and thinking about what he was doing. Clearly there are times when this NO! is overridden by external circumstances, such as the accounts of having been raped given by Dolores and Ella (and in Dolores' case, nearly murdered) in Chapter 4.

NO! IN RELATIONSHIP

Vivienne's discussion of her letter to Geoff, also discussed in Chapter 4 is, however, an example of a woman using her potentially explosive, cutting aggressive energies in a morally engaged and relational way. The result is not safe or comfortable: Vivienne's letter 'uncontains' the aggression which had settled into destructive amalgams and patterns in the relationship. In this uncontained state, aggression could have easily become caught up in divisive, melancholic amalgams, but Vivienne's account provides a series of clues about why this did not occur. First, she considered at length how she felt and what she thought about her marriage to Geoff before writing the letter. Second, the letter she wrote was not full of blame and resentment – it simply said what was not working for her, and left Geoff the space to respond to that, allowing for his previous history of answering honestly, even when to do so would be painful or awkward. Above all though, Vivienne's descriptions imply a fight with herself about what to do. And this is a fight which she sees through until her answer is clear. She then uses her own aggressive energies to cut free of her own fantasies of dependency and helplessness. This is important – Vivienne does not just fight endlessly with herself. She knows when that process has gone as far as it can go, and she knows that the next step is to involve the Other in the fight.

Again, aggressive energies are not the enemy of relationship. They are a crucial aspect of the glue which holds a relationship together. Vivienne's description of her letter to Geoff was a second-round contribution, as was a story from Jane about a similar moment in the development of her relationship.

Jane: Not long after I moved in with my then boyfriend (in my mid-twenties), a huge row blew up over the simplest thing. One day he opened the fridge and said 'there's no orange juice'. Me: 'yes, that's right' (hair on back of neck starting to stand up, having watched my mum wait on my dad hand, foot and finger for years). Him: 'but couldn't you have got some when you went shopping?' Me (starting to feel scared and sick and jelly-like): 'Yes, I could have if you had reminded me to get it. I don't drink orange juice, so you need to remind me if you need it'. Him: 'surely you must have noticed that I was running out?' Me: 'no, I don't drink orange juice, so it's not something I notice or think about. I'm happy to get it for you, but you are the one who uses it, and you need to tell me if you want me to get some'. This row went on (off and on) for three days. I remember sitting on the bus, going to work in the dark one morning thinking, 'well, that's that I suppose. The briefest cohabitation in the history of relationships'. But I knew I couldn't give in. Just because I'm female doesn't mean that I come ready made to manage the lives of everyone around me, take total responsibility for their needs and think about what they could run out of, before it happens. Stuff that. Anyway, the row was awful. It felt like I was being cruel to a fluffy, cute, brown-eyed animal. I felt so guilty, like a mass murderer or something. He couldn't believe that I could be so unsupportive, so unreasonable. I knew that if I gave in on this one, I was finished. We had to sort out the fact that I wasn't his mum and wasn't prepared to have one of those relationships where fifteen years later you just count him as one of the kids. He's just someone else who you have to manage because you are the only grownup around. I wanted a man who could act like a father when we got to that bit, not someone who was going to be too busy with his work while I drowned in a sea of domestic crap. I could just picture it – years of seething resentment and dead of cancer by the time I was sixty. Eventually we got through it. I knew I had to hold my ground and just hope that we could keep at each other for long enough to sort it out. Without the capacity to do that, we would never have lasted.

Like Vivienne, Jane knows that sometimes love means taking a fight right down to the wire. Note, however, that also like Vivienne, she manages to keep her aggression and toughness relatively free of revenge or fear. Jane is not pre-emptively attacking, or nasty for the sake of it. She knows that she has to find out what is real in the relationship, sooner rather than later. In spite of fearing that her actions might end the relationship, Jane is aware that (again, like Vivienne) if she does not fight, the relationship is over anyway.

For Jane (or Vivienne) to have made a melancholic turn in relation to the losses and violences of identity formation would have meant continuing to internalise the struggle with her relationship interminably, keeping all the energy of the fight and aggression to herself. In doing so, important energies would have been kept out of the relationship, steadily starving it of aliveness and commitment. Melancholic fantasies about how the relationship used to be, or still could be (one day, if only he loved me . . .), accumulate. This turn towards a melancholic position involves a backing-away from muscular tussles. It is often driven by a fear-born sense of despair that the Other may not want or be able to fight fairly, or that the two parties are not able to hang in through the tussle and use it to learn something about themselves and their desires. I suggest that these melancholic turns which are so much part of the performance of recognisable femininity can become murderous resentment, which then appears in images such as the two women's dreams discussed earlier. The resultant desire is to finally unleash the resentment and get away with it.

Instead, both Jane and Vivienne use connective amalgams of their aggressive energies to say a NO! which calls for an honest response from their partner. And again, in both cases there is a willingness to use aggression and clarity to strip away the fantasies and assumptions about what the Other could or should provide. In this way it is possible to weather loss and disappointment in order to discover what holds when the relationship seems to be coming apart.

TURNING TO JELLY

Note also how Jane has a strong, fearful physical reaction as she realises the level of difference which is emerging between her and her boyfriend and starts to position herself in order to hold her line in relation to it. Mary made a similar point about her reactions to her own aggressive energies in a first-round contribution to the project.

> **Mary:** There are lots of different images of aggressions and angers for me. There's pushing people off a high building, exploding in their face (just when they think I've given up), imploding into a black hole and taking the whole damn galaxy with me, stabbing them a million times, nuclear-vaporisation of the entire planet, and so on. What comes out of my mouth as I watch this happen inside myself and feel my neck spasm is either: 'that's fine', or, if I'm doing well it's: 'could we, perhaps, consider an alternative (please)?' By then I am usually wobbly inside and close to tears.

Mary's initial comments imply that for her, aggressive energies and fantasies are familiar and comfortable. But her final comments indicate the extent of the gap between her inner life and her capacity to stand up for herself. Again, I would suggest that the absence of any cultural narratives which connect the fragments of women's energies with agency and identity make it difficult for a woman to negotiate this gap.

Nonetheless, Mary offered a further contribution in which she discusses how an aggressive fantasy was an initial step in a longer process of learning how to stand up for herself. Interestingly, this contribution was a revenge fantasy, whose object was to make a spectacle of another woman. This was a woman who had been undermining her and treating her with contempt in the company of her peers at work for some time. As a young woman, new to the adult workforce, Mary had put up with this, hoping it would 'blow over', but it had not. Eventually it became intolerable and Mary's 'snap' came in the form of an aggressive fantasy.

> **Mary:** I was still stinging from Cheryl's last swipe at me, thinking over how I could have avoided it, or managed it better when I got this image. In it, I had a pelvis which would rotate so that my vagina faced in any direction – like a gun turret on a tank. I'd be able to use my insides to squeeze together a nice ball of menstrual blood and fire it at Cheryl so it would splat in her face – in public with the rest of our peers present – and knock her off her silly high heels! She'd be wearing one of those ugly tight little-girl outfits she seemed to have a wardrobe full of. I'd like to say that after that I never looked back. Not true, but I have learnt over the years to look after myself a bit better, and giving myself permission to think about dropping heavy things on people, blowing them up, and so on has helped a lot.

Mary was able to turn her work situation into a heroic cartoon strip and through that explore a fantasy of launching an amalgam of attacking aggressive energies on Cheryl. Note, however, that Mary positions this image as a single step in a journey. Making use of these energies in relationship is profoundly difficult for women but, as Mary describes it, being able to have such fantasies can be an important part of coming to be able to 'look after oneself a bit better'. I wonder what would happen if Miss Baxter had enough internal space to imagine attacking her boy pupils in this way, or some representative of the school system who was policing her performance of her role.

THE XENAVERSE AND THE DICE MAN

Doris also made a second-round contribution in which she describes her struggle to link an awareness of her own aggressive energies and fantasies to the day-to-day world.

Doris: In the last year I've developed a fascination for the now completed series 'Xena, Warrior Princess'. When it was being screened on broadcast TV I ignored it because there's this big lesbian cult following of the show – a sort of knee jerk reaction on my part not to watch (you know, like all lesbians are supposed to like listening to k.d. laing). Anyway, I have cable now and they screen these fests of cult shows and I accidentally tuned in one 'Xenarama' and was hooked. Apart from the fact that it really is an extraordinary show in terms of what it does with women, what I was hooked by was the Xena character – she is a character disallowed, or even unthinkable, previous to this. An anti-heroine, a woman who for ten years after the sacking of her village went on a crazed rampage at the head of an army (or many armies) – often referred to as 'destroyer of nations' killing thousands of people for pleasure – serious pleasure. Then (previous to the show's curtain raiser) she has a blacker than black dark night of the soul and sets out in search of redemption. In a constant struggle with her dark side, the one that takes pleasure in causing pain and death, she is at the same time battling the many minions of untold evil in her path towards the light (and, you would have to say, enjoying every minute of it). What struck me most was the actress Lucy Lawless's interpretation of the role – honestly, I have never seen a woman on screen look so happy wielding a sword and killing things. Most female superheroes have this sort of 'well if I have to, I will' attitude to killing – Xena as performed by Lucy Lawless, with her 'kill 'em all' war cry unsheathes her sword with such glee it's absolutely infectious. The show is an amazing foray into women's expressions of rage – there's a lot of other women in the Xenaverse with a penchant for feats of arms – whether it's in the cause of enlightenment or a crazed lunge for power. And sooo entertaining. You should see the Xena sand play pit I've made of my office in the vain pursuit of an answer to the question of what to do with the rage – it's almost an installation.

The Xenaverse looks as if it may offer a vehicle for engaging with aggressive energies. It even suggests that there is a link between aggression and the processes of developing morality and identity. But what is missing is what Haraway refers to when she says that '[s]elf-knowledge requires a semiotic-material technology to link meanings and bodies' (1997: 288). The missing semiotic-material technology is the knowledge that aggressive energies are secretly about connection, but the structure of femininity makes it extremely difficult to access these potentials.

I reintroduce the quotation from Samuels, used in Chapter 1, which articulates clearly this connective potential in aggressive fantasy:

> Aggressive fantasy promotes a vital style of consciousness . . . Aggressive fantasy has much to do with our desire to know; it is not, in itself, completely bloodstained and unreflective. . . . Aggressive fantasy can bring into play that interpersonal separation without which the word 'relationship' would have no meaning. In this sense, aggressive fantasy may want to make contact, get in touch, relate. . . . Aggressive fantasy forces an individual to consider the conduct of personal relations. When one fantasises an aggressive response to one's desires on the part of the other, one is learning something about that other as a being with a different but similar existence to one's own. Without aggressive fantasy, there would simply be no cause for concern about other people and so aggressive fantasy points beyond ruthlessness to discover the reality and mystery of persons. 'It is only when intense aggressiveness exists between two individuals that love can arise.'
>
> (1989: 208–209, quoting Storr)

Earlier I offered an interpretation of the two women's dreams from Chapter 1. That reading suggested that these dreams depicted explosive and attacking amalgams of aggression which are usually dispersed in the structure and performance of femininity. Viewed through these dreams, the Xena character provides a vehicle for repeated explorations of the ways in which various amalgams of aggression can play out in the world. Xena refuses to use her aggressive energies to anchor any kind of a space for the Other, let alone a safe one. But, unlike the two women's dreams discussed earlier, the moral learning embedded in aggressive fantasies and energies is touched on (which is what gives the series its interest), but is largely lost. Basically, there is no problem with Xena doing what she can do and getting away with it.

It is thrilling to see a woman depicted in Xenaverse terms, but the gap between it and ordinary, relational life and struggles with agency too easily becomes the object of cultural manipulation. Xena is much more hands-on than Rider Haggard's Ayesha, yet both stories depict women who are cartoon-like in their power. The problem with both is that their power is not subject to the kinds of difficulties which Walkerdine's Miss Baxter vignette illustrated in Chapter 1. Power is complex, and women's power and aggressive energies are particularly susceptible to having their value reassigned according to how and where the individual woman is positioned discursively.

This is what is usually missing from the mytho-poetic explorations of images of powerful women.

These mythic, heroic figures of women appear to offer a turn towards a gender identity based on mourning, rather than melancholia, but there is a sleight of hand involved. In reality, such moves (and the development of the kind of agency they entail) are paradoxically only possible at points where agency is failing. These moments are often accompanied (as described in Chapter 4) by extreme despair and a sense of abject helplessness. In other words, the kind of agency which matters, the kind which can *really* turn a melancholic identity structure into a livelier one based on mourning, does not arise in places where one feels in control or able to move easily.

The Xenaverse does not provide Doris with real clues about what to do with the rage because it does not engage in a sustained way with the tension, desperation and sense of helplessness which accompany ordinary women's aggressive energies. These kinds of unbearable tensions are what Vivienne and Jane exemplified when they used their aggressive energies to challenge their relationships. The processes of drawing the love, connection and agency out of aggressive energies is painful and often involves the breakdown or surrender of what one previously thought mattered enormously, whether that is a relationship, or an aspect of one's inner life or identity. Only under those kinds of pressures does it really *matter* whether aggressive energies have a *telos* of morality and connection.

Sara expressed this kind of desperate, helpless place in her second-round contribution.

Sara: I remember (fairly clearly) the day I was knocked down. I was feeling depressed/apart from/numb. I decided I would walk across a busy road without looking and if I got to the other side alive I would do my best to live for others. When I was knocked down I felt OK. It was too sudden to hurt and I was still numbish – not at all upset. The next day I was sore. The young man who knocked me down came to see me with his mum and dad and a box of chocs. I told him it was my fault – I said I wasn't used to all the traffic. I signed something saying it wasn't his fault. They thanked me and I was glad it wasn't him who might have killed me. He and his family were very nice. Suicide has always been an option. I call it my 'Dice Man' solution. If I get out of this, I live. I throw a mental dice.

This is a very different use of aggressive energy. In this context, I read Sara as describing a psychological place of extreme depression and despair in which she has become trapped and numb in a melancholic, lifeless state. The Dice Man gamble uses the Other to try to break that state open. From this perspective, walking out into the traffic is an attempt to externalise aggressive energies and collide with those externalised energies.

The psychological component of Sara's actions might be that she is trying to feel (as her own) the aggressive energies which she is externalising. She might be trying to find a way of undoing herself, of using the hard, fast-moving surfaces of the outside world to break open the trap of her identity, when what is needed is for her to develop a sense of the hard, fast-moving surfaces within her. It is these surfaces which, if owned as qualities of hers, might enable her to rage against melancholic identity structures and refuse to join the parts of herself and the world around her which are already dead. In the same way that von Franz needed to make the murderous burglar in her dream serve her creativity, Sara might be trying to make the hard, mobile parts of her feminine identity structure work for her, rather than needing to collide with them in the outside world. She might need to develop a sense of being able to knock down what gets in her way in order to move against the 'apart from/numb' state which she describes. Again, note how the energies which are disavowed include aggression and impulses towards powerful mobility.

THE MAJOR PSYCHOPATH AROUND HERE IS ME . . .

Developing this sense of the hard, sharp or explosive qualities of one's personality is, as we have seen, extremely difficult for women, as it involves stepping outside of cognisable identity into realms of uninhabitable helplessness. Yet the material which arises in women's inner lives demands this move. One of Ella's first-round contributions describes her struggle to come to terms with what might be called her 'inner psychopath'.

> **Ella:** My knee jerk anger against men (which is largely unreasonable and certainly unhelpful in the move towards world peace) is going to give me a hell of a spiritual hoop to jump through. Sometimes I have to ask myself who the hell I think I am – if I analyse my speech there is plenty of viciousness. There but for the Grace of God go I, and not by a long way either. But why am I so keen to be the good guy, sorry person? 'Well, Ella, you didn't change the world but at least you kept your hands clean'. I don't know, but it doesn't help anyone, that's for sure. I'm beginning to suspect that the major psychopath around here is me.

Again, the dilemma for a woman facing her own aggressive energies is the temptation to construct herself exclusively as the victim of these energies, and avoid responsibility for them. Indeed, Ella implies that while parts of her want to offload responsibility for destructive and vicious amalgams of aggressive energies onto men, part of her knows that to do so is fraudulent. In Chapter 3 I used a quotation from David Cooper's introduction to Foucault's *Madness and Civilization* to discuss the losses involved in turning away from the abject, mad, monstrous parts of ourselves:

> We chose to conjure up this disease [of madness] in order to evade a certain moment of our own existence – the moment of disturbance, of penetrating vision into the depths of ourselves, that we prefer to externalise into others. Others are elected to live out of the chaos that we refuse to confront in ourselves. By this means we escape a certain anxiety, but only at a price that is as immense as it is unrecognised.
>
> (Cooper, 1995: viii)

Ella's comments suggest that she is aware of her own struggle *not* to externalise her own disturbance (the disturbance that is actually her). While part of her very much wants to be rid of the chaos and undone states which aggressive energies bring with them, I suggest that Ella is also aware that the price of doing so would be unacceptable. In Chapter 6, Jenny's goblin of self-hatred repeatedly smashed the glass room of her safe, secure world by reintroducing desire, aggression, rage and, ultimately, a sense of personal boundaries. Similarly, Ella cannot be rid of her chaos without losing her own desire, aliveness and the possibility of a penetrating vision into herself and those around her.

What is seen through the kind of penetrating vision on offer here may not be comfortable but it can, in the way of Jane's morphing animal faces in Chapter 3, provide important information about how the margins of one's consciousness experience the world. Those margins, where the performance of intelligible identity is less well regulated, can offer a richness of perception which is usually filtered out by the fantasy of the unified and coherent 'I'. If Ella were able to rid herself of these parts of her interiority she would lose the grounds for developing her own sense of morality and the potential to take up the connective *telos* of her own aggressive energies.

One of Dolores' second-round comments also took up the theme of questioning what Ella referred to as her knee-jerk anger against men.

Dolores: While I was reading your thesis a little scenario occurred that I paid attention to because I was reading it. Recently I was visiting some friends; the woman has led a very independent life. Like me, she has no particular axe to grind (need to feel angry and victimised on a personal level) but like me, I guess she has some anger at that amorphous thing I can only call 'the patriarchy'. This is what happened: Male dog is out of control and must be 'snipped'. He comes home after the op. very sorry for himself and us girls, I have to say, we aren't terribly sympathetic. We go, 'oh, poor Snowy' but in tones of merriment!! Husband comes home, puts dog on lap for cuddling, says with tones of genuine sympathy, 'oh poor boy, I know how you feel'. We are still chuckling. I thought, neither of us is a heartless bitch so why are we laughing because the dog has lost his balls? Later, the husband says to me, 'oh they (wife and daughters) are always ganging up on me and bossing me around'. I said, 'well, Dave, at least they haven't had you snipped!' He laughed and then said darkly, 'well they might as well have done!' I told my friend later and we laughed! And I notice, that I'm grinning as I type this. It's not really that funny but I'm laughing from a sort of inner delight. Dave is a nice guy, it's nothing personal at all, it's just representative of something that we carry around with us from cradle to grave, that we have to carry all this stuff about not being good enough and then we see some representative of the supposedly glorious and superior sex brought low and we have to laugh. It's at times like this you begin to get a hint of the extent of the damage.

Dolores notes how she almost automatically gets caught in a sadistic, vengeful fantasy. By picking the fantasy up, and bringing it to consciousness, however, she starts to explore what she describes as her 'inner delight' at Dave's uncomfortable identification with the desexed male dog. As Dolores becomes aware of this cruel pleasure, it flips over and she starts to question how it comes to operate automatically in her. As she explores that, her understanding broadens and becomes sadder, more compassionate, seeing gender warfare as a mark of damage. This echoes the way in which Isla's fantasy of raping the rapist (Chapter 4) revealed something of the Otherness of the Other. In Dolores' case, conscious exploration of her aggressive fantasy revealed something about the Otherness within her.

Again, as with Ella's comments, my sense is that Dolores knows that the automatic, sadistic, gender warfare position may be pleasurable, but it involves a turn towards a melancholia-based metaphysics of presence. Such a move offers the pleasure of feeling safe and certain that there is a 'glorious and superior' Other sex (even if one hates them) against whom one has scored a point. But the scoring of this point is a pyrrhic victory: it actually entrenches the fantasy of the power of the Other.

Women's explorations of their own aggressive fantasies and energies question the nature of the Other's power not through a sense of being able to 'beat' them, but through the knowledge that what sustains the Other's feared power is partly one's own anxieties about using one's own knife-like, or explosive aggressions in order to see the Other more clearly. This parallels what Garner realised in her fencing bout in Chapter 1. By engaging her aggressive energies in fights which were about the art of fighting well, rather than simply about applying brute force in order to win, she learnt important things about her own mind and body. Likewise, when reflected upon from outside a 'lose–win' frame of reference, the aggressive energies which arise in Dolores' story become connective. They turn away from familiar gender positions, with their known powers and fantasies about the Other. As she turns away from these fantasies, Dolores opens up the question of gender as damage, which invites a move into the metaphysics of absence, engaging with unknown but enlivening, decentring desires and senses of identity.

Dolores' move in some ways parallels the object relations move to the depressive position, but it seems to me that much is lost if it is assumed to be just that. First, the notion of the 'depressive position' originates from a mother and baby-centred discourse which is predicated on the exclusion (or at the very least, bracketing) of adult women's aggressive, desirous and demanding energies. These are the kinds of energies Dolores is discussing, and using a tool to understand them which is fashioned through their exclusion cannot work. Object relations is also steeped in a metaphysics of presence: the importance of the maternal presence, the container, the emphasis on coming to know the meaning of desires, its traditional emphasis on heterosexuality and parenthood as developmental goals, and so on. Again, it makes little sense to use a concept which is the product of a conservative identity discourse to explore radical notions such as gender as the product of damage, and the decentring desires which destabilise socially recognisable identity.

Dolores articulated another aspect of the importance of trying to move from a gender identity based on melancholia to one based on mourning when writing about her own experience of the 60s' and 70s' arguments about women's agency as penis envy.

Dolores: Now, on the subject of women's aggression and agency: This morning, thinking about what I would write, I remembered how, in the 60s' and early 70s' before women's studies etc took hold, every thought that a woman expressed that was authentic and that stepped beyond the corset of what was 'appropriate feminine behaviour' was labelled penis envy! If I had a dollar for every time I was accused by some wanker of having that or a castration complex, I'd be a rich woman! Freud has a lot to answer for! But it was an effective way of silencing women. Now I'm happy to see that you don't bother to mention it but it was terribly influential because it did turn you back to arguing about whether that was true instead of getting on and moving forward. One day on a nudist beach in South Australia, it occurred to me that if anyone should feel insecure about their genitals it was men not the other way round and that it was extremely unlikely that I had unconsciously ever wanted to have one, and that what I was angry about was the inequality of power.

Dolores is discussing women's aggressive energies and agency, and as she does so she moves from an account of futile, energy-sapping arguments about women's supposed penis envy to an image of male vulnerability which introduces questions about male power.

FANTASIES OF MASCULINITY

One reading of this move is that gathering back the aggressive energies and agency which were wasted on futile arguments in previous decades required the capacity to cut through cultural fantasies about male power. What is revealed when she does so is an image of a naked man, whose genitals render him highly vulnerable. In a similar way Segal questions the psychoanalytic notion that men fear women because they appear castrated. She suggests (through the work of Susan Lurie) instead, that men fear women and construct them as castrated because women are not castrated despite the fact that they have no penis (1994: 137). Waldby spells out the cultural fantasies which lie behind this system of fears:

> The culture's privileging of masculinity means that the hegemonic bodily imago of masculinity conforms with his status as sovereign ego, the destroyer, and that of women with the correlative status of the one who is made to conform to this ego, the destroyed. The male body is understood as phallic and impenetrable, as a war-body simultaneously armed and armoured, equipped for victory. The female body is its opposite, permeable and receptive, able to absorb all this violence. In other words, boundary difference is displaced outwards from (imaginary) genital difference. The fantasy of the always hard and ready penis/phallus characterises the entire surface of the male body, while the fantasy of the soft accommodating and rather indeterminate vagina is synecdochal for the entire feminine body.
>
> (1995: 268)

As Dolores' reflections suggest, however, one look at the male body when it is not sexually aroused (in other words, as it is most of the time) gives the lie to this cultural fantasy. It takes a certain use of aggressive energies to be clear-eyed enough to see this because it involves a refusal to evade (as Cooper suggests above) a disturbing moment of interiority. What is being seen is that the eroticised melancholic fantasies about gender, which form such an important part of cognisable personhood, are simply hollow performances of dressing up and displaying differences, while simultaneously using them to evade the terrifying chaos and madness which lies at the edges of identity.

Women's aggressive fantasies disrupt this melancholic imaginal field, demanding that notions of passivity and activity, penetrability and vulner-ability be reconsidered. Indeed, Segal uses Jean Laplanche's question '[i]s penetration more active than receiving the penis?' (1994: 243) to question the ideological basis of the Freudian narrative which links activity and passivity to fantasies about sexual difference. Again, Courtin's reaction to her rapists involved a refusal of the cultural fantasy that an erect penis signifies a phallic, powerful and impenetrable male body. She was able to hold onto the know-ledge that attached to the erections were a couple of frightened, pathetic, useless bullies.

INNER AND OUTER EXPERIENCE

While writing this book, I have wondered what a parallel account of the experiences of masculinity might show. What are the kinds of images at the edges of male identity, how does it break down and under what conditions? Are these zones populated by images of catastrophic collapses, explosions and physical attacks of various forms as they are for women? How do the decentred metaphysics of absence-based desires which are available on these margins manifest themselves? How and where do men eroticise the distances they have to fabricate from the injurious terms and violences of identity formation? Exactly how much freedom does the traditional association of aggression with masculinity give individual men to engage with these vio-lences and their attendant amalgams of aggression? What factors influence those freedoms, both in terms of their development, and the ways in which they play out, circumstance by circumstance, identity position by identity position? The questions are endless, and while I am interested in them as they arise in work with male analysands, my sense is that exploring them system-atically, in the kind of countertransferential way I have with women's aggres-sive fantasies and energies, would produce different results if the researcher were a man, or group of men.

Whatever might emerge from such a project, I would imagine that it would strike the same problem I have struggled with throughout this book, which is how to link deeply felt, personal struggles with interiority to wider, external issues of cultural fantasies about gender and the range of inequalities that are predicated upon those fantasies. My use of the concept of an identity based on gender mourning and/or melancholia is an attempt to create such a link. But behind it lies Walkerdine's critical psychological approach in which power is viewed as not being a static or simple entity – it is a series of dynamics which fluctuate within ranges so that:

> girls and women do not take up *any* position in *any* discourse. Their signification as girls and women matters. It means that the positions available to them exist *only* within certain limits. These limits are material

– not in the sense that they are directly *caused* by the materiality of the female body, but certainly by the limits within which that body can signify in current discursive practices.

(Walkerdine, 1990: 14, original italics)

To use Walkerdine's language, the particular pressures which incline a woman towards a melancholic identity structure operate through the ways in which femininity is used as a signifier in current discursive practices. Femininity brings with it two sets of melancholic gradients. First, there are those gradients which determine where and how girls and women can position themselves in social discourse. This is what Miss Baxter was up against in the vignette in Chapter 1. Her role was defined through a system which used femininity and associated fantasies about unconditionally containing, nurturing environments in ways which determined how Miss Baxter could afford to see herself and what was happening around her. Again, this is where the perspective I am offering differs from that of object relations: Miss Baxter's predicament, and that of many women, calls for a model which engages with the way that the psychological is always shot through with identity politics. These politics are not abstract matters: they create gradients, flows and no-go zones within women's internal landscapes and bodies. Such material can be analysed as aspects of interiority (without turning sessions into political discussions as a substitute for analysis) provided interiority is seen as both highly personal, private, and potentially meaningful, and, simultaneously, arising out of a socially determined 'I-slot'.

Second, there are the inner processes of how these gradients are felt, how they are lived, and the kinds of experiences and images which accompany women's struggles to engage with them. Actually, this distinction between inner and outer is deeply problematic, even as it is unavoidable. The cultural 'I-slots' in which we come to live our lives constrain our self-reflexivity, even as that self-reflexivity provides us with the means to examine how the processes of identity formation have fashioned us. My response to the falsehood of this distinction is to use Jung's dissociationist heritage which offers simultaneous access to the 'I', which I experience myself to be, and the 'Not-I within', which is excluded from identity in order for identity to exist. This 'Not-I within', as I am using it, includes both material which could potentially be assimilated into a liveable identity (and is approachable through developmentally based depth psychologies), as well as levels of inner Otherness which are cultural. These culturally defined inner Othernesses (in other words, the possible identities which must be excluded for culturally recognisable identity to exist) are much more difficult to engage with because of the ways in which they threaten individual and social identity as outlined in the preceding chapters. Of course, the possibilities of unravelling or shattering of identity which are associated with these excluded realms means that that which is Other to cognisable personhood is both the object of fascination and terror, and also the margin where desire becomes possible.

But this distinction between the 'I' and the 'Not-I' is also inadequate, even as it struggles to express something about the human condition.[1] As Nancy Mairs suggests:

> The utterance of an 'I' immediately calls into being its opposite, the 'not-I,' Western discourse being unequipped to conceive 'that which is neither "I" nor "not-I," ' 'that which is both "I" and "not-I," ' or some other permutation which language doesn't permit me to speak. The 'not-I' is, by definition, other.
>
> (1997: 299)

The permutations of identity which are of most interest to me are essentially unspeakable. They lie in the realms of the metaphysics of absence, beyond development psychologies, beyond dualisms such as 'I' and 'Not-I', but this is where language fails. Hence my need to resort to unsatisfactory oversimplifications which distort, even as they (hopefully) point beyond their own limitations. Again, however, the value of the psychoanalytic endeavour is that it '*depends on* a process of theoretical collapse' (Bersani, 1986: 3, original italics). In this collapse something of the nature of the unconscious may be revealed. My attempts at engaging with women's aggressive energies has shown, above all else, that even as these energies collapse, explode or evade all the terms which I have attempted to use to explore them, they can (as suggested in Chapter 4) act as the gateway to the reality and mystery of persons.

Shildrick summarises Derrida's notion of the self in a way which sheds light on this:

> Not only does representation precede meaning, but the primary term is both literally meaningless without the margins of its own discourse, and unable to erase the trace of its others. What that means in terms of the subject is that the self does not precede its differentiation from the other – the multiple others homogenised here into a single category – *but is founded in the very project of setting boundaries.*
>
> (italics added)

[. . . thus . . .]

> The 'I', the supposedly sovereign, timeless and self-identical individual of liberal humanist discourse is exposed as (1) just another signifier reliant for even provisional definition on its other, the 'you', and (2) as radically incorporating the trace of that other which will always frustrate the claim to purity and autonomy of the primary term.
>
> (Shildrick, 1997: 151)

We are unable to erase the trace of our Others, the cultural 'Not-I' which is both our inner Otherness, and through that, our portal to the outer Otherness of the world. The self is a product of the processes which set its boundaries – the losses which attend the formation of identity. Rather than trying to rid oneself of the marks of these losses, Derrida's view suggests that concentrating on the Otherness which defines us would be more meaningful. This is the basis of my interest in Jung's dissociationist heritage since the reading of it proposed in Chapter 2 offers a way of moving beyond the specific Other of the 'object relations mother' out towards the Otherness of identity production without getting caught up in the grand-narrative aspects of Jung's system of thought. Paying attention to the 'Not-I within' so that its character can emerge over time reveals something of the traces of these bigger, wider Others within us, a process which can be radically destabilising. Yet it can also be a great relief and joy to discover that one's interiority is a 'community of souls', with all the tensions and creativity that can offer.

AGGRESSIVE ENERGIES AND THE CALL TO CITIZENSHIP

A second-round comment from Vivienne amplifies the struggle with unresolvable inner plurality and how it can come to be recognised as the substance of a woman's life and her connection to the world.

> **Vivienne:** If I were at home in my body there'd be almost nothing I couldn't do. I suppose I'd have a quite fabulous sex life. I probably wouldn't have married Geoffrey in the first place. Perhaps I wouldn't be anxious and neurotic and fearing failure. Perhaps I'd be articulate and not so fuzzy too. I think I'd be full of confidence and would dare to do exactly what I want to do. I'd just get the vision and take the steps. But ... perhaps it wouldn't be so interesting or interested. If I'd been at home in my body I mightn't have had a therapy. I mightn't have had all those low rumbling fears and guilts and got involved with the multiculturalism and minority rights movements. I might have been so engrossed in material existence that I mightn't have noticed diversity and depth. I might have just merged into bourgeois society and mainstream life and been forever surface and trivial. I might never have thought about land and body, encountered aboriginal depths, involved myself in pagan meditations or how I can re-negotiate with Pan/Dionysos. If I hadn't been in exile I couldn't have made the wonderful and terrible journey back.

If Vivienne were able to create the illusion of what Shildrick describes as 'the supposedly sovereign, timeless and self-identical individual of liberal human-ist discourse' she would, perhaps, have been more comfortable. She would have been able to blend in with mainstream society more effectively, but as she says, she might not have noticed diversity and depth. Above all she would not have been brought into relationship with her culture's 'Not-I' through issues of multiculturalism and minority rights. Nor would she have been brought into contact with her own inner Othernesses, her own 'Not-I within', a process which she describes as a wonderful and terrible journey back from exile. She would have missed out not only on living the liveable life within her, but also on mourning the unlived and unliveable lives within her. Through that acceptance of loss and process of mourning, Vivienne becomes more of who she is.

Note how part of what stops Vivienne fitting in with bourgeois society is that she is not at home in her body. She is unable to 'live' her body in such a way as to disperse or naturalise the injurious terms which call her into being. Instead, she is fuzzy, anxious and neurotic. Again, as Redfearn (1994) sug-gests, the body is the gateway to the 'Not-I within' and its sufferings call us back again and again to the chaos and madness which would otherwise displace onto others, both individually and culturally.

Ella also took up the theme of identity and politics in her second-round re-sponse in which she quotes from what she believed to be Nelson Mandela's inaugural speech in 1994. In fact this speech is not by Mandela (see note 2 for further explanation), but what matters in this context is how Ella used what she believed to be a speech by Mandela to move around in her inner landscape in important ways. In order to retain the spirit of Ella's comments and their implications, I will refer to the text she quotes from as 'the speech':

> Our deepest fear is not that we are inadequate. Our deepest fear is that we are powerful beyond measure. It is our light, not our darkness that frightens us. We ask ourselves, who am I to be brilliant, gorgeous, talented and fabulous? Actually, who are you not to be?
>
> You are a child of God. Your playing small doesn't benefit the world. There's nothing enlightening about shrinking so that other people won't feel insecure around you. We were born to make manifest the glory of God that is within us. It's not just in some of us, it's in all of us. It's in everyone!
>
> And as we let our light shine, we unconsciously give other people the permission to do the same. As we are liberated from our own fear, our presence automatically liberates others.

Ella then describes how she feels about this speech.

> **Ella:** . . . the ultimate call to be a citizen. I can't slide down into suicide and tidy myself away, I have something to do and maybe I'll never see the light in me, I'll just have to take it on trust/risk being deluded.
>
> I can run the 'becoming visible' scenario with this internal 'light on': there's no violent splattering. Now there's a thing. It's also no co-incidence that when Mandela overcame his hatred of the prison guards, he overcame his anger. I am not trying to equate my emotional problems with those of this great soul, but making a sort of parallel as to why I'm attracted to and repelled by the speech.

The speech can be read as an articulation of the power of aggressive energies in the way that Garner used her aggressive energies in Chapter 1 to access a vibrant, connective aliveness in herself and in others. The speech calls the listener to engage with, and take responsibility for their own strong energies, their own vibrant, aggressive desires to push on, generate change, and live themselves as fully as possible. As Courtin suggested, also in Chapter 1, these strong energies often get caught up in amalgams of emotions which render them negative, neurotic and I-based. She lists the characteristics of energy coming from such a negative state of mind as: 'it comes from a huge sense of I, it comes from fear, it's narrow, it's a sense of separateness, and it wants to harm' (Courtin, interviewed by Rachel Kohn, 2003).

The speech, like Garner's story, outlines the opposite position, where aggressive energies are expressed with a minimal sense of I, very little fear, great breadth of vision and willingness to engage as fully as possible, without the desire to harm herself or the Other. From this place, aggression becomes a point of connection and expansion. It becomes a vehicle for supporting the Other by demanding that they live their aliveness fully. This is what I heard in Lizzie's anorexic battlefield image – a rageful plea that someone help her live her aggressive energies and explosive desires for change and, through that, discover that they are love.

Ella, like Vivienne, takes these questions out into the arena of citizenship, into relationships which offer the kind of possibilities that Samuels is suggesting when he writes that: '[t]o be authentically aggressive, angry in the belly, and still be able to be part of social and political processes, is a psychological and ethical goal of the highest order' (1993: 57). Ella hears the speech as the ultimate call to citizenship, the ultimate call to stop privatising her aggressive energies and put them at the service of relationships (in the way Vivienne and Jane did in their relationships above).

The speech suggests that individuals can channel their aggressive energies into the formation of relationships and community, offering them out as part of what drives political processes, with all the terrors and joys associated with that. But the way in which aggression is being channelled is important: it is being moved out of self-serving, fearful amalgams, into creative connective ones, and that demands trust. As Ella puts it, 'I have something to do and maybe I'll never see the light in me, I'll just have to take it on trust/risk being deluded'. And this is the point about connective amalgams of aggression: they rarely feel strong or clear. More often they get caught up in struggles with neurotic fears, which force them back underground. When they are eventually expressed, it may be in ways which are initially less than helpful, needing thought and support from others to help them find their form. These kinds of connective amalgams of aggression carry the haunting uncertainty of Ella's self-doubt – they are unsettled and unsettling, decentring and open-ing. The imagery associated with aggressive energies and fantasies provides a vehicle for this because, as we have seen, these energies collide with the place where blissful, *jouissante* desires and longings become unsettling, instigating moral considerations and explorations of difference.

Again, such energies offer the choice to move towards an identity based on mourning, rather than the *status quo* position, which is based on melancholia. Hence the effect of the speech on Ella at the level of her comment that 'I can't slide down into suicide and tidy myself away'. The speech externalises the aggressive reactions to the losses and injuries of identity. It demands that the listener, to use Butler's language, rage against the dead in order not to join them. It demands that one serve the living and life, even if that means being undone in the process, hence Ella's ambivalence towards the speech. The kinds of vital possibilities which aggressive energies offer are both attractive in their vibrancy, and repellent because their unravelling, spontaneous, vast-ness threatens to flood the ego with abject inner Otherness which is usually cordoned off.

Ella's second response is that if she reruns the visibility experiment from Chapter 5 with the 'internal light' (which she glimpses through the speech) switched on, there is no violent splattering. I suggest that through her reading of the speech, the disavowed aggressive energies which would normally be folded down into her flesh and dispersed throughout her performance of identity (and femininity in particular) have been gathered together. The energy in them, which would otherwise become explosive, has been focused into the form of an inner light. This is made possible because as she reads the speech, Ella views her own aggressive energies through the speech's call to citizenship. Through what Ella believes to be Nelson Mandela's eyes, her aggressive energies belong to the outer world. In fact the world needs them, needs the love and the rage and the fight that they contain. The Other's feared judgement does not cut in, and so there is no need for an explosion. Note also that by gathering up her aggressive energies and having them reframed in this radical way, Ella also gives her self-hating committee the slip.

Through the way Ella engages with what she believes to be Mandela's speech, her aggressive energies come to be seen as something which reveals the trace (in Derrida's sense) of the Other – the Otherness of the processes of identity formation which, if raged at and mourned, turns out to be connective, rather than divisive. This is the inner Otherness to which Jung's dissociationist heritage offers clinical access.

Women's aggressive energies have within them possibilities for vitality, agency and love. These possibilities are often presented as self-hateful, unsettling or disturbing fragments of inner life. By taking the time and space to explore these elements of 'Not-I within', aggressive energies can sometimes be brought into amalgams which are almost invariably profoundly uncomfortable, but are often deeply enriching. Without these energies and fantasies we are less than half alive.

Notes

1 A different way of looking at aggression

1 The sensibility behind this comment, and indeed the whole book, is drawn from Andrew Samuels where he writes: 'To be authentically aggressive, angry in the belly, and still be able to be part of social and political processes, is a psychological and ethical goal of the highest order' (1993: 57). This quote will be returned to in the final chapter.

2 The theorising of aggression usually centres on the nature/nurture debate, which comes down to the following questions: given a specific discipline's definition of aggression, are some people more aggressive than others, and if so why? Are variations circumstantial, innate, or both? And are the identified differences a result of biology, psychology, evolution, socialisation or some mixture of these and/or other factors (and how could we tell)? The various answers offered by different disciplines usually refer to biology, experimental psychology, primatology, ethology or anthropology as grounds for their authority.

Regardless of academic discipline, the assumption is generally made that with respect to humans, males are much more aggressive than females although, as Sayers points out, the anthropologist Konrad Lorenz:

> argued that there were no consistent differences between the sexes as regards aggression. Indeed, he maintained that in so far as the evolution of biologically based aggressiveness had been fostered by the needs of 'brood defence', so females, including human females, were often more aggressive than males.
>
> (1982: 72)

Sayers goes on to argue that the extenders of Lorenz's work reversed this argument so that biology 'makes' males more aggressive than females. This was then used as the basis for concluding that male societal domination is biologically determined, and patriarchy the 'natural' order (Sayers, 1982: 72–73).

The work of depth psychologists such as Erich Fromm (1997), Anthony Storr (1998) and Rollo May (1998) either argues for this latter position, or takes it for granted, as can be seen by the scant or non-existent attention paid to women's aggression in their texts. This is, however, largely due to the way aggression is defined by these authors, so that women's aggression is rendered invisible.

Psychologically influenced sociobiological thought comes to similar conclusions (see John Renfrew, 1997, for a contemporary biopsychosocial example) and only engages with the question of women's premenstrual, hormonally related aggression, or with women as victims of aggression. Women's aggression is regarded as an aberration. Again, however, Sayers' comments provide some context to this. She critiques the basic propositions of sociobiology, commenting that they rest on what the biologist Stephen Jay Gould called 'crude biological determinism' (1982: 71). Likewise, the psychology used to support this field is usually crudely deterministic behaviourism, which unquestioningly accepts the ideological premises that underpin its supposedly empirical methodology.

A body of feminist critique has developed dealing with the assumptions in these psychological models, their methodologies and quality of argument. Carol Tavris, for example, points out the logical error of interpreting evidence that women are less likely to be aggressive than men (under similar, but limited conditions) as supporting a generalisable, oppositional structure whereby men 'are aggressive' and women 'are not aggressive' (1992: 91). Erica Burman also provides a powerful critique of the ideology, research practices and reasoning of developmental psychology (1997), and many of her criticisms can be applied to the kind of experimental psychology most aggression theorists rely upon. Likewise, most of the papers in *The Gender and Psychology Reader* (edited by McVicker Clinchy and Norem, 1998) directly or indirectly question the epistemological authority of experimental psychology. Furthermore, Siann (1985) and Selg (1975) raise questions about the nature of aggression and the assumptions commonly built into the methodologies of studies on aggression.

The practice of justifying a notion of 'natural' male dominance, based on innate aggression and its capacity to structure primate societies is core to much aggression theory. Sayers takes this to task, pointing out that:

> Comparison of various baboon societies indicates that dominance hierarchies among these primates is a learned response to situations in which space, cover and food are limited (Bleier, 1976). Dominance hierarchies appear where foraging for food is problematic and complicated by the presence of many predators, but do not appear in habitats where food is more plentiful and predators less of a menace (Leibowitz 1975; Donelson and Gullahorn 1977). If, as this data indicates, dominance behaviour is a learned phenomenon among non-human primates, then it is more than likely also to be learned among humans – that is, a response to environmental and societal factors rather than mechanistically determined by biology
>
> (Sayers, 1982, 74–75).

This untangling of assumptions about dominance, masculinity and aggression is important because it is part of what has traditionally closed off discussion of women's aggression by rendering it trivial. The academic assumption has been that what does not matter in the competitive struggle for dominance does not matter at all and can be ignored; part of this assumption is that women's experiences of their own aggression are irrelevant to the competitive struggle and hence of no significant interest. But as Anne Campbell argues (1993), this is simply a result of choosing an exclusively instrumental model of aggression (which fits with male socialisation) and ignoring expressive aggression (which fits with female socialisation).

Whether the primatological research Sayers quotes to support her argument is definitive or not, the point stands that dominance, masculinity and aggression are not *necessarily* entwined and inseparable. Sayers expands on this, unravelling the dubious assumptions, methods and conclusions of writers like Claiborne, Goldberg and Wilson by pointing out the common practice of relying on:

> false analogies between the social organization of primate societies and that of pre-colonial and industrial societies in order to claim that [patriarchal]

organization is essentially constant as far as male dominance is concerned and that male dominance must therefore be biologically determined. They also have to assume that dominance behaviour – whether it is that of guiding troop movements (in baboon societies), wage earning, occupying high-status occupations, or political activity is essentially aggressive in nature. They have to assume this in order to argue that male domination is dictated by men's greater biological propensity for aggression . . .

In fact, however, the evidence for a linkage between dominance and aggression even in baboon societies is far from clear. Indeed it is reported (Pilbeam 1973) that the dominant male in one troop – as measured by standard ethological criteria of frequency of completed successful matings, and influence on troop movements – was far less aggressive and, indeed, frequently lost fights with a younger and more vigorous adult male.

It is also not at all clear that human dominance behaviour, at least as measured by occupational success, is dependant on aggression and related psychological characteristics

(Sayers, 1982: 81).

I have quoted Sayers at length because of the importance of her work in undermining traditional biological and ethological fantasies about gender differences and aggression. Also of relevance is the work done by Frans De Waal, whose publications are listed at http://www.psychology.emory.edu/Faculty/dewaalpub.html. De Waal's work explores conflict resolution tactics in primate societies and provides an account of the strong roles of females in that process. See De Waal's article in *Scientific American*, March 1995, 82–88, which can be found at: http://www.worldpolicy.org/globalrights/sexorient/bonobos.html.

From a clinical perspective, there are further problems with the notion of aggression. Robert Mizen points out that there is a lack of clarity about what is meant by 'violence' (2003: 285), which he takes to be a subset of aggression. My argument is that there has also been a lack of clarity about the clinical concept of aggression, with problematic ethological research forming the basis of much of that misunderstanding. Mizen also provided a useful summary of the views of Freud, Klein and Jung on aggression and suggests that it can be argued that, in Jung's view, aggression has instinctual origins, but does not have its origins in one single instinct (2003: 290).

3 A number of authors have tackled aspects of the question of women's aggressive acts. Kirsta (1994) and Pearson (1998) provide systematic accounts of women's aggressive behaviour, but Campbell's (1993) work provides the strongest psychological account through her inclusion of women's and men's accounts of their experiences of their own and other people's aggression.

Alongside these are a range of more popular accounts by Fillion (1996); Lumby (1997); Denfeld (1997); Wurtzel (1998), and fictional or ironic renderings by Zahavi (1992) and Sacks (1998). But none of these seeks to provide an account of the *meanings, contexts and interiorities* of women's aggression. While each commentator (Campbell and Zahavi in particular, in spite of their different genres) may elucidate significant parts of the puzzle as to how to think about women's aggression, none of them works through the contradictory notion of femininity and aggression as mutually exclusive, yet paradoxically, unconsciously and often tragically entwined in Western culture. It is this last group of concerns that this book seeks to explore, since, as Valerie Walkerdine points out ' "[g]ood girls" are not always good – but where and how is their badness lived?' (1990: 103).

4 Active imagination is defined by Samuels, Shorter and Plaut in the following terms:

Jung used the term in 1935 to describe a process of dreaming with open eyes (CW, 6, para. 723n). At the outset one concentrates on a specific point, mood, picture or event, then allows a chain of associated fantasies to develop and gradually take on a dramatic character. Thereafter the images have a life of their own and develop according to their own logic. Conscious doubt must be overcome and allowance made for whatever falls into consciousness as a consequence.

Psychologically, this creates a new situation. Previously unrelated contents become more or less clear and articulate. Since feeling is roused, the conscious ego is stimulated to react more immediately and directly than is the case with dreams. . . .

Active imagination is to be contrasted with day-dreaming which is more or less of one's own invention and remains on the surface of personal and daily experience. Active imagination is the opposite of conscious invention.

(Samuels, Shorter and Plaut, 1986: 9)

5 Sherry Salman (2003: 245–246) provides a particularly telling image of the kinds of ghosts which I am gesturing towards:

Jung early on pointed out that when we deny the autonomy of any complex, much less of archetypal affect, trying to 'assimilate' it, eat it, and make it 'one of our own,' we are engaging in . . . a magical solution that is doomed eventually to fail. It is unsettling to observe how easily in our analytic practice and training, what we often find left behind after a therapeutic meal of such ego-satisfying interpretations, are still the Furies. They live on in their Athenian disguises, as child protectors, patron goddesses of the 'cult of the inner child' to which so many contemporary therapists and patients have fallen prey, identifying with the Furies or their victims, through a relentless, reductive pursuit of the never-ending, unfinished business of childhood.

6 Giles Clark, personal communication.

2 The *telos* of aggression: a post-Jungian perspective

1 The direction in which I will be taking my analysis of this kind of material is, however, very different to Kalsched's.
2 I take this use of the term 'self-hater' from Demaris Wehr's 1987 *Jung and Feminism*, where on pages 18 and 19 she uses the work of Doris Lessing to introduce the term and explore its meaning. Wehr's work also drew my attention to Lessing's comments, which I quote here.
3 This section of the book owes a heavy debt to Bram Dijkstra's fascinating and highly recommended work on images of 'evil' women in the art of the end of the nineteenth century and the beginning of the twentieth century. The images used here are from Dijkstra's *Idols of Perversity: Fantasies of Feminine Evil in Fin-de-Siècle Culture* and are reproduced with the permission of the author.
4 Philosophically, Jung's notion of archetype is neo-Platonic in origin, but it is his (problematic) subjectivist interpretation of Kant, as identified by Marilyn Nagy (1991: 74) and Roger Brooke (1993: 75), that enabled him to collapse together the external world and the categories of perception, making the external world, as Brooke says, a creation of the subject (1993: 75). To that end, Jung relied on Schopenhauer first for his reading of Kant and second for the development of a notion of blind (directionless) but unitive Will underlying all existence (Nagy, 1991: 74, 234). Von Hartmann's ideas are used to introduce meaning and *telos* to

this unitive layer of existence (Nagy, 1991: 234) and thus flesh out the concept into something we are more familiar with as the traditional reading of archetype.

5 Jung makes a distinction between archetypes (as ahistorical and universal) and archetypal images (as culturally inflected and temporal), and a traditional analysis of the Salome/Ayesha stories might be that they are simply culture- and period-specific images of universal and eternal patterns. That separation obscures too much of the politics which are packed into such images, and also the politics involved in choosing to view them in this way. My point is not that political analysis is an alternative to depth psychology, but that psychology is always and already full of unconscious politics. If those political processes are made conscious and engaged with, they can lead to a deepening of psychology; they can also lead to a more inclusive psychology, which is more respectful of difference. Obviously I am taking my lead from Samuels' work in this.

6 There is clearly a problem with this formulation which is that the opposition between an 'I' and a 'Not-I Within' is oversimplistic and false. In fact there are a spectrum of positions which language does not recognise, and this is a point which I will return to in Chapter 7. Meanwhile, in the absence of a better language through which to describe the phenomena which interest me, I will use the oppositional terms 'I' and 'Not-I' as a form of dissociationist shorthand.

7 But note, this move leaves Jung's concern for an ethical base to analytical psychology intact.

8 I am aware of Jacqueline Rose's critical stance towards Jung's work in *The Haunting of Sylvia Plath* (1991). Nonetheless, her work remains important to me, and I use it to amplify something in Jung's work on the grounds that often contradictory things have to be acknowledged as both being true, even if that creates an uncomfortable and untidy state of affairs.

9 I am also aware of the significant differences between the Hammer film version of *She*, and Rider Haggard's book. The book takes place in Africa, the film in Palestine, and the approach to Ayesha's kingdom is by water in the book, not across a desert as in the film. Kallikrates comes to a different end, and the roles of almost all of the other characters are changed in significant ways (especially Ustane and Billali). Most importantly, however, Ayesha is much, much wiser and cleverer in the book, having her own sophisticated philosophy of life. My overlapping of the two is, however, legitimate because they both revolve around a woman who is 'She Who Must Be Obeyed' and something of her personality carries over into the 1970s' film. Somehow, as a teenager, I totally missed the 'boy's own adventure' theme which dominates the film, and was transfixed by the idea of 'She Who Must Be Obeyed', much as Jung appears to have been when he met her through Rider Haggard's text.

10 Nina's comments can be read as an exploration of what Samuels calls the need for gender certainty and gender confusion (1989: 75–76).

11 Raya Jones provides useful clarification of the clash of cultures between the analytical and the metatheoretical (social constructionist) underpinnings of critical psychology, which are at stake at this point:

> Whereas analytical psychology pertains to intra-individual dynamical structures, which could be externalised in dreams, visions, myths, etc., social constructionism pertains to the supra-individual power structures, immanent in discursive practices, which are internalised in people's 'private' discourse; e.g., in one's thoughts about oneself. . . . Varela and Harré (1996) contend that the assumption that 'human nature is biological, it is lived psychologically, and therefore is social' is incompatible with the view, which they endorse, that

'human nature is cultural, it is lived socially, and therefore it is psychological' (p.137).

(Jones, 2003: 359)

Jones engages with this discursive difference through the work of Bakhtin, with particular reference to his work on the dialogical act. My interest in this discursive clash is different and focuses on its clinical implications. Specifically, I believe that embedded in this clash are ways of using the psychoanalytic process to access levels of distress and patterns of energy which have traditionally been excluded in order to stabilise and make viable the psychoanalytic project itself. Hence my interest in using Jung's dissociationist heritage to engage with the space between the analytical and the critical since the psyche, at times, experiences both the social dimensions and the biological dimensions of its humanness as alien, inner otherness. My suggestion is that both the analytic and critical discourses gesture towards these important facets of what it is to be human, and that the analytic challenge is to find a way of honouring these apparently irreconcilable dimensions of experience, because they both have their 'truth'.

12 In his exploration of alternative images to 'the child' in psychoanalysis Christopher Hauke takes a similar position. Hauke points out that '. . . infancy, childcare, and the family are socially constructed and not the "natural" phenomena that psychoanalysis so often assumes' (2003: 63). He goes on to suggest that the

> focus in the industrialized West has turned upon *ourselves and each other: what remains for humanity is the puzzle of nature that is our relationship with each other and with our inner fantasies.* 'L'enfer c'est les autres.' It is *other people* and our relationships with them that is the stuff of therapy today. It is our inner and outer, social and psychological, intercourse and discourse, that seems to be the true concern of psychotherapy.
>
> Therefore, this is not just a 'culture of narcissism' as sometimes suggested. It is more a sort of 'culture of socialism' if you like! But a 'culture of relationship' carries less baggage. It therefore needs to include far more attention to, and eventually new theorising about, our social relationships according to a discourse that resonates with contemporary life. This would require far more of a focus on our experience of each other in the here and now and far less of an emphasis on *explanations* of such experiences
>
> (2003: 66, original italics).

I read Hauke's analysis as pointing to a need to place our experience of inner and outer Otherness at the centre of psychoanalysis, with our clinical and theoretical activities designed to amplify and engage with the mystery, pleasures and terrors of that. Such an approach demands the bringing together of seemingly incompatible discourses to try to express the contradictory facets of human experience. Reducing the analytic interaction to a single discourse, for example, that of the baby and mother, or child and parent cannot suffice to this task.

3 Identity nightmares and a methodology in the madness

1 This point is drawn from Andrew Samuels' *Political Psyche* (1993: 128).
2 In order to put the power of this quote in its context, I will quote Rose's preceding comments:

> What distinguishes psychoanalysis from sociological accounts of gender (hence for me the fundamental impasse in Nancy Chodorow's work) is that

whereas for the latter, the internalization of norms is assumed roughly to work, the basic premise and indeed starting point for psychoanalysis is that it does not. The unconscious constantly reveals the 'failure' of identity. Because there is no continuity of psychic life, so there is no stability of sexual identity, no position for women (or for men) which is ever simply achieved. Nor does psychoanalysis see such 'failure' as a special-case inability or an individual deviancy from the norm. 'Failure' is not a moment to be regretted in a process of adaptation, or development into normality, which ideally takes its course (some of the earliest critics of Freud, such as Ernest Jones, did, however, give an account of development in just these terms). Instead 'failure' is something endlessly repeated and relived moment by moment throughout our individual histories. It appears not only in the symptom, but in dreams, in slips of the tongue and in forms of sexual pleasure which are pushed to the sidelines of the norm. Feminism's affinity with psychoanalysis rests above all, I would argue, with this recognition that there is a resistance to identity which lies at the very heart of psychic life.

(Rose, 1990: 232)

3 Hauke distinguishes Jung's view of the unconscious from other, more reductive views, pointing out that instead of emphasising past causes:

the Jungian position emphasises the understanding of phenomena – including social conditions – by asking 'Where is this heading? What are these conditions – or "symptoms" – leading us towards?'

(2000: 57)

4 These images of psychological landscapes and ways of engaging with them clinically owe a huge debt to both Giles Clark and Peter Fullerton. As clinical supervisors they have both been unstintingly generous and supportive of my work, for which I am deeply grateful.

5 While I cannot give detailed descriptions of the women participants' backgrounds (for reasons of confidentiality), it is possible, however, to indicate the overall demographic patterns among the 14 contributors, and the tables which follow provide that information. All information applies to the point in time at which women made their initial contributions to the project.

Primary ethnic group with which participant identifies

Anglo-Saxon   = 7
Celtic   = 4
Northern European   = 1
Southern European   = 2

Participant's age group

20–29 years   = 1
30–39 years   = 4
40–49 years   = 5
50–59 years   = 3
60–69 years   = 1

Participant's description of their family background

Working-class   = 9
Middle-class   = 5

Had the participant or their parents migrated between countries?

Yes	= 10
No	= 4

What level of education did the participant receive?

School Certificate or equivalent	= 3
Higher School Certificate or equivalent	= 4
Tertiary Education	= 7

Is the participant in a partnership relationship?

Yes	= 11
No	= 3

Does the participant identify as heterosexual or as lesbian?

Heterosexual	= 10
Lesbian	= 4

Does the participant have children?

Yes	= 6
No	= 8

6 The value of psychoanalytic theory is in terms of its notion of the unconscious, in particular the way in which it provides space for human irrationality, undercutting the notion of the unitary subject and entwining cognition and affect (Henriques *et al.*, 1998: 205). Again, this is important as it provides a potential route for exploring women's aggressive fantasies and impulses, which usually lie outside of rationality and coherent subjecthood.

7 Feminists argue instead that theoretical knowledge is a kind of practical knowledge, thus countering the common assumption that women's knowledge, which is often practical, is second rate. Feminist theory of knowledge also assumes that all knowledge is essentially social and that our values inform what we classify as knowledge (Tanesini, 1999: 12). Gerda Siann makes a similar point when she argues that her examination of the theories of aggression shows that people define aggression according to their situation (culture, era and academic discipline) as well as their value system and temperamental disposition (1985: 225).

To the reader who is familiar with feminist standpoint theory, it might look as if I am working from that model. In fact I am simultaneously drawing on aspects of standpoint theory and trying to move beyond it. Tanesini summarises the relevant principles of standpoint theory:

> in recent years some feminists have claimed that experience can be a useful tool for epistemology as long as it is not understood as giving us an immediate and infallible access to the object of knowledge. Starting from experience is a sound starting point of inquiry if it is understood as a matter [of] starting from a perspective which is inevitably partial and subject to revision. The problem encountered by earlier versions of standpoint epistemology can be avoided if we acknowledge differences among women.
>
> (1999: 156–157)

This broad deployment of standpoint theory avoids a descent into relativism, and implies a critique of traditional notions of objectivity. If Tanesini's comments about *difference among women* are extended to include the notion of psycho-analytic, inner plurality (so that there are differences *within each individual woman*), this reading also resolves the issue which Shildrick raises about Hart-stock's standpoint theory's erroneously assuming a unified subject (1997: 158). In effect, this incorporates the pluralism of post-modernism-informed feminism, without abandoning feminist politics, which Seyla Benhabib fears as an inevitable consequence of such a marriage. Thus, while this project is not specifically based on standpoint theory, engaging with the material which emerged in it leads to the question that Haraway raises:

> Many currents in feminism attempt to theorize grounds for trusting especially the vantage points of the subjugated; there is good reason to believe vision is better from below the brilliant space platforms of the powerful . . . But *how* to see from below is a problem requiring at least as much skill with bodies and language, with the mediations of vision, as the 'highest' technoscientific visualizations.
>
> (1997: 286, original italics)

In Haraway's terms, this project necessitated the development not only of a view from the marginalised aggressive fantasies of women, but also an explor-ation of how this vision operates and what it offers both feminism and depth psychology.

8 See Tanesini (1999: 223) for a discussion of this aspect of Irigaray's work. Also Segal criticises both Kristeva and Irigaray on account of their essentialism (Segal, 1987: 132–133) and elsewhere criticises Irigaray, arguing that '[s]he bypasses rather than explores women's complex psychic compulsions and resistances in relation to phallocentric assumptions of sexual difference; bypasses rather than contests their cultural and political backing' (Segal, 1994: 154). Likewise Lisa Jardine comments that Irigaray's text, which is supposed to speak a deeply female language, is as impenetrable to many women as it was intended to be for men (1989: 67).

9 Stanley and Wise outline feminist tactics which entail:

> recognition of the reflexivity of the feminist researcher *in* her research as an active and busily constructing agent; insistence that the 'objects' of research are also subjects in their own right as much as researchers are subjects of theirs (and objects of other people's); acceptance that the researcher is on the same critical plane as those she researches and not somehow intellectually superior; and, most fundamental of all, no opinion, belief or other construc-tion of events or persons, no matter from whom this derives, should be taken as a representation of 'reality' but rather treated as a motivated construction or version to be subject to critical feminist analytical inquiry.
>
> (1993: 200)

10 Thomä and Cheshire make a similar point in their criticism of developmentally influenced psychotherapies:

> The tendency to trace the causes of psychological disturbances further and further back into the past has become stronger over the decades . . . as if an individual's fate were determined in the first months of life or even in the intra-uterine phase – and this not as a result of inheritance by some genetic code, but because of presumed environmental influences. It is almost as

if some neo-Calvinist had revived a psychobiological doctrine of 'predestination'.

(1991: 418)

11 Lloyd is careful in her use of terms and points out that the lines of association between the categories of masculinity and male, and femininity and female, are not those of simple or static equivalence. At the same time, the category female does not stand completely independently from the cultural concept of femininity. Thus while the meanings attached to femininity as a descriptive cultural category do not immediately apply to all women, such meanings are entwined in the prescriptive practices which determine what counts socially as intelligible womanhood.

12 Interestingly, the traditional Jungian view of a woman's animus is that it is often represented as a group of men; for example, an image of a jury, providing a harsh internal commentary.

13 Samuels, Shorter and Plaut say the following about Jung's method of amplification in *A Critical Dictionary of Jungian Analysis*:

Jung regarded amplification as the basis of his synthetic method. . . . He stated its aim was to make both explicit and ample what is revealed by the unconscious [for example] of the dreamer. This then enables the dreamer to see it as unique but of universal significance, a synthesis of personal and collective patterns.

(1986: 16)

14 Clearly, there are dimensions of these kinds of internal narratives which call for an object relations-based exploration, and authors such as Judith Mitrani (2001) provide thoughtful and heartful examples of how this can be done. I want to stay with a different track which is to keep the focus on the powerful perceptions which might be embedded in the disagreeable thoughts which provoke the self-hater's attack.

4 Transgressing rational identity

1 I return to this notion of femininity (and thus gender) as fetish in Chapter 5's section 'Fashion and Otherness'.

2 I have kept Nina's turn of phrase here, taking her to mean 'like no other physical body could' when she writes 'no body'.

3 When I think about what life might be like for the parts of the personality which are rendered Other, and experienced (by the 'I') as uninhabitable, I think of the title characters in Tom Stoppard's *Rosencrantz and Guildenstern are Dead* (see Sales, 1988). Stoppard's play explores the perspective of the sidelined characters, scripted for premature oblivion by the dominant narrative, much as I imagine the 'I' would often like to do with the threatening 'Not-I within'. As with Stoppard's characters, they can seem like a dispensable sub-plot from the perspective of the narrating Hamlet/'I'. Yet engaging with these characters from within their own world tells an important story about the realm of the 'Not-I within', the realm which is marginalised for the 'I' to exist. Just as the absurd cruelty and nauseating incoherence of Hamlet's world is all the more apparent from the perspective of Rosencrantz and Guildenstern, so too is the madness of the discourse of coherent identity.

4 Despair is a big factor here: 'nothing will make any difference' and 'I haven't got what this is going to take' set the tone. The countertransferencial sense of being

overwhelmed by such paralysed amalgams of aggression (and this kind of defeat often does have an aggressively, monolithically stuck air about it) can be hard work to stay with over long periods of time. An image which I use within myself at this point is that if I were to set off in a plane flying a perfectly easterly course from Sydney and follow the lines of latitude around the planet exactly, I would, fuel permitting, eventually end up back in Sydney. No matter how many times I did it, the result would always be the same. If, however, I changed my course, even by only a few fractions of a radian of a degree, and held to that variation whenever I could while circling the earth many times, I would end up in quite a different place. These are the tiny degrees of agency I am trying to spot in my analysand, and bear in mind until they can find them for themselves.

5 'Custard, Darling?' can be found, along with other images by Margot Bandola (including this book's cover image called 'Woman with Spanner') at http.// www.cannsdownpress.co.uk/artM.A.htm.

5 Explosive visibility

1 Lloyd writes that for Rousseau:

> Women symbolise a desired closeness to Nature which, in a sense, they never leave. . . . Rousseau sees [women] as a potential source of disorder, as needing to be tamed by Reason. . . . But they are also, through their very closeness to Nature, objects of adulation and an inspiration to virtue.
>
> (1993: 63)

> Female closeness to Nature enables woman to function as moral exemplar; she is both what Reason leaves behind and that to which it aspires. But it is men who make Rousseau's journey from corrupted Reason to Nature. It is they who enact the full drama of Reason's transformation so that it reflects and enhances true human nature. Rousseau's women never really make the journey; for them, unlike men, closeness to Nature is a natural state, not an achievement of Reason.
>
> (1993: 64)

> The containment of women in the domestic domain helped control the destructive effects of passion on civil society, while yet preserving it as an important dimension of human well-being . . . [Rousseau saw the civil and domestic] spheres as intersecting in ways that gave women a role in the development and preservation of good forms of public life, in which they themselves did not directly participate. The private was for Rousseau a domain of private virtue, free of the falseness and corruption of public life, under the reign of women close to Nature. And it was not merely a retreat for men from the corruption of contemporary society; it was also the nursery of good citizens who would transform public life.
>
> (1993: 77–78)

2 When doing this exercise as part of a workshop I usually run it some way into the day, so that people have had a chance to get comfortable with each other. It is also useful to take the group through a body-focused meditation before doing the exercise.

3 Again, this could simply be read as a distinction between personal complexes and psychological splits, and a collective unconscious, archetypal realm. My choice is not to use that language and those concepts because I want to stay with options which support political analysis.

4 This idea of fashion as a laboratory for experimenting with the emergent sensibilities around the display of feminine anti-matter came from Dr Leon Petchkovsky.

6 Eating disorders and the *telos* of aggression

1 In this chapter I use the female pronoun mainly to indicate the fact that the ratio of women and girls to men and boys who develop eating disorders is given as varying between 15:1 and 20:1. Also, the subject of the book is women's aggressive fantasies.
2 Melanie Katzman suggests that, when trying to answer the question of who develops eating disorders and why, it is not gender that matters, but rather the issue of experiencing oneself as relatively powerful or powerless (Katzman, 1997).
3 BMI (Body Mass Index) is a ratio of weight in kilograms divided by height in metres squared and a BMI between 19 and 25 is generally considered healthy. An example of a BMI of 13 is someone who is 162 centimetres tall and weighs 34 kilograms (i.e., 5 feet 4 inches tall and weighs 5 stone 5 pounds) or 177 centimetres tall/41 kilograms (i.e., 5 feet 10 inches/6 stone 6 pounds).
4 It is worth noting that alexithymia gets very much worse with starvation. With analysands who are extreme restrictors I try to agree a deal with them whereby they (minimally) drink a cup of milky coffee 30 minutes or so before their session, as it can make a significant difference to their degree of emotional and cognitive availability in the session.
5 When I tell the lion story as part of a presentation, I usually call the lion 'he'. This is intended to depict the (usually female) person with anorexia's sense of these kind of ferocious energies as being a long way away from her conscious position.
6 This image is taken from the work of two colleagues who both arrived at the image of anorexia as a cell independently of each other, Dr Jill Welbourne, and Robyn Townsend.
7 One of the few places where I have seen a link made between women's overeating and aggression or anger is in Bunny Epstein's 'Women's Anger and Compulsive Overeating' (1994). From the point of view of this book, the problem with Epstein's paper is that being based on Winnicott's work, its objectives are to bring anger and aggression back into the realms of attachment, rather than to explore them as aspects of passion, which need to be experienced in their own right. I see Winnicott's link between aggression and attachment as short-circuiting out the kind of passion which would lead to a very different kind of love and attachment.
8 My thanks to Dr Jill Welbourne and her patient for this image.

7 Aggressive energies and relationships

1 I wish to thank Dirk Felleman for pointing this out to me.
2 Ella used this text to illustrate her point in good faith believing, as many people do, that it was from Mandela's inaugural speech. Indeed, a number of websites substantiate the text as Mandela's speech.
    In fact it was not, as indicated at the website:

    http://www.marianne.com/
        If you like the quote, you'll love the book . . .
        Several years ago, this paragraph from *A Return To Love* began popping up everywhere, attributed to Nelson Mandela's 1994 Inaugural Address. As honoured as I would be had President Mandela quoted my words, indeed he

did not. I have no idea where that story came from, but I am gratified that the paragraph has come to mean so much to so many people.

From *A Return To Love* by Marianne Williamson

© 1992 (Paperback; pp 190–191)

In order to preserve the tone of Ella's relationship to the text, I have referred to it as 'the speech', since while it is not a speech by Mandela, Ella's response to it is based on the assumption that it was. What I want to convey is how Ella's experience of her own aggressive energies changed when she experienced those energies through what she believes to be the eyes of a great political leader.

Bibliography

Acker, J., Barry, K. and Esseveld, J. (1991) 'Objectivity and Truth: Problems in Doing Feminist Research', in M. Fonow and J. Cook (eds.), *Beyond Methodology: Feminist Scholarship as Lived Research*, Bloomington and Indianapolis: Indiana University Press.

Ainley, R. (1998) 'Watching the Detectors: Control and the Panopticon', in R. Ainley (ed.), *New Frontiers of Space, Bodies and Gender*, London: Routledge.

Appignanesi, L. and Forrester, J. (1993) *Freud's Women*, London: Virago.

Ardener, S. (1993) 'An Introduction' in S. Ardener (ed.), *Women and Space: Ground Rules and Social Maps*, Oxford and Providence: Berg Publishers.

Austen, J. (1987) *Pride and Prejudice*, Harmondsworth: Penguin Classics. (First published in 1813.)

Austin, S. (2003) 'Psychoanalytic Infant Observation and the Shadow of Containment', *The International Journal of Critical Psychology*, Issue 7, pp. 102–125.

Australian Bureau of Statistics (ABS) (1997) '3102.0 "Longer lives, fewer babies", 26/05/1997. Online at: http://www.abs.gov.au/Ausstats/abs@.nsf/e5cb0b45f4547cc4ca25697500217f47/64031d28db62f60dca2568a90013622e!OpenDocument (accessed 1 November 2004).

Badinter, E. (1981) *Mother Love: Myth and Reality*, New York: Macmillan Publishing. (First published in French by Flammarion, Paris.)

Bair, D. (2003) *Jung: A Biography*, Boston: Little, Brown and Company.

Benjamin, J. (1988) *The Bonds of Love: Psychoanalysis, Feminism and the Problem of Domination*, New York: Pantheon.

Benjamin, J. (1998) *Shadow of the Other: Intersubjectivity and Gender in Psychoanalysis*, New York: Routledge.

Bersani, L. (1986) *The Freudian Body: Psychoanalysis and Art*, New York: Columbia University Press.

Best, S. (1995) 'Sexualizing Space', in E. Grosz and E. Probyn (eds.), *Sexy Bodies: the Strange Carnalities of Feminism*, London and New York: Routledge.

Bordo, S. (1997) 'The Body and the Reproduction of Femininity', in K. Conboy, N. Medina and S. Stanbury (eds.), *Writing on the Body: Female Embodiment and Feminist Theory*, New York: Columbia University Press.

Brinton Perera, S. (1981) *Descent to the Goddess*, Toronto: Inner City Books.

Brooke, R. (1993) *Jung and Phenomenology*, London: Routledge. (First published in 1991.)

Brunner, C. (1986) *Anima as Fate*, Dallas: Spring Publications (Originally published in

German with a preface written by C. G. Jung in 1959. First published in English in Zurich in 1963.)

Burman, E. (1997) *Deconstructing Developmental Psychology*, London: Routledge. (First published in 1994.)

Butler, J. (1990) *Gender Trouble: Feminism and the Subversion of Identity*, New York: Routledge.

Butler, J. (1997) *The Psychic Life of Power: Theories in Subjection*, Stanford: Stanford University Press.

Cameron, D. (1994/95) 'Just Say No: the Empire of Assertiveness', *Trouble And Strife*, 29/30, Winter, pp. 8–13.

Campbell, A. (1993) *Men, Women, and Aggression*, New York: Basic Books.

Carrette, J. (1994) 'The Language of Archetypes: a Conspiracy in Psychological Theory', *Harvest*, Vol. 40.

Claremont de Castillejo, I. (1973) *Knowing Woman: a Feminine Psychology*, New York: Harper and Row.

Cooper, D. (1995) 'Introduction', to M. Foucault, *Madness and Civilization: A History of Insanity in the Age of Reason*, London: Routledge. (Foucault's text was first published in 1967.)

Courtin, R. (2003) 'Chasing Robina', transcript of interview with Rachel Kohn on *The Spirit of Things*. Sydney: ABC Radio 13/07/2003. Online. at http://www.abc.net.au/rn/relig/spirit/stories/s897932.html (accessed 19 July 2003).

Cowan, L. (1994) 'Dismantling the Animus'. Online at *The Jung Page* Khttp://www.cgjungpage.org/index.php?option=content&task=view&id=105K (accessed 6 November 2004).

Cowie, E. (1993) 'Pornography and Fantasy: Psychoanalytic Perspectives', in L. Segal and M. McIntosh (eds.), *Sex Exposed: Sexuality and the Pornography Debate*, New Brunswick: Rutgers University Press.

Denfeld, R. (1997) *Kill the Body, the Head Will Fall: A Closer Look at Women, Violence, and Aggression*, London: Vintage.

Dijkstra, B. (1986) *Idols of Perversity: Fantasies of Feminine Evil in Fin-de-Siècle Culture*, Oxford: Oxford University Press.

Doane, J. and Hodges, D. (1992) *From Klein to Kristeva: Psychoanalytic Feminism and the Search for the 'Good Enough' Mother*, Ann Arbor: The University of Michigan Press.

Douglas, C. (1990) *The Woman in the Mirror: Analytical Psychology and the Feminine*, Boston: Sigo.

Duker, M. and Slade, R. (1992) *Anorexia Nervosa and Bulimia: How to Help*, Milton Keynes: Open University Press. (First published 1988.)

Epstein, B. (1994) 'Women's Anger and Compulsive Eating', in M. Lawrence (ed.), *Fed Up and Hungry*, London: The Women's Press. (First published 1987.)

Fillion, K. (1996) *Lip Service: The Myth of Female Virtue in Love, Sex and Friendship*, Australia: HarperCollins.

Flower MacCannell, J. (1992) '*Jouissance*', in E. Wright (ed.), *Feminism and Psychoanalysis: a Critical Dictionary*, Oxford: Blackwell.

Fonow, M. and Cook, J. (eds.) (1991) *Beyond Methodology: Feminist Scholarship as Lived Research*, Bloomington: Indiana University Press.

Foucault, M. (1973) *The Order of Things*, New York: Random House. (First published 1973.)

Foucault, M. (1980) 'Introduction', in *Herculine Barbin, Being the Recently Discovered Memoirs of a Nineteenth-Century French Hermaphrodite*, Brighton: Harvester.

Foucault, M. (1990) *The History of Sexuality*, Vol. 1: *an Introduction*, Harmondsworth: Penguin. (First published 1976.)

Foucault, M. (1990a) *The Care of the Self: the History of Sexuality*, Vol. 3, Harmondsworth: Penguin. (First published 1984.)

Foucault, M. (1992) *The Use of Pleasure: the History of Sexuality*, Vol. 2, Harmondsworth: Penguin. (First published 1984.)

Foucault, M. (1995) *Madness and Civilization: a History of Insanity in the Age of Reason*, London: Routledge. (First published 1967.)

Fromm, E. (1997) *The Anatomy of Human Destructiveness*, London: Pimlico. (First published 1974.)

Fuery, P. (1995) *Theories of Desire*, Melbourne: Melbourne University Press.

Gamman, L. and Makinen, M. (1994) *Female Fetishism: a New Look*, London: Lawrence & Wishart.

Garner, H. (2001) 'The Feel of Steel' in *The Feel of Steel*, Sydney: Picador.

Garner, H. (2001a) 'The Feel of Steel 2' in *The Feel of Steel*, Sydney: Picador.

Gatens, M. (1991) *Feminism and Philosophy: Perspectives on Difference and Equality*, Cambridge: Polity Press.

Grosz, E. (1994) *Volatile Bodies*, Australia: Allen and Unwin.

Grosz, E. (1995) *Space, Time and Perversion*, Sydney: Allen and Unwin.

Guirand, F. (1987) 'Greek Mythology', in *New Larousse Encyclopedia of Mythology*, London: Hamlyn.

Haraway, D. (1997) 'The Persistence of Vision', in K. Conboy, N. Medina and S. Stanbury (eds.), *Writing on the Body: Female Embodiment and Feminist Theory*, New York: Columbia University Press.

Hart, D. (1997) 'The Classical Jungian School', in P. Young-Eisendrath and T. Dawson (eds.), *The Cambridge Companion to Jung*, Cambridge: Cambridge University Press.

Hartman, G. (1994) *The Franco Prussian War or Jung as a Dissociationist*. Online at *The Jung Page* http://www.cgjungpage.org/index.php?option=content&task=view&id=139 (accessed 21 November 2004).

Hartstock, N. (1987) 'Rethinking Modernism: Minority vs. Majority Theories', *Cultural Critique*, Vol. 7.

Hauke, C. (2000) *Jung and the Postmodern: the Interpretation of Realities*, London: Routledge.

Hauke, C. (2003) 'Uneasy Ghosts: Theories of the Child and the Crisis in Psychoanalysis', in R. Withers (ed.), *Controversies in Analytical Psychology*, London: Brunner-Routledge.

Haule, J. (1992) 'From Somnambulism to the Archetypes: the French Roots of Jung's Split with Freud', in R. Papadopoulos (ed.), *Carl Gustav Jung: Critical Assessments*, Vol. 1, London: Routledge.

Henriques, J., Hollway, W., Urwin, C., Venn, C. and Walkerdine, V. (1998) *Changing the Subject: Psychology, Social Regulation and Subjectivity*, London: Routledge. (First published in 1984.)

Hillman, J. (1992) 'Therapy, Dreams and the Imaginal', in R. Papadopoulos (ed.), *Carl Gustav Jung: Critical Assessments*, Vol. III, London: Routledge.

Hinshelwood, R. (1991) *A Dictionary of Kleinian Thought*, London: Free Association Books Ltd. (First published in 1989.)

Hinshelwood, R. (2002) 'Applying the Observational Method: Observing Organisations', in A. Briggs (ed.), *Surviving Space: Papers on Infant Observation*, London: Karnac.

Jardine, L. (1989) 'The Politics of Impenetrability', in T. Brennan (ed.), *Between Feminism and Psychoanalysis*, London: Routledge.

Jones, R. (2003) 'Between the Analytical and the Critical: Implications for Theorizing the Self', *The Journal of Analytical Psychology*, Issue 48, pp. 355–370.

Jung, C. (1977) *Memories, Dreams, Reflections*, London: Fontana. (First published in 1963.)

Jung, C. (1981) 'Woman in Europe', in H. Read, M. Fordham and G. Adler (eds.), *C.G. Jung: the Collected Works*, Vol. 10 – *Civilization in Transition*, London: Routledge and Kegan Paul. (First published in German in 1927.)

Jung, C. (1986) 'Preface', in C. Brunner (ed.), *Anima As Fate*, Dallas: Spring Publications. (Originally published in German with a preface written by C. G. Jung in 1959. First published in English in Zurich in 1963.)

Jung, C. (1998) *Visions: Notes on the Seminar Given in 1930–1934*, C. Douglas (ed.), Vol. II, London: Routledge.

Kalsched, D. (1996) *The Inner World of Trauma*, London: Routledge.

Kalsched, D. (1998) 'Archetypal Affect, Anxiety and Defence in Patients who have Suffered Early Trauma', in A. Casement (ed.), *Post-Jungians Today: Key Papers in Contemporary Analytical Psychotherapy*, London: Routledge.

Katzman, M. (1997) 'Getting the Difference Right: it's Power not Gender that Matters', *European Eating Disorders Review*, Vol. 5, No. 2.

Kimbles, S. (2003) 'Cultural Complexes and Collective Shadow Processes', in J. Beebe (ed.), *Terror, Violence and the Impulse to Destroy*, Canada: Daimon Verlag.

Kirkland, G. (1986) *Dancing on My Grave: an Autobiography*, New York: Doubleday.

Kirsta, A. (1994) *Deadlier Than the Male: Violence and Aggression in Women*, London: HarperCollins.

Klein, M. (1989) *The Psycho-analysis of Children*, trans. A. Stratchey, London: Virago. (First published in 1932.)

Kristeva, J. (1982) *Powers of Horror: an Essay on Abjection*, trans. L. Roudiez, New York: Columbia University Press.

Kugler, P. (1993) 'The "Subject" of Dreams 1', *Dreaming, The Association for the Study of Dreams*, Vol. 3, No. 2. Online at *The Jung Page* http://www.cgjungpage.org/index.php?option=content&task=view&id=242 (accessed 21 November 2004).

Lacan, J. (1982) 'God and the *Jouissance* of the Woman. A Love Letter', in J. Mitchell and J. Rose (eds.), *Feminine Sexuality: Jacques Lacan and the école freudienne*, London: Norton. (First published in 1975.)

Lacan, J. (1982a), 'Feminine Sexuality in Psychoanalytic Doctrine', in J. Mitchell and J. Rose (eds.), *Feminine Sexuality: Jacques Lacan and the école freudienne*, London: Norton. (First published in 1975.)

Lessing, D. (1969), *The Four-gated City*, New York: Bantam Books.

Leys, R. (1992) 'Jung, and the Limits of Association', in R. Papadopoulos (ed.), *Carl Gustav Jung: Critical Assessments*, Vol. 1, London: Routledge.

Lloyd, G. (1993) *The Man of Reason: 'Male' and 'Female' in Western Philosophy*, London: Routledge. (First published in 1984.)

Loach, L. (1993) 'Bad Girls: Women who Use Pornography', in L. Segal and M.

McIntosh (eds.), *Sex Exposed: Sexuality and the Pornography Debate*, New Brunswick: Rutgers University Press.

Lumby, C. (1997) *Bad Girls: the Media, Sex and Feminism in the 90s*, Australia: Allen and Unwin.

Lunbeck, E. (1994) *The Psychiatric Persuasion: Knowledge, Gender and Power in Modern America*, Princeton: Princeton University Press.

McVicker Clinchy, B. and Norem, J. (eds.) (1998) *The Gender and Psychology Reader*, New York: New York University Press.

Mairs, N. (1997) 'Carnal acts', in K. Conboy, N. Medina and S. Stanbury (eds.), *Writing on the Body: Female Embodiment and Feminist Theory*, New York: Columbia University Press.

Marcus, J. (2001) *The Indomitable Miss Pink: a Life in Anthropology*, Sydney: UNSW Press.

May, R. (1998) *Power and Innocence: a Search for the Sources of Violence*, New York: Norton. (First published in 1972.)

Meir C. (1992) 'The Theory of Complexes', in R. Papadopoulos (ed.), *Carl Gustav Jung: Critical Assessments*, Vol. 2, London: Routledge.

Menzies, I. (1970) *The Function of Social Systems as a Defence Against Anxiety – A Report on a Study of the Nursing Service of a General Hospital*, London: The Tavistock Institute of Human Relations. (First published in *Human Relations*, 1959)

Merck, M. (1993) *Perversions: Deviant Readings*, London: Virago.

Miller, D. (1990) 'An Other Jung and an Other . . .', in K. Barnaby and P. D'Acierno (eds.), *C. G. Jung and the Humanities: Toward a Hermeneutics of Culture*, London: Routledge.

Mitchell, J. (1974) *Psychoanalysis and Feminism*, London: Pelican.

Mitchell, J. (ed.) (1986) *The Selected Melanie Klein*, Harmondsworth: Penguin.

Mitrani, J. (2001) *Ordinary People and Extra-Ordinary Protections*, Hove: Brunner-Routledge.

Mizen, R. (2003) 'A Contribution Towards an Analytic Theory of Violence', *The Journal of Analytical Psychology*, Issue 48, pp. 285–305.

Modleski, T. (1984) *Loving with a Vengeance: Mass-produced Fantasies for Women*, New York: Methuen. (First published in 1982.)

Morgan, H., Purgold, J. and Welbourne, J. (1983) 'Management and Outcome in Anorexia Nervosa: a Standardised Prognostic Study', *British Journal of Psychiatry*, Vol. 143, September.

Morgan, H., and Russell, G. (1975) 'Value of Family Background and Clinical Features as Predictors of Long-term Outcome in Anorexia Nervosa: Four-year Follow-up Study of 41 Patients', *Psychological Medicine*, 5(4) Vol. 5, Issue 4.

Nagy, M. (1991) *Philosophical Issues in the Psychology of C. G. Jung*, Albany: State University of New York.

Noll, R. (1992) 'Multiple Personality, Dissociation and C.G. Jung's Complex Theory', in R. Papadopoulos (ed.), *Carl Gustav Jung: Critical Assessments*, Vol. 2, London: Routledge.

North Shore Temple Emmanuel (eds.) (1997) *Or Chadash*, Sydney: North Shore Temple Emmanuel.

Papadopoulos, R. (1992) 'Jung and the Concept of the Other', in R. Papadopoulos (ed.), *Carl Gustav Jung: Critical Assessments*, Vol. 1, London: Routledge.

Parker, R. (1996) *Torn in Two: the Experience of Maternal Ambivalence*, London: Virago. (First published in 1995.)

Pearson, P. (1998) *When She was Bad: Violent Women and the Myth of Innocence*, London: Virago.

Redfearn, J. (1992) *The Exploding Self: the Creative and Destructive Nucleus of the Personality*, Illinois: Chiron Publications.

Redfearn, J. (1994) 'Introducing Subpersonality Theory: a Clarification of the Theory of Object Relations and of Complexes, with Special Reference to the I/Not-I Gateway', *Journal of Analytical Psychology*, Vol. 39, pp. 283–310.

Renfrew, J. (1997) *Aggression and its Causes: a Biopsychosocial Approach*, Oxford: Oxford University Press.

Rider Haggard, H. (1888) *She*, London: Longmans, Green and Company.

Rose, J. (1990) 'Femininity and its Discontents', in T. Lovell (ed.), *British Feminist Thought: A Reader*, Oxford: Blackwell.

Rose, J. (1991) *The Haunting of Sylvia Plath*, London: Virago.

Rowland, S. (2002) *Jung: a Feminist Revision*, Cambridge: Polity.

Rowland, S. (2005) *Jung as a Writer*, London: Brunner-Routledge.

Russo, M. (1986) 'Female Grotesques: Carnival and Theory', in T. de Laurentis (ed.), *Feminist Studies: Critical Studies*, Bloomington: Indiana University Press.

Sacks, J. (1998) *Nice*, London: Pan Books.

Sales, R. (1988) *Tom Stoppard: Rosencrantz and Guildenstern are Dead*, Harmondsworth: Penguin.

Salman, S. (2003) 'Blood Payments', in J. Beebe (ed.), *Terror, Violence and the Impulse to Destroy*, Canada: Daimon Verlag.

Samuels, A. (1989) *The Plural Psyche*, London: Routledge.

Samuels, A. (1993) *The Political Psyche*, London: Routledge.

Samuels, A. (1997) 'Introduction: Jung and the Post Jungians', in P. Young-Eisendrath and T. Dawson (eds.), *The Cambridge Companion to Jung*, Cambridge: Cambridge University Press.

Samuels, A. (2000) 'Post Jungian Dialogues', in *Psychoanalytic Dialogues*, Vol. 10, No. 3, pp. 403–424.

Samuels, A., Shorter, B. and Plaut, F. (1986) *A Critical Dictionary of Jungian Analysis*, London: Routledge & Kegan Paul.

Sayers, J. (1982) *Biological Politics: Feminist and Anti-feminist Perspectives*, London: Tavistock Publications.

Sayers, J. (1986) *Sexual Contradictions: Psychology, Psychoanalysis, and Feminism*, London: Tavistock Publications.

Scheman, N. (1997) 'Queering the Center by Centering the Queer: Reflections on Transsexuals and Secular Jews', in D. Tietjens Meyers (ed.), *Feminists Rethink The Self*, Colorado: Westview Press.

Segal, L. (1987) *Is the Future Female? Troubled Thoughts on Contemporary Feminism*, London: Virago.

Segal, L. (1993) 'Sweet Sorrows, Painful Pleasures: Pornography and the Perils of Heterosexual Desire', in L. Segal and M. McIntosh (eds.), *Sex Exposed: Sexuality and the Pornography Debate*, New Brunswick: Rutgers University Press.

Segal, L. (1994) *Straight Sex: the Politics of Pleasure*, London: Virago Press.

Selg, H. (1975) *The Making of Human Aggression*, London: Quartet Books.

Shamdasani, S. (1990) 'A Woman Called Frank', *Spring: a Journal of Archetype and Culture*, Issue 50, pp. 26–56.

Shamdasani, S. (1998) 'From Geneva to Zürich: Jung and French Switzerland', *The Journal of Analytical Psychology*, Vol. 43, No. 1, pp. 115–126.

Shamdasani, S. (2003) *Jung and the Making of Modern Psychology: the Dream of a Science*, Cambridge: University Press.

Shildrick, M. (1997) *Leaky Bodies and Boundaries: Feminism, Postmodernism and (Bio)Ethics*, London: Routledge.

Siann, G. (1985) *Accounting for Aggression: Perspectives on Aggression and Violence*, London: George Allen & Unwin.

Spivak, G. (1988) *In Other Worlds: Essays in Cultural Politics*, London: Routledge.

Stanley, L. and Wise, S. (1983) ' "Back to the Personal" or: Our Attempt to Construct "Feminist Research" ', in G. Bowles and R. Duelli Klein (eds.), *Theories of Women's Studies*, London: Routledge & Kegan Paul.

Stanley, L. and Wise, S. (1993) *Breaking Out Again: Feminist Ontology and Epistemology*, London: Routledge. (First published in 1983.)

Storr, A. (1998) *Human Aggression*, Harmondsworth: Penguin. (First published in 1968.)

Tanesini, A. (1999) *An Introduction to Feminist Epistemologies*, Oxford: Blackwell.

Tavris, C. (1992) *The Mismeasure of Woman*, New York: Simon & Shuster.

Taylor, C. (1989) *Sources of the Self*, Gateshead: Athenæum Press.

Thomä, H. and Cheshire, N. (1991) 'Freud's *Nachträglichkeit* and Strachey's "Deferred Action": Trauma, Constructions and the Direction of Causality', *The International Review of Psycho-Analysis*, Vol. 18, Part 3, pp. 407–427.

Tietjens Meyers, D. (1997) 'Emotion and Heterodox Moral Perception: an Essay in Moral Social Psychology', in D. Tietjens Meyers (ed.), *Feminists Rethink The Self*, Colorado: Westview Press.

von Franz, M. (1988) *The Way of the Dream*, Canada: Best Printing Company.

Waldby, C. (1995) 'Destruction: Boundary Erotics and Refigurations of the Heterosexual Male Body', in E. Grosz and E. Probyn (eds.), *Sexy Bodies: the Strange Carnalities of Feminism*, London: Routledge.

Walkerdine, V. (1990) *Schoolgirl Fictions*, London: Verso.

Warner, M. (1994) *Managing Monsters: Six Myths of Our Time – The Reith Lectures*, London: Vintage.

Wehr, D. (1987) *Jung and Feminism: Liberating Archetypes*, Massachusetts: Beacon Press.

Williams, L. (1989) *Hard Core: Power, Pleasure and the 'Frenzy of the Visible'*, Berkeley: University of California Press.

Winnicott, D. (1949) 'Hate in the Counter-Transference', *International Journal of Psychoanalysis*, 30, pp. 69–70.

Winnicott, D. (1958) *Collected Papers: Paediatrics to Psycho-Analysis*, London: Tavistock.

Winnicott, D. (1986) 'This Feminism', in *Home is Where We Start From: Essays by a Psychoanalyst*, Harmondsworth: Penguin. (Draft of a talk given in 1964.)

Winterson, J. (1985) *Oranges Are Not the Only Fruit*, London: Pandora.

Woodward, K. (1996) 'Anger . . . and Anger: from Freud to Feminism', in J. O'Neill (ed.), *Freud and the Passions*, Pennsylvania: Pennsylvania State University Press.

Wurtzel, E. (1998) *Bitch: In Praise of Difficult Women*, London: Quartet Books.

Young-Eisendrath, P. and Wiedeman, F. (1987) *Female Authority: Empowering Women Through Psychotherapy*, New York: The Guilford Press.

Young-Eisendrath, P. (1997) 'Gender and Contrasexuality: Jung's Contribution and Beyond', in P. Young-Eisendrath and T. Dawson (eds.), *The Cambridge Companion to Jung*, Cambridge: Cambridge University Press.

Young, I. M. (1990) 'Throwing Like a Girl', in *Throwing Like a Girl and Other Essays in Feminist Philosophy and Social Theory*, Bloomington and Indiana: Indiana University Press.

Zahavi, H. (1992) *Dirty Weekend*, London: Flamingo. (First published in 1991.)

Index